PROBLEMS IN MACROECONOMIC THEORY

Solutions to Exercises
from Thomas J. Sargent's
Macroeconomic Theory, Second Edition

PROBLEMS IN MACROECONOMIC THEORY

Solutions to Exercises from Thomas J. Sargent's *Macroeconomic Theory, Second Edition*

CHARLES H. WHITEMAN
Department of Economics
University of Iowa
Iowa City, Iowa

ACADEMIC PRESS, INC.
Harcourt Brace Jovanovich, Publishers
San Diego New York Berkeley Boston
London Sydney Tokyo Toronto

ACADEMIC PRESS, INC.
San Diego, California 92101

United Kingdom Edition published by
ACADEMIC PRESS LIMITED
24-28 Oval Road, London NW1 7DX

Library of Congress Cataloging-in-Publication Data

Whiteman, Charles H.
Problems in macroeconomic theory.

1. Macroeconomics. 2. Macroeconomics – Problems, exercises, etc. I. Sargent, Thomas J. Macroeconomic theory. II. Title.
HB172.5.S27 1987 Suppl. 2 339 87-17398
ISBN 0-12-619752-0 (pbk.)

PRINTED IN THE UNITED STATES OF AMERICA
89 90 91 92 93 9 8 7 6 5 4 3 2

CONTENTS

Preface

A good way to begin learning about macroeconomics is to read Thomas Sargent's Macroeconomic Theory. To learn how to do macroeconomics, especially "Rational Expectations Macroeconomics," one should read Sargent's text again, and do the exercises it provides. That was my learning procedure, and it is one I have used, perhaps forced, on students for nearly a decade. Beginning with a distinctly pleasant three year tenure as Sargent's Teaching Assistant at The University of Minnesota, and continuing more recently at The University of Iowa, I have been telling students that to understand Macroeconomic Theory, it is necessary to do the problems in Macroeconomic Theory. Successful completion of an exercise from the text does not merely verify that the student understands the material -- it indicates that he or she has wrestled with the intricacies of a model, has learned a little bit about which alleys are blind and which are not, and has had to think a little bit about the "big picture" and how the tools used to solve the problem might be applied in other contexts.

While "Do the problems" is good advice, it plants a seed which grows into "I have done the problems, but have I done them correctly?" After having my advice come back to haunt me in this way a number of times, I began assembling the solutions contained in this book. I have always provided students with as many of the solutions as I had, and I have advised them to spend some time on each problem and to write out the candidate answer before looking at the solution. Unfortunately, this exercise working strategy is not time consistent (see Chapter XV), so I can only hope that some precommitment to it can be induced by associating peeking with substantial guilt. Often, there are important but subtle lessons in the working of an exercise which are not learned when the solution is read immediately after the problem is posed.

While many of the exercises are quite challenging, there are large rewards to solving them. Most of the exercises have been used as examination questions at Minnesota and Iowa. Several exercises grew out of recently published journal articles. Many contain useful, little-known results. Once, after I had passed out copies of several of the new exercises, a member of the class asked "our assignment is to read this, right?" I had rather more in mind, but a mere reading would have had a positive marginal product. I hope the users of this book will find the solutions even more useful.

Early versions of the solutions circulated at Minnesota, Iowa, and, I understand, elsewhere. I have received numerous comments on them over the years; the first came from Rusdu Saracoglu when I was the student and he was the TA. Later, Ian Bain helped make several solutions much clearer than they otherwise would have been, and Larry Christiano and Tom Doan set me straight on a number of problems. Jim Hamilton provided helpful comments on several chapters, and Robert Rosenman forced me to clarify my thinking on a number of the issues treated here. I am sure that there were other contributors whom I am forgetting to thank, just as I am sure that there were comments to which I should have listened, and did not; suggestions which I should have followed and did not. Thus for the "bugs" which remain, for unnecessarily complicated solutions, I claim sole responsibility.

A number of graduate students at Iowa have helped me assemble these solutions. Diana Wisner, Chris Blair, Subir Chakrabarti, Barry Sopher,

Cheng-Zhong Qin, and Scott Simkins have all left their marks on various editions of the manuscript. Scott's influence on this edition has been large; he has helped improve the presentation in a number of places, and he has helped edit and proofread the entire manuscript.

I would like to thank the Instructional Support Services Office at The University of Iowa for helping me produce this book. Phyllis Irwin orchestrated the production of the typescript, and Cindy Woods and Julie Skog efficiently typed the rather involved text reproduced here. Linda Knowling drew the figures.

Finally, I wish to acknowledge a large debt to Thomas Sargent; he sparked my interest in the practicing and preaching of Macroeconomic Theory, and in the solving of these problems. I hope he thinks I got them right.

Charles H. Whiteman
Durham, North Carolina

CHAPTER II

THE KEYNESIAN MODEL

EXERCISES

1. Take a simple version of the Keynesian model described above, one with $\pi(M + B)/p$ excluded from the consumption function.

A. Describe the behavior of the model (i.e., the response of all endogenous variables to jumps in each of the exogenous variables) where the endogenous variables are taken to be Y, N, C, I, r, and M, while the exogenous variables are G, T, π, w, p, and K.

B. Describe the behavior of the model where the endogenous variables are Y, N, C, I, p, and M and the exogenous variables are G, T, K, π, w, and r.

2. Take a simple version of the classical model. Describe the behavior of the model where the endogenous variables are Y, N, C, I, w, r, and M, while the exogenous variables are G, T, π, p, and K.

3. Consider an economy described by the following equations.

$Y/K = A(N/K)^{1.10}$	(production function. Bodkin and Klein, 1967)
$N/K = \beta_0(w/p)^{\beta_1}$	$\beta_1 < 0$ (demand function for labor)
$I = I(r)$	$I' < 0$
$C = C(Y - T)$	$0 < C' < 1$

$$C + I + G = Y$$

$$M/p = m(r,Y,W) \qquad m_r < 0,\ m_Y > 0,\ m_W = 1$$

$$W = ((M + B)/p) + K.$$

The endogenous variables are:

Y = GNP
C = consumption
N = employment
r = interest rate
p = the price level
W = real wealth held by the public.
I = investment

The exogenous variables are:

K = the capital stock
w = the money wage
T = tax collections
G = government expenditures, a flow
M = the money stock, a liability of the government
B = stock of government interest bearing bonds.

Government bonds are like savings deposits, having a variable interest rate and fixed nominal value. Describe the effects on Y, N, P, and r of:

A. An increase in the money supply brought about by an open-market operation, i.e., $dM = -dB$.

B. A once-and-for-all increase in the money supply caused by a one-time government money bonus to veterans, i.e., $dM > 0$, $dB = 0$.

C. A once-and-for-all increase in the stock of outstanding government bonds, caused by a one-time gift of some new government bonds to veterans, i.e., $dB > 0$, $dM = 0$.

4. Consider the following macroeconomic model:

$$Y = F(K,N) \qquad F_K, F_N > 0;\ F_{KK}, F_{NN} < 0,\ F_{KN} > 0$$

$$w/p = F_N$$

$$N^S = N^S(\frac{w}{p}, r - \pi) \qquad N^S_{w/p} > 0,\ N^S_{r-\pi} > 0$$

$$N = N^S$$

$$I = I(r - \pi) \qquad I' < 0$$

$$C = C(Y - T) \qquad 0 < C' < 1$$

$$C + I + G = Y$$

$$M/p = m(r,Y) \qquad m_r < 0,\ m_Y > 0$$

where Y is GNP, K is the capital stock, N is employment, w is the money wage, N^S is the supply of labor, p is the price level, r is the interest rate, π is the anticipated inflation rate, I is investment, C is consumption, G is government expenditures, and T is taxes net of transfers. The endogenous variables are Y, N, N^S, w, p, r, C, and I. The exogenous variables are M, K, G, T, and π.

A. Describe the effects on Y, p, r, and N of: (1) an increase in M, (2) an increase in G with T constant, and (3) an increase in π. Does an increase in π leave the real rate of interest unchanged?

B. Suppose that the government finances its deficit by printing bonds and/or money. At the equilibrium values of the variables that satisfy the above equations are we assured that the public will be willing to accumulate new bonds and/or money at exactly that rate at which the government is creating it? Explain.

5. Consider an economy described by the IS-LM diagram in Figure 6. Here (Y_e, r_e) is an equilibrium output-interest rate pair. Consider now the situation at (Y_e, r_1).

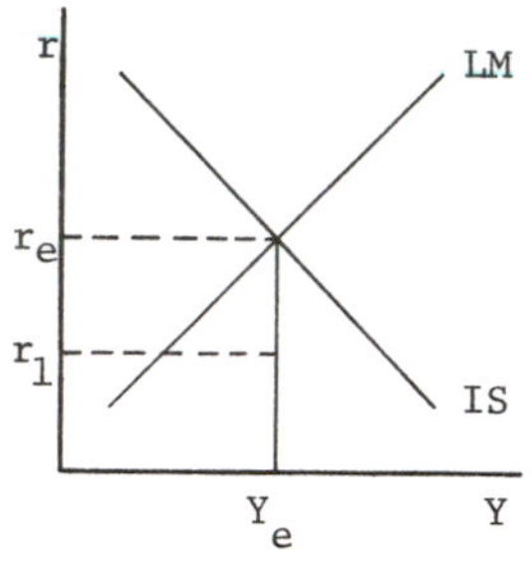

Figure 6

A. Is there an excess supply or an excess demand for money at (Y_e, r_1)?

B. Is there an excess supply or an excess demand for output at (Y_e, r_1)?

C. Are your answers to (A) and (B) consistent with Walras' law?

6. Assume an economy in which money matters; the monetary authority can influence the interest rate, real output and employment, and the price level at any moment in time. Also, the firms of this economy are price takers, at least in the labor market, so the marginal product of labor and the real wage are equal at every moment. Now, suppose that a constant-purchasing-power law is passed, a law that requires all firms to compensate employees for any change in the commodity price level by increasing money wages proportionately. What is the significance of this new law for the monetary authority? Is it still able to influence real output and employment, the interest rate, and the price level?

7. There is a country whose government is financing all of its expenditures by means of money creation. All money is the liability of the government, there being no commercial banks. The government acts to

keep its rate of real expenditures G constant over time at the real rate $G = \bar{G}$. Accordingly, money creation is governed by

$$\frac{dM}{dt}/p(t) = \bar{G}$$

where M is the money supply and p the price index. Suppose that real output is constant over time and that actual and expected inflation at each moment both equal (dM/dt)/M(t). Since $\bar{G}$ is a nonnegligible proportion of the country's GNP, this country has been experiencing a high rate of inflation. It also happens that the government has prohibited residents of this country from holding money and other assets of any foreign countries.

A. How would you find the maximum rate of expenditures that the government can finance by money creation?

B. Assume that $\bar{G}$ is initially lower than the maximum G described in (A), and that the rate of money creation is correspondingly lower than the rate needed to maximize G. Explain whether abandoning the restriction on holding of foreign assets would make it easier or harder for the government to finance its expenditures at the same real rate $\bar{G}$ by money creation.

C. Assuming that it would still be possible to finance $\bar{G}$ by money creation if the prohibition on holding foreign assets were eliminated, would the equilibrium rate of inflation be higher or lower than initially?

8. Consider the following model of a small country.

$Y = F(N,K)$	$F_N, F_K, F_{NK} > 0; F_{NN}, F_{KK} < 0$ production function
$w/p = F_N$	marginal equality for employment

$I = I(r)$	$I' < 0$	investment schedule
$X = X(t)$	$X_t < 0$	export schedule
$t = \frac{e \cdot p}{p^*}$		definition of terms of trade
$C = c(Y - T)$	$0 < c' < 1$	consumption function
$C + I + G + X = Y$		equilibrium condition in market for domestic good
$M/p = m(r,Y)$	$m_r < 0$, $m_Y > 0$	portfolio equilibrium condition.

Here Y is GNP, N is employment, K is capital, I investment, C consumption, X exports, M the money supply, r the interest rate, p the price level in this country (measured in dollars per unit domestic good), p* the price level in the rest-of-the world (measured in pounds per unit rest-of-the-world good), t the terms of trade (measured in rest-of-the-world good per unit domestic good), and e is the exchange rate measured in pounds per dollar (it is the price of dollars measured in foreign currency). Notice that exports decline when t rises. The domestic interest rate r must equal the world interest rate and hence is exogenous. The other exogenous variables are K, w, p*, G, T, and either M or e. The endogenous variables are Y, N, p, I, C, X, t, and either e or M.

A. Consider a regime in which the government pegs the exchange rate e at some arbitrary level, so that e is exogenous and M is endogenous. In this fixed exchange-rate regime, analyze the effects on the endogenous variables of:

(i) an increase in G;

(ii) an increase in the exchange rate e;

(iii) an increase in w.

B. Consider a flexible exchange rate regime in which the government sets M exogenously and permits e to be endogenous. Analyze the effects on the endogenous variables of:

(i) an increase in G;

(ii) an increase in M;

(iii) an increase in w.

9. What are the units of the following variables: π, w, N, p, Y, C, I, G, K, M, B, (M + B)/p, ((M + B)/p)π?

10. Keynes liked to measure real GNP in terms of "wage units," i.e., he liked to work with the variable pY/w. What are the units of this variable?

11. Some classical economists assert that there can be no such thing as "cost-push" inflation. Discuss.

SOLUTIONS

1. A simple Keynesian model is given by

$$Y = F(N,K) \qquad F_N,\ F_K > 0;\ F_{NN},\ F_{KK} < 0;\ F_{NK} > 0 \tag{1}$$

$$\frac{w}{p} = F_N(N,K) \tag{2}$$

$$I = I(r - \pi) \qquad I' < 0 \tag{3}$$

$$C = c(Y - T) \qquad 0 < c' < 1 \tag{4}$$

$$C + I + G + \delta K = Y \tag{5}$$

$$\frac{M}{p} = m(r,Y) \qquad m_r < 0 < m_Y.$$

Taking total differentials and setting $dK = 0$, obtain:

$$dY = F_N dN \tag{1'}$$

$$\frac{w}{P}\left(\frac{dw}{w} - \frac{dp}{p}\right) = F_{NN}dN, \text{ or } \frac{dw}{w} - \frac{dp}{p} = \frac{F_{NN}}{F_N}\, dN \tag{2'}$$

$$dI = I'dr - I'd\pi \tag{3'}$$

$$dC = c'dY - c'dT \tag{4'}$$

$$dC + dI + dG = dY \tag{5'}$$

$$\frac{M}{p}\left(\frac{dM}{M} - \frac{dp}{p}\right) = m_r dr + m_Y dY. \tag{6'}$$

A. The endogenous variables are Y, N, C, I, r, and M. The exogenous variables are G, T, π, w, p, and K. Note first that (2') is a <u>reduced form</u> for dN. Combining (1') and (2') yields a reduced form for dY:

$$\frac{dw}{w} - \frac{dp}{p} = \frac{F_{NN}}{F_N^2}dY. \tag{A}$$

Solution of (A) for dY and substitution into (4') yields a reduced form for dC:

$$dC = c'\frac{F_N^2}{F_{NN}}(\frac{dw}{w} - \frac{dp}{p}) - c'dT. \tag{B}$$

Use of (A) and (B) in (5') gives a reduced form for dI:

$$dI = \frac{F_N^2}{F_{NN}}(\frac{dw}{w} - \frac{dp}{p}) - c'\frac{F_N^2}{F_{NN}}(\frac{dw}{w} - \frac{dp}{p}) + c'dT - dG$$

$$dI = (1 - c')\frac{F_N^2}{F_{NN}}(\frac{dw}{w} - \frac{dp}{p}) + c'dT - dG. \tag{C}$$

Notice that (C) can be used in (3') to obtain a reduced form for dr which can in turn be used to produce a reduced form for dM from (6').

ANALYSIS:

(i) For $dG > 0$: (2') implies $dN = 0$; (A) implies $dY = 0$; (B) implies $dC = 0$; (C) implies $dI < 0$, or (5') implies $dI = -dG < 0$; (3') implies $dr > 0$; (6') implies $dM < 0$.

(ii) For $dT > 0$: (A) implies $dY = 0$; (1') implies $dN = 0$; (B) implies $dC < 0$; (C) implies $dI > 0$. Notice that (5') implies $dC = -dI$. (3') implies $dr < 0$; (6') implies $dM > 0$.

(iii) For $d\pi > 0$: (A) implies $dY = 0$; (1') implies $dN = 0$; (B) implies $dC = 0$; (C) implies $dI = 0$; (3') implies $dr = d\pi > 0$; (6') implies $dM < 0$.

(iv) For $dw > 0$: (A) implies $dY < 0$; (1') or (2') implies $dN < 0$; (B) implies $dC < 0$; (C) implies $dI < 0$; (3') implies $dr > 0$; (6') implies $dM < 0$.

(v) For $dp > 0$: (A) implies $dY > 0$; (1') or (2') implies $dN > 0$; (B) implies $dC > 0$; (C) implies $dI > 0$; (3') implies $dr < 0$; (6') implies $dM > 0$.

B. The endogenous variables are Y, N, C, I, p and M. The exogenous variables are G, T, π, r, K, and w. Notice that (3') is a reduced form for dI. Now (3'), (4'), (5') combine to yield

$$dG + c'dY - c'dT + I'dr - I'd\pi = dY$$

or

$$\frac{dG}{1 - c'} - \frac{c'dT}{1 - c'} + \frac{I'}{1 - c'}dr - \frac{I'}{1 - c'}d\pi = dY \tag{D}$$

which is a reduced form for dY. Once dY is known (from (D)), (1') yields a reduced form for dN and (A) gives a reduced form for dp. These results, combined with (6'), yield a reduced form for dM.

<u>ANALYSIS</u>:

(i) For $dG > 0$: (D) implies $dY > 0$; (1') implies $dN > 0$; (A) implies $dp > 0$; (4') implies $dC > 0$; (3') implies $dI = 0$; (6') implies $dM > 0$.

(ii) For $dT > 0$: (D) implies $dY < 0$; (1') implies $dN < 0$; (A) implies $dp < 0$; (3') implies $dI = 0$; (4') implies $dC < 0$; (6') implies $dM < 0$.

(iii) For $d\pi > 0$: (3') implies $dI > 0$; (D) implies $dY > 0$; (1') implies $dN > 0$; (A) implies $dp > 0$; (4') implies $dC > 0$; (5') implies $dM > 0$.

(iv) For $dw > 0$: (D) implies $dY = 0$; (1') implies $dN = 0$; (3') implies $dI = 0$; (2') implies $dp > 0$. Notice that $\frac{dp}{p} = \frac{dw}{w}$. (6') implies $dM > 0$.

(v) For $dr > 0$: (D) implies $dY < 0$; (1') implies $dN < 0$; (3') implies $dI < 0$; (4') implies $dC < 0$; (A) implies $dp < 0$; (6') implies $dM < 0$.

* * *

2. A simple classical model is given by

$$Y = F(N,K) \qquad F_N, F_K, F_{NK} > 0; F_{NN}, F_{KK} < 0. \tag{1}$$

$$\frac{w}{p} = F_N(N,K) = \xi \tag{2}$$

$$N = N^s(\frac{w}{p}) \qquad N^{s'} > 0 \tag{3}$$

$$I = I(r - \pi) \qquad I' < 0 \tag{4}$$

$$C = c(Y - T) \qquad 0 < c' < 1 \tag{5}$$

$$C + I + G + \delta K = Y \tag{6}$$

$$\frac{M}{p} = m(r,Y) \qquad m_r < 0, m_Y > 0. \tag{7}$$

Taking total differentials and setting $dK = 0$, obtain:

$$dY = F_N dN \tag{1'}$$

$$\frac{dw}{w} - \frac{dp}{p} = \frac{F_{NN}}{F_N}dN = \frac{d\xi}{F_N} \qquad (\text{since } F_{NN}dN = d\xi) \tag{2'}$$

$$dN = N^{s'}F_N(\frac{dw}{w} - \frac{dp}{p}) = N^{s'}d\xi \tag{3'}$$

$$dI = I'dr - I'd\pi \tag{4'}$$

$$dC = c'dY - c'dT \tag{5'}$$

$$dC + dI + dG = dY \tag{6'}$$

$$\frac{M}{p}(\frac{dM}{M} - \frac{dp}{p}) = m_r dr + m_Y dY. \tag{7'}$$

The endogenous variables are Y, N, C, I, w, r and M. The exogenous variables are G, T, π, p and K. Notice that (2') and (3') combine to yield

$$dN = N^{s'}F_{NN}dN$$

which is uniquely solved by $dN = 0$ if the system was initially in equilibrium. But then (2') implies $\frac{dw}{w} = \frac{dp}{p}$ and (1') implies $dY = 0$.

Then (5') implies $dC = -c'dT$, and (6') implies $-c'dT + I'dr - I'd\pi + dG = 0$. This can be expressed as follows:

$$\frac{dw}{w} = \frac{dp}{p} \tag{A}$$

$$dC = -c'dT \tag{B}$$

$$I'dr = c'dT + I'd\pi - dG. \tag{C}$$

Also notice that (6') implies

$$dI = -dC - dG = c'dT - dG. \tag{D}$$

ANALYSIS:

(i) For $dG > 0$: $dY = dN = 0$. (A) implies $dw = 0$; (B) implies $dC = 0$; (D) implies $dI = -dG < 0$; (C) implies $dr > 0$; (7') implies $dM < 0$.

(ii) For $dT > 0$: $dY = dN = 0$. (A) implies $dw = 0$; (B) implies $dC < 0$; (D) implies $dI > 0$; (C) implies $dr < 0$; (7') implies $dM > 0$.

(iii) For $d\pi > 0$: $dY = dN = 0$. (A) implies $dw = 0$; (B) implies $dC = 0$; (D) implies $dI = 0$; (C) implies $dr = d\pi > 0$; (7') implies $dM < 0$.

(iv) For $dp > 0$: $dY = dN = 0$. (A) implies $dw > 0$; (B) implies $dC = 0$; (C) implies $dr = 0$; (D) implies $dI = 0$; (7') implies $dM > 0$.

* * *

3. The model is:

$$Y = AN^{1.1}/K^{.1} \tag{1}$$

$$N = \beta_0 K\left(\frac{w}{p}\right)^{\beta_1} \tag{2}$$

$$I = I(r) \tag{3}$$

$$C = C(Y - T) \tag{4}$$

$$C + I + G = Y \tag{5}$$

$$M/p = m(r,Y,W) \tag{6}$$

$$W = \frac{M + B}{p} + K. \tag{7}$$

First, note that N can be eliminated from the system by using (2) in (1).

$$Y = A[\beta_0 K(\frac{W}{p})^{\beta_1}]^{1.1}/K^{.1}$$

$$= A[\beta_0(\frac{W}{p})^{\beta_1}]^{1.1}K.$$

Now let $A(\beta_0)^{1.1} = \alpha_0$ and let $\beta_1(1.1) = \alpha_1$. Then

$$Y = \alpha_0(\frac{W}{p})^{\alpha_1}K.$$

Setting dK = 0, we have

$$dY = \frac{\alpha_1 Y}{(w/p)} d(\frac{W}{p}) = \alpha_1 Y(\frac{p}{w})(\frac{W}{p})(\frac{dw}{w} - \frac{dp}{p})$$

$$dY = \alpha_1 Y(\frac{dw}{w} - \frac{dp}{p}).$$

Second, solve (7) for $\frac{M}{p}$ and use this in (6):

$$W - \frac{B}{p} - K = m(r,Y,W);$$

taking the total differential and letting dK = 0, obtain

$$dW - \frac{B}{p}(\frac{dB}{B} - \frac{dp}{p}) = m_r dr + m_Y dY + dW \quad \text{(recall that } m_W = 1).$$

Then

$$\frac{B}{p}(\frac{dp}{p} - \frac{dB}{B}) = m_r dr + m_Y dY,$$

which eliminates M from the system. Third, take the total differentials of the remaining equations ((3),(4) and (5)), setting $dG = dT = dw = 0$. (We are not asked to analyze the effects of changes in G, T, w.) Obtain

$$dY = -\alpha_1 Y\frac{dp}{p} \qquad (\alpha_1 < 0) \tag{A}$$

$$dI = I'dr \tag{B}$$

$$dC = C'dY \tag{C}$$

$$dC + dI = dY \tag{D}$$

$$\frac{B}{p}\left(\frac{dp}{p} - \frac{dB}{B}\right) = m_r dr + m_Y dY. \tag{E}$$

The "IS" curve is given by B, C, and D:

$$C'dY + I'dr = dY$$

$$dr = \frac{1 - C'}{I'}dY$$

which is downward sloping in the (r,Y) plane (since $\frac{dr}{dY} = \frac{1 - C'}{I'} < 0$). The "LB" curve is given by A and E:

$$\frac{B}{p}\left(\frac{-dY}{\alpha_1 Y} - \frac{dB}{B}\right) = m_r dr + m_Y dY,$$

$$\frac{1}{m_r}\left[\left(-m_Y - \frac{B}{p}\frac{1}{\alpha_1 Y}\right)dY - \frac{dB}{p}\right] = dr.$$

The slope of this curve in the (r,Y) plane,

$$\left.\frac{dr}{dY}\right|_{dB=0} = \frac{1}{m_r}\left(-m_Y - \frac{B}{p\alpha_1 Y}\right),$$

is of ambiguous sign. A stability analysis which mimics the one in Section II.2 of the text reveals that the slope of the LB curve must be greater than that of the IS curve. But this leaves open the possibility that the LB curve slopes downward. Moreover, since

$$\left.\frac{dr}{dB}\right|_{dY=0} = -\frac{1}{m_r p} > 0,$$

an increase in B unambiguously shifts the LB curve to the left. The "IS" curve and an upward-sloping "LB" curve are shown in Figure 7.

ANALYSIS:

A. For $dB < 0$: The LB curve shifts right, so $dr < 0$ and $dY > 0$. Then (1) implies that $dN > 0$. (A) implies $dp > 0$. (If the LB curve slopes downward, but is not as steep as the IS curve, these results are reversed.)

B. For $dM > 0$, $dB = 0$: Neither the "IS" or the "LB" curve shifts; no variable which we are considering changes. (Note that $m_W = 1$ in (6): the increase in M increases wealth, but has no other effect.)

C. For $dB > 0$, $dM = 0$: The LB curve shifts left, so $dr > 0$, $dY < 0$ and $dN < 0$. (A) implies $dp < 0$. (If the LB curve slopes downward, but is not as steep as the IS curve, these results are reversed.)

* * *

4. The model is

$$Y = F(N,K) \tag{1}$$

$$\frac{W}{p} = F_N \tag{2}$$

$$N = N(\frac{W}{p}, r - \pi) \tag{3}$$

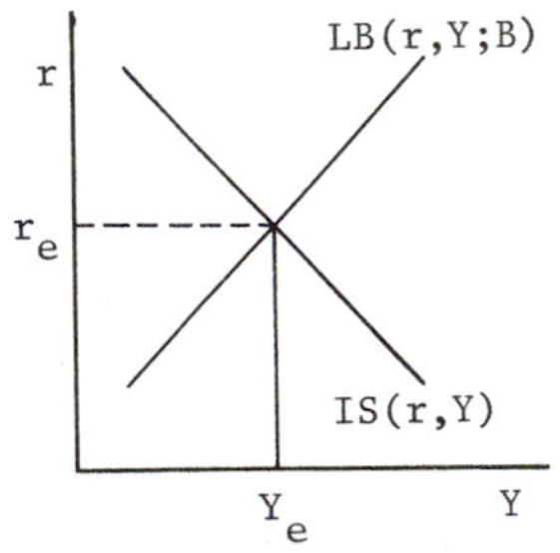

Figure 7

$$I = I(r - \pi) \tag{4}$$

$$C = C(Y - T) \tag{5}$$

$$Y = C + I + G \tag{6}$$

$$\frac{M}{p} = m(r,Y). \tag{7}$$

Taking total differentials and setting $dK = dT = 0$, we have

$$dY = F_N dN \tag{1'}$$

$$d(\frac{W}{p}) = F_{NN} dN \tag{2'}$$

$$dN = N_1 d(\frac{W}{p}) + N_2 dr - N_2 d\pi \qquad (N_1 = N^S_{W/p},\ N_2 = N^S_{r-\pi}) \tag{3'}$$

$$dI = I'dr - I'd\pi \tag{4'}$$

$$dC = C'dY - C'dT \tag{5'}$$

$$dY = dC + dI + dG \tag{6'}$$

$$\frac{M}{p}(\frac{dM}{M} - \frac{dp}{p}) = m_r dr + m_Y dY. \tag{7'}$$

Notice first that (2') and (3') can be reduced to one equation in dN and dr by eliminating $d(\frac{W}{p})$: using (2') and (3'), obtain

$$dN = N_1 F_{NN} dN + N_2 dr - N_2 d\pi$$

or

$$dN = \frac{N_2}{1 - N_1 F_{NN}}(dr - d\pi).$$

This expression can be used in the production function to obtain a relationship between dY and dr:

$$dY = \frac{F_N N_2}{1 - N_1 F_{NN}}(dr - d\pi). \tag{E}$$

This is the total differential of a curve in the (r,Y) plane which we will label $E(r,Y;\ \pi)$. Since $F_N N_2/(1 - N_1 F_{NN}) > 0$, it is upward sloping.

Equations (4'), (5'), and (6') can be combined to yield the familiar IS curve:

$$dY = \frac{I'(dr - d\pi)}{1 - C'} + \frac{1}{1 - C'}dG \qquad \text{(IS)}$$

which is downward sloping in the (r,Y) plane since $I'/(1 - C') < 0$. Increases in G shift this curve to the right. The $E(r,Y;\pi)$ and $IS(r,Y; G,\pi)$ curves are shown together in Figure 8.

ANALYSIS:

A. (1) For $dM > 0$: Neither curve shifts so $dY = dr = 0$. Then (1') implies $dN = 0$; (2') implies $d(\frac{W}{p}) = 0$; (4') implies $dI = 0$; (5') implies $dC = 0$. (7') implies $\frac{dp}{p} = \frac{dM}{M} > 0$, so $\frac{dw}{w} = \frac{dp}{p} = \frac{dM}{M} > 0$.

(2) For $dG > 0$: The IS curve shifts right, so $dY > 0$ and $dr > 0$. Then (1') implies $dN > 0$; (2') implies $d(\frac{W}{p}) < 0$; (4') implies $dI < 0$; (5') implies $dC > 0$; (7') implies the sign of dp is indeterminate.

(3) It will be convenient to find the reduced form for dr. Using the IS curve in $E(r,Y; \pi)$, obtain

$$\left(\frac{I'}{1 - C'} - \frac{F_N N_2}{1 - N_1 F_{NN}}\right)(dr - d\pi) = \frac{-1}{1 - C'}dG.$$

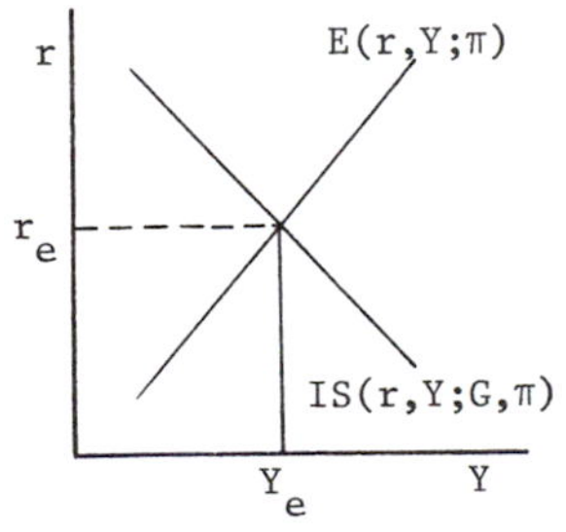

Figure 8

Suppose $d\pi > 0$ and $dG = 0$. Then $dr = d\pi$, so an increase in π leaves the real rate of interest unchanged. Then the IS curve yields $dY = 0$. So (1') implies $dN = 0$; (2') implies $d(\frac{W}{p}) = 0$; (4') implies $dI = 0$; (5') implies $dC = 0$; (7') implies $dP > 0$.

B. Yes. See Macroeconomic Theory, pp. 26-29.

* * *

5. A. Excess demand for money. (Note $r_1 < r_e$ implies $m(r_1,Y_e) > m(r_e,Y_e)$, an excess demand for money.)

B. Excess demand for output. (Note $r_1 < r_e$ implies $C(Y_e) + I(r_1 - \pi) + G > C(Y_e) + I(r_e - \pi) + G$, an excess demand for output.)

C. Yes; there are two distinct constraints at work here, one for stocks, another for flows. Because agents face a (stock) balance sheet constraint, the excess demand for money is offset by excess supplies of bonds and equities:

$$\frac{M^D}{p} - \frac{M}{P} = \frac{B - B^D}{p} + \frac{V - V^D}{p}.$$

Agents also face the (flow) budget constraint

$$C + S = Y_D \ (Y_D = \text{disposable income}).$$

By virtue of this constraint, the excess demand for goods is offset by the excess flow supply of assets:

$$Y_A - Y = [\dot{K} + \frac{\dot{M}}{p} + \frac{\dot{B}}{p} - S].$$

See Section II.7 of Macroeconomic Theory.

* * *

6. Consider the following model,

$$Y = F(N,K) \qquad F_N,\ F_K,\ F_{NK} > 0;\ F_{NN},\ F_{KK} < 0$$

$$\frac{W}{p} = F_N$$

$$I = I(r) \qquad I' < 0$$

$$C = c(Y) \qquad 0 < c' < 1$$

$$C + I + G = Y$$

$$\frac{M}{p} = m(r,Y)$$

in which both money and fiscal policy matter. Further, suppose $\frac{W}{p} = \eta$ (a constant amount of purchasing power). Then $d\eta = d(\frac{W}{p}) = 0$. Then $F_{NN}dN = 0$ (for $dK = 0$). Hence $dY = 0$. Then $dC = 0$. The remaining equations are $dI = I'dr$, $dI + dG = 0$, and $d(\frac{M}{p}) = m_r dr$.

The model is thus reduced to

$$dI = I'dr$$

$$dI = -dG \tag{A}$$

$$d(\frac{M}{p}) = \frac{M}{p}(\frac{dM}{M} - \frac{dp}{p}) = m_r dr$$

so

$$\frac{-dG}{I'} = dr \tag{B}$$

and

$$\frac{M}{p}(\frac{dM}{M} - \frac{dp}{p}) = m_r(\frac{-dG}{I'})$$

so

$$\frac{p^2}{M}(\frac{dM}{p} + \frac{m_r}{I'}dG) = dp. \tag{C}$$

Hence, (B) is the reduced form for r: only changes in G affect r. (A) is the reduced form for I: only changes in G affect I. (C) is the reduced form for p: only changes in M and G affect p. The monetary authority can only affect the price level (and hence, the nominal wage).

* * *

7. Suppose the commodity demand sector equations for this economy are given by

$$I = I(r - \pi) \qquad I' < 0$$

$$C = c(Y) \qquad 0 < c' < 1$$

$$Y = C + I + G.$$

In this case, the constancy of Y and G ensures that I and thus the real rate of interest $r - \pi$ are constant.

A. Now

$$\overline{G} = p^{-1}(dM/dt) = (M/p)M^{-1}(dM/dt)$$

$$= (M/p)(\dot{M}/M).$$

Suppose

$$\frac{M}{p} = m(r,Y).$$

Then

$$\frac{dm(r,y)}{dt} = \dot{m} = \frac{M}{p}\left[\frac{\dot{M}}{M} - \frac{\dot{p}}{p}\right]$$

which implies

$$\frac{\dot{M}}{M} = \frac{\dot{p}}{p} + \frac{\dot{m}}{m}.$$

Since r and Y are both constant, M/p is constant and $\dot{m} = 0$. Since actual and expected inflation are equal, $\dot{p}/p = \pi$. Thus

$$\bar{G} = m(r,Y)\pi.$$

Notice that the nominal rate of interest r can be written

$$r = (r - \pi) + \pi = \rho + \pi,$$

where ρ is the real rate. Thus the above condition becomes

$$\bar{G} = m(\rho + \pi,Y)\pi.$$

Assuming $m_{rr} \leq 0$, the maximum G is found by differentiating this expression with respect to π and setting the result to zero:

$$d\bar{G}/d\pi = m(\rho + \pi,Y) + \pi m_r = 0$$

or

$$1 = -(\pi/m)(\partial m/\partial \pi).$$

Thus to maximize $\bar{G}$, the government should inflate to the point where the inflation elasticity of the demand for real balances is unity.

B. Financing government expenditures becomes more difficult when the "capital controls" are lifted. To see this, denote the nominal foreign money supply ("pounds") by F and the exchange rate (dollars per pound) by e. Then the supply of real balances is $(M + eF)/p$, while the demand continues to be described by $m(r,Y)$. Now

$$\bar{G} = p^{-1}dM/dt = p^{-1}d(pm(r,y) - eF)/dt$$
$$= p^{-1}(p\dot{m} + m\dot{p} - e\dot{F} - \dot{e}F).$$

When r and Y are constant, $\dot{m} = 0$. Suppose also that the foreign money supply is not growing, so that $\dot{F} = 0$. Then

$$\bar{G} = m(\dot{p}/p) - \dot{e}(F/p)$$
$$= m(r,Y)\pi - \dot{e}F/p$$

when $\dot{p}/p = \pi$. When there is depreciation ($\dot{e} > 0$), it is clear that it becomes more difficult to finance expenditures by money creation, as there is now flight to the foreign currency which must be offset.

C. It is clear from the above argument that if the previous maximum $\bar{G}$ can still be financed, the inflation rate necessary to do so will be higher, since now

$$\pi m = \bar{G} + \dot{e}F/p.$$

* * *

8. The model is:

$$Y = F(N,K) \quad (1)$$
$$\frac{w}{p} = F_N \quad (2)$$
$$I = I(r) \quad (3)$$
$$X = X(t) \qquad X' < 0 \quad (4)$$
$$t = (p^*)^{-1}ep \quad (5)$$
$$C = c(Y - T) \quad (6)$$
$$C + I + G + X = Y \quad (7)$$
$$\frac{M}{p} = m(r,Y). \quad (8)$$

Take total differentials, setting $dK = dT = dr = dp^* = 0$ (we are not called upon to analyze the effects of changes in these exogenous variables):

$$dY = F_N dN \tag{1'}$$

$$F_N\left(\frac{dw}{w} - \frac{dp}{p}\right) = F_{NN} dN \tag{2'}$$

$$dI - I'dr = 0 \tag{3'}$$

$$dX = X'dt \tag{4'}$$

$$dt = (p^*)^{-1}(edp + pde) \tag{5'}$$

$$dC = c'dY \tag{6'}$$

$$dC + dG + dI + dX = dY \tag{7'}$$

$$\frac{M}{p}\left(\frac{dM}{M} - \frac{dp}{p}\right) = m_Y dY. \tag{8'}$$

Equations (1') and (2') give (AS), the aggregate supply curve in differential form:

$$dY = -\frac{1}{p}\frac{F_N^2}{F_{NN}}dp + \frac{1}{w}\frac{F_N^2}{F_{NN}}dw; \tag{AS}$$

$$\frac{\partial Y}{\partial p}\bigg|_{AS} = -\frac{1}{p}\frac{F_N^2}{F_{NN}} > 0,$$

so the aggregate supply curve is upward sloping in the (p,Y) plane. Notice also that

$$\frac{\partial Y}{\partial w}\bigg|_{AS} = \frac{1}{w}\frac{F_N^2}{F_{NN}} < 0$$

so increases in w shift the AS curve left. If M is exogenous, (8') is one equation (call it PB) in dY and dp:

$$\frac{\partial Y}{\partial p}\bigg|_{PB} = \frac{-M}{m_Y p^2} < 0,$$

so the PB curve is downward sloping in the (p,Y) plane. Notice also that

$$\frac{\partial Y}{\partial M}\bigg|_{PB} = \frac{1}{m_Y p} > 0$$

so increases in M shift the PB curve right.

When M is exogenous, one uses (AS) and (PB) to determine equilibrium. The AS and PB curves are shown together in Figure 9.

When e is exogenous, (3') thru (7') give a sort of aggregate demand curve as follows: Note that (3') implies $dI = 0$, while (4') and (5') yield

$$dX = \frac{X'}{p*}(edp + pde).$$

Use this and (6') and (7') to obtain (AD'):

$$c'dY + dG + \frac{X'}{p*}(edp + pde) = dY$$

or

$$\frac{dG}{1 - c'} + \frac{X'e}{(1 - c')p*}dp + \frac{X'p}{(1 - c')p*}de = dY; \qquad \text{(AD')}$$

$$\left.\frac{\partial Y}{\partial p}\right|_{AD'} = \frac{X'e}{(1 - c')p*} < 0$$

so the AD' curve is downward sloping in the (p,Y) plane. Notice also that

$$\left.\frac{\partial Y}{\partial G}\right|_{AD'} = 1/(1 - c') > 0$$

so increases in G shift (AD') to the right, and

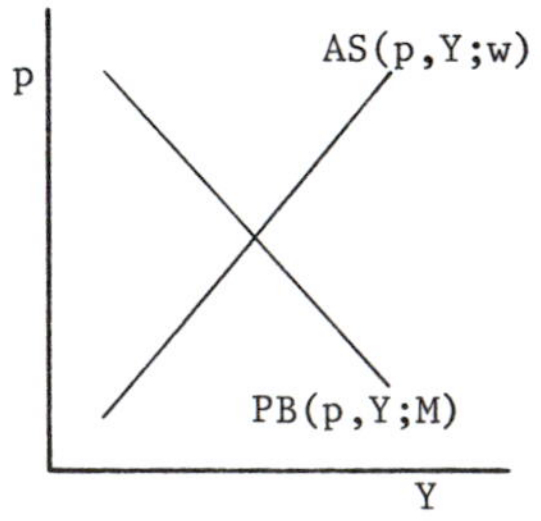

Figure 9

$$\frac{\partial Y}{\partial e}\bigg|_{AD'} = \frac{X'p}{(1 - c')p^*} < 0$$

so increases in e shift (AD') to the left. When e is exogenous, one uses (AS) and (AD') to determine equilibrium. The AS and AD' curves are shown together in Figure 10.

ANALYSIS:

A. For e exogenous, use Figure 10.

(i) For $dG > 0$: (AD') shifts right, so $dp > 0$ and $dY > 0$. (1') implies $dN > 0$; (6') implies $dC > 0$ and $dC < dY$; (8') implies $dM > 0$; (5') implies $dt > 0$; (4') implies $dX < 0$.

(ii) For $de > 0$: (AD') shifts left, so $dp < 0$ and $dY < 0$. (1') implies $dN < 0$; (6') implies $dC < 0$; (5') implies $dt > 0$; (7') implies $dX < 0$; (8') implies $dM < 0$.

(iii) For $dw > 0$: (AS) shifts left, so $dp > 0$ and $dY < 0$. (1') implies $dN < 0$; (6') implies $dC < 0$; (5') implies $dt > 0$; (4') implies $dX < 0$; (8') implies the sign of dM is indeterminate.

B. For M exogenous, use Figure 9.

(i) For $dG > 0$: Neither curve shifts, so $dp = dY = 0$. (1') implies $dN = 0$; (6') implies $dC = 0$; (7') implies $dX < 0$; (4') implies $dt > 0$; (5') implies $de > 0$.

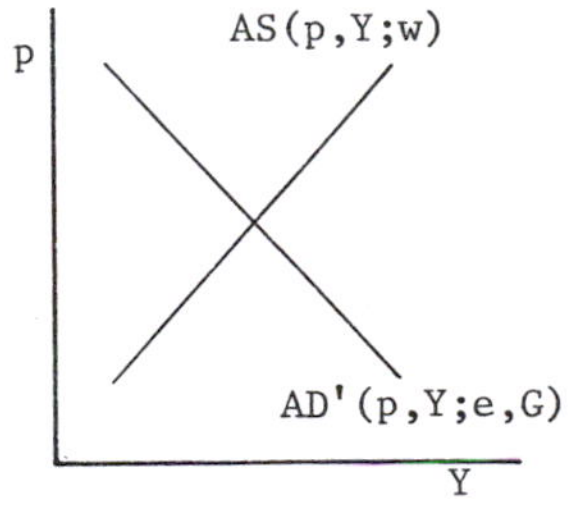

Figure 10

(ii) For $dM > 0$: (PB) shifts right, so $dp > 0$ and $dY > 0$. (1') implies $dN > 0$; (6') implies $dC > 0$ and $dC < dY$; (7') implies $dX > 0$; (4') implies $dt < 0$; (5') implies $de < 0$.

(iii) For $dw > 0$: (AS) shifts left, so $dp > 0$ and $dY < 0$. (1') implies $dN < 0$; (6') implies $dY < dC < 0$; (7') implies $dX < 0$; (4') implies $dt > 0$; (5') implies the sign of de is indeterminate.

* * *

9. The units are as follows.

Variable	Units
π	Pure number per unit time
w	(Dollars per person) per unit time
N	Persons
p	Dollars per good
Y	Goods per unit time
C	Goods per unit time
I	Goods per unit time
G	Goods per unit time
K	Goods
M	Dollars
B	Dollars
$\frac{M + B}{p}$	Goods
$\frac{M + B}{p}\pi$	Goods per unit time

* * *

10. The units are:

$$\frac{pY}{w} = \frac{\$}{\text{good}} \cdot \frac{\text{good}}{\text{time}} \cdot \frac{1}{\frac{\$}{\text{person} \cdot \text{time}}} = \text{persons.}$$

* * *

11. Consider the simple classical model

$$Y = F(N,K) \qquad F_{NN}, F_{KK} < 0 < F_N, F_K, F_{KN} \tag{1}$$

$$w/p = F_N \tag{2}$$

$$N = N^S(w/p) \qquad N^{S'} > 0 \tag{3}$$

$$I = I(r) \qquad I' < 0 \tag{4}$$

$$C = c(Y) \tag{5}$$

$$C + I + G = Y \tag{6}$$

$$\frac{M}{p} = m(r,Y) \qquad m_r < 0 < m_Y. \tag{7}$$

The exogenous variables are K, G, and M, while the endogenous variables are Y, N, p, w, I, C and r. Equations (1), (2), and (3) determine Y and N. The aggregate supply curve is vertical. Equations (4), (5), (6), and (7) give rise to an aggregate demand curve which is downward sloping in the (p,Y) plane. "Inflation" (taken, here, to be a jump in p at a point in time) only occurs when one of the exogenous aggregate demand variables, M or G, is increased. Since there is no exogenous variable z associated with the aggregate supply curve such that $dY/dz < 0$, there is no "supply side" inflation. Mechanically, there is no "cost-push" inflation in this model. The real reason classical economists can make this assertion is that "cost-push" inflation is supposed to be caused by exogenous increases in prices of factors of production--phenomena which can occur only when markets are not perfect. But the basic tenet of the classical model is that markets <u>do</u> clear: evidence is found in (3).

"Cost-push" inflation occurs in a Keynesian model when the (exogenous) money wage is increased.

CHAPTER III

TOBIN'S DYNAMIC AGGREGATIVE MODEL

EXERCISES

1. Consider an economy described by the following equations:

$$Y = F(K,N) \qquad \text{with } F_K, F_N, F_{KN} > 0; F_{NN}, F_{KK} < 0$$

$$\frac{w}{p} = F_N$$

$$r = F_K$$

$$C = C(Y - T) \qquad \text{with } 0 < C' < 1$$

$$Y = C + I + G$$

$$\frac{M}{p} = H(r, C + I) \qquad \text{with } H_r < 0, H_{C+I} > 0.$$

Here Y is GNP, N employment, K capital, w the money wage, p the price level, C consumption, I investment, T taxes net of transfers, G government purchases, and M the money supply. The exogenous variables are K, M, G, T, and w. The endogenous variables are Y, N, C, I, r, and p. Describe the effects on all six endogenous variables of:

A. an increase in M achieved via an open-market operation;

B. an increase in T;

C. an increase in G.

2. Consider an economy described by the following equations:

$$Y = F(K, N) \qquad \text{with } F_K, F_N, F_{KN} > 0 > F_{NN}, F_{KK} \text{ (production function)}$$

$\frac{w}{p} = F_N$ (marginal equality for employment)

$r = F_K$ (marginal equality for capital)

$C = C(Y_D)$ with $0 < C' < 1$ (consumption function)

$Y_D = Y - T$

$C + I + G = Y$

$\frac{M}{p} = m(r, Y_D)$ with $m_r < 0$, $m_{Y_D} > 0$ (portfolio equilibrium condition).

The endogenous variables are:

Y = GNP	C = consumption
N = employment	r = interest rate
p = the price level	Y_D = disposable income
I = investment	

The exogenous variables are:

K = the capital stock	M = the money stock, a liability of the government
w = the money wage	
T = tax collections	G = government expenditures

Describe the effects on the endogenous variables of:

A. an increase in the money wage;

B. an increase in government expenditure;

C. an increase in tax collections.

SOLUTIONS

1. The model is given by

$$Y = F(K,N) \qquad F_K, F_N, F_{KN} > 0;\ F_{NN}, F_{KK} < 0 \tag{1}$$

$$\frac{w}{p} = F_N \tag{2}$$

$$r = F_K \tag{3}$$

$$C = C(Y - T) \qquad 0 < C' < 1 \tag{4}$$

$$Y = C + I + G \tag{5}$$

$$\frac{M}{p} = H(r, C + I) \qquad H_r < 0,\ H_{C+I} > 0. \tag{6}$$

Note that substituting (5) into (6) gives

$$\frac{M}{p} = H(r, Y - G).$$

Take total differentials and set $dK = dw = 0$ to obtain

$$dY = F_N dN \tag{1'}$$

$$d\left(\frac{w}{p}\right) = F_{NN}dN = F_N\left(\frac{dw}{w} - \frac{dp}{p}\right) = -\frac{F_N}{p}dp \tag{2'}$$

$$dr = F_{KN}dN \tag{3'}$$

$$dC = C'dY - C'dT \tag{4'}$$

$$dY = dC + dI + dG \tag{5'}$$

$$\frac{M}{p}\left(\frac{dM}{M} - \frac{dp}{p}\right) = H_r dr + H_2 dY - H_2 dG. \tag{6'}$$

Equations (1') and (3') give the KE curve:

$$dr = \frac{F_{KN}}{F_N}dY. \tag{KE}$$

Since $\left.\frac{\partial r}{\partial Y}\right|_{KE} = \frac{F_{KN}}{F_N} > 0$, the KE curve is upward sloping in the (r,Y) plane. Equation (2') yields

$$- \frac{dp}{p} = \frac{F_{NN}}{F_N} dN$$

which can be rewritten (using (1')) as

$$- \frac{dp}{p} = \frac{F_{NN}}{F_N^2} dY. \tag{7}$$

Equation (7) can be used in (6') to obtain the differential of the LM' curve:

$$\frac{M}{p}\left(\frac{dM}{M} + \frac{F_{NN}}{F_N^2} dY\right) = H_r dr + H_2 dY - H_2 dG$$

or

$$\frac{1}{H_r}\left[\frac{M}{p}\frac{dM}{M} + \left(\frac{M}{p}\frac{F_{NN}}{F_N^2} - H_2\right)dY + H_2 dG\right] = dr. \tag{LM'}$$

Note that

$$\frac{\partial r}{\partial Y}\bigg|_{LM'} = \frac{1}{H_r}\left(\frac{M}{p}\frac{F_{NN}}{F_N^2} - H_2\right) > 0,$$

so the LM' curve is also upward sloping in the (r,Y) plane. In addition,

$$\frac{\partial r}{\partial M}\bigg|_{LM'} = \frac{1}{H_r p} < 0,$$

so the LM' curve shifts right with increases in M, and

$$\frac{\partial r}{\partial G}\bigg|_{LM'} = \frac{H_2}{H_r} < 0,$$

so the LM' curve shifts right as G increases. The LM' and KE curves are shown together in Figure 3. The LM' curve is assumed to be steeper than the KE curve to assure stability of the system.

ANALYSIS:

A. If $dM > 0$ and $dM = -dB$, then the LM' curve shifts right, so $dY > 0$ and $dr > 0$. (1') implies $dN > 0$; (2') implies $dp > 0$; (4') implies $dC > 0$ and $dC < dY$; (5') implies $dI > 0$.

B. If $dT > 0$, neither curve shifts and $dY = dr = 0$. (1') implies $dN = 0$; (2') implies $dp = 0$; (4') implies $dC < 0$; (5') implies $dI > 0$.

C. If $dG > 0$, then the LM' curve shifts right, so $dY > 0$ and $dr > 0$. (1') implies $dN > 0$; (2') implies $dp > 0$; (4') implies $dC > 0$ and $dC < dY$; (5') implies that the sign of dI is indeterminate.

* * *

2. The model is given by

$$Y = F(N,K) \qquad F_K,\ F_N,\ F_{KN} > 0;\ F_{NN},\ F_{KK} < 0 \tag{1}$$

$$\frac{W}{P} = F_N \tag{2}$$

$$r = F_K \tag{3}$$

$$C = C(Y_D) \qquad 0 < C' < 1 \tag{4}$$

$$Y_D = Y - T \tag{5}$$

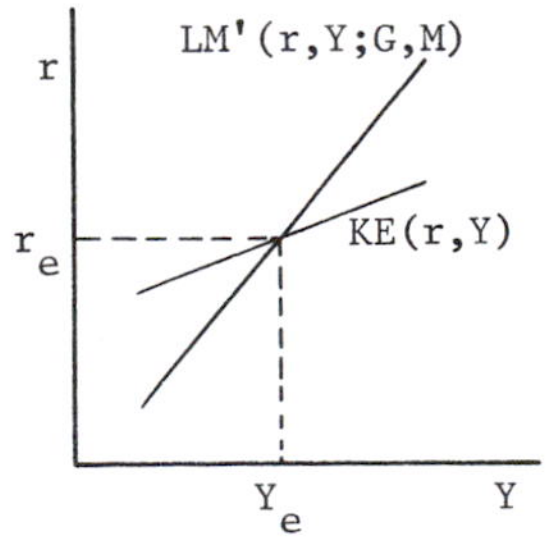

Figure 3

$$C + I + G = Y \tag{6}$$

$$\frac{M}{p} = m(r, Y_D) \qquad m_r < 0,\ m_{Y_D} > 0. \tag{7}$$

Take total differentials and set dK = 0 to obtain

$$dY = F_N dN \tag{1'}$$

$$F_N\left(\frac{dw}{w} - \frac{dp}{p}\right) = F_{NN} dN \tag{2'}$$

$$dr = F_{KN} dN \tag{3'}$$

$$dC = C' dY_D = C' dY - C' dT \tag{4'}$$

$$dY_D = dY - dT \tag{5'}$$

$$dC + dI + dG = dY \tag{6'}$$

$$\frac{M}{p}\left(\frac{dM}{M} - \frac{dp}{p}\right) = m_r dr + m_{Y_D} dY_D = m_r dr + m_{Y_D}(dY - dT). \tag{7'}$$

Equations (1') and (3') give the KE curve:

$$dr = \frac{F_{KN}}{F_N} dY. \tag{KE}$$

The KE curve is upward-sloping in the (r,Y) plane. Equations (1'), (2'), and (7') give the LM curve: (1') and (2') yield

$$\frac{dw}{w} - \frac{dp}{p} = \frac{F_{NN}}{F_N^2} dY.$$

Use this result in (7') to obtain:

$$\frac{M}{p}\left(\frac{dM}{M} + \frac{F_{NN}}{F_N^2} dY - \frac{dw}{w}\right) = m_r dr + m_{Y_D} dY - m_{Y_D} dT$$

or

$$\frac{1}{m_r}\left[\frac{dM}{p} - \left(\frac{M}{p}\right)\frac{dw}{w} + \left(\frac{M}{p}\frac{F_{NN}}{F_N^2} - m_{Y_D}\right)dY + m_{Y_D} dT\right] = dr. \tag{LM}$$

Note that

$$\frac{\partial r}{\partial Y}\bigg|_{LM} = (m_r)^{-1}\left(\frac{M}{p}\frac{F_{NN}}{F_N^2} - m_{Y_D}\right) > 0$$

so the LM curve is upward sloping in the (r,Y) plane. Note also that

$$\frac{\partial r}{\partial M}\bigg|_{LM} = (m_r p)^{-1} < 0$$

so the LM curve shifts right with increases in M,

$$\frac{\partial r}{\partial w}\bigg|_{LM} = -M(m_r wp)^{-1} > 0$$

so the LM curve shifts left with increases in w, and

$$\frac{\partial r}{\partial T}\bigg|_{LM} = m_{Y_D}(m_r)^{-1} < 0$$

so the LM curve shifts right with increases in T. The LM and KE curves are shown together in Figure 4 under the usual stability assumption that the LM curve is sloped more steeply than the KE curve.

ANALYSIS:

A. If $dw > 0$, the LM curve shifts left, so $dY < 0$ and $dr < 0$. (1') implies $dN < 0$; (4') implies $dY_D < 0$ and $dC < 0$; (6') implies $dI < 0$. The sign of dp is indeterminate.

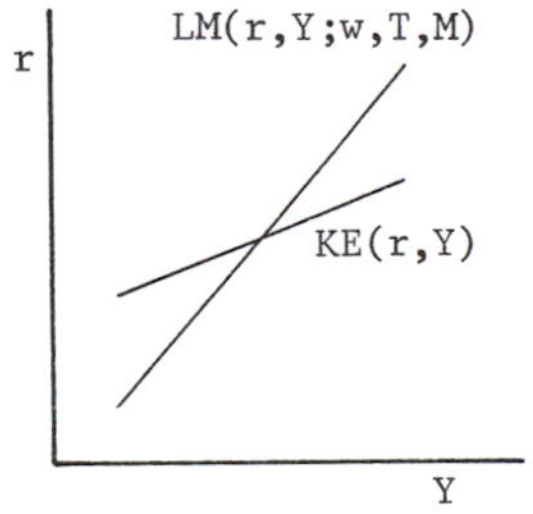

Figure 4

B. If $dG > 0$, neither curve shifts, so $dY = dr = 0$. (1') implies $dN = 0$; (2') implies $dp = 0$; (4') implies $dC = 0$; (5') implies $dY_D = 0$; (6') implies $dI = -dG$.

C. If $dT > 0$, the LM curve shifts right, so $dr > 0$ and $dY > 0$. (1') implies $dN > 0$; (2') implies $dp > 0$. The signs of dY_D, dC, and dI depend on unspecified assumptions about the magnitudes of

$$\frac{F_{KN}}{F_N} \quad \text{and} \quad \frac{m_{Y_D}}{m_r}\left[\frac{M}{p}\left(\frac{F_{NN}}{F_N^2}\right) - m_{Y_D}\right]^{-1}.$$

CHAPTER V

DYNAMIC ANALYSIS OF A KEYNESIAN MODEL

EXERCISES

1. Under both adaptive expectations and perfect foresight, perform a dynamic analysis of Tobin's dynamic aggregative model, formed by substituting for Equation (3) the equation

$$r + \delta - \pi = f(\lambda) - \lambda f'(\lambda).$$

Now instantaneous equilibrium occurs at the intersection of the KE and LM curves, while steady-state equilibrium occurs at the intersection of the KE curve and y^* line.

2. For both adaptive expectations and perfect foresight, analyze the dynamics of the model when the Phillips curve is modified to assume the form

$$\frac{\dot{w}}{w} = h\left(\frac{N}{N^S}\right) + \alpha\pi, \qquad h' > 0,\ h(1) = 0,\ 0 < \alpha < 1.$$

SOLUTIONS

1. The model is

$$y = f(\lambda) \qquad \lambda=\lambda(y),\ \lambda'=1/f',\ f' > 0,\ f'' < 0 \tag{1}$$

$$\frac{w}{p} = f'(\lambda) \tag{2}$$

$$r + \delta - \pi = f(\lambda) - \lambda f'(\lambda) \tag{3}$$

$$c = z(y - \tilde{t} - \delta) \tag{4}$$

$$y = c + i + g + \delta \tag{5}$$

$$\frac{M}{pK} = m(r,y) \tag{6}$$

$$\frac{\dot{w}}{w} = h\left(\frac{N}{N^s}\right) + \pi \tag{7}$$

$$\frac{\dot{N}^s(t)}{N^s(t)} = n \tag{8}$$

$$K(t) = K(\tau) + \int_\tau^t i(s)K(s)ds \tag{9}$$

$$\dot{\pi} = \beta\left(\frac{\dot{p}}{p} - \pi\right) \qquad \beta > 0. \tag{10}$$

The exogenous variables are $w(\tau)$, $\pi(\tau)$, $K(\tau)$, and $M(t)$, $g(t)$, $\tilde{t}(t)$, for $t \geq \tau$. Set $\delta = \tilde{t} = 0$ for convenience. The steady-state output-capital ratio, y^*, is given by $y^* = c + n + g$, or

$$y^* = \frac{(n + g)}{1 - z}.$$

Using $\lambda = \lambda(y)$ in (3), the KE curve is given by

$$r - \pi = y - \frac{\lambda}{\lambda'}. \tag{KE}$$

Along this schedule,

$$\frac{\partial r}{\partial y} = 1 - \left[\frac{(\lambda')^2 - \lambda\lambda''}{(\lambda')^2}\right] = \frac{\lambda\lambda''}{\lambda'\lambda'} > 0.$$

Thus (KE) slopes upward in the (r,y) plane. Notice further that $\frac{\partial r}{\partial \pi} = 1$

along KE.

To derive the LM curve, solve (2) for p, use the result in (6), and rearrange to get

$$\frac{M}{wK} = \lambda'(y)m(r,y). \tag{LM}$$

Along this schedule, $\frac{\partial r}{\partial y} > 0$ so the LM curve slopes upward. Further, $\frac{\partial y}{\partial M} > 0$, so the LM curve shifts right with increases in M. As in Chapter III, assume the LM curve is steeper than the KE curve.

Starting from a steady state in which $\frac{\dot{M}}{M} - n = \frac{\dot{p}}{p} = \frac{\dot{w}}{w} = 0$, consider the consequences of an increase in M which leaves $\frac{\dot{M}}{M}$ unaltered. Assume for the moment that $\beta = \pi = 0$, and that g is constant. Thus expectations are "naively adaptive," and the central authorities adjust G to compensate for any changes in K: $\frac{d}{dt}(\frac{G}{K}) = 0$. An unexpected increase in M shifts the LM curve right, so the momentary r and y exceed the steady-state values of r and y. Notice that the increase in M does not affect the KE curve. Notice further that di = dy - dc - dg = (1 - z)dy > 0. Thus,

$$\dot{r}\Big|_{\substack{LM \\ \dot{y}=0}} = \frac{m}{m_r}\left(\frac{\dot{M}}{M} - i - \frac{\dot{w}}{w}\right)$$

is positive since now $i > n = \dot{M}/M$ and $dy > 0$ implies $d\lambda > 0$ which implies $dN = Kd\lambda + \lambda dK = Kd\lambda > 0$ and $N > N^S$ so $\dot{w}/w = h(N/N^S) > 0$. Thus, the LM curve moves upward (left) through time. Now consider the first instant at which the momentary equilibrium interest rate coincides with the steady-state one: $\dot{M}/M = n = i$, but while λ is back to its steady state level, $N/N^S = \lambda K/N^S$ exceeds unity since K has grown at a rate i which exceeded the growth rate n of N^S ever since the increase in M. Thus, at this "first crossing," $\dot{w}/w = h(N/N^S) > 0$ and the LM curve continues to move left. Assuming that the system is dynamically stable, r and y initially increase in response to the increase in M, and then display damped oscillations about their steady-state levels.

As was the case with the Keynesian model, the analysis is much more complicated when $\beta > 0$. However, the comments in the last few paragraphs of Section V.1 of Macroeconomic Theory apply. The LM curve will now be shifting toward an intersection at y^* with a KE curve associated with a positive rate of expected inflation. When the KE and LM curves intersect at y^*, wages will be rising even faster than they would have been had π been zero throughout. Assuming dynamic stability (notice π must fall and eventually become negative for a time), the final resting place for all variables will be the same as if π had been zero throughout.

Under perfect foresight, the analysis in Section V.2 of Macroeconomic Theory applies: history determines N at each point in time. Thus λ is inherited from the past, as is Y. Given Y, C is determined by $C = zY$, and, given g, $i = y - c - g$. Since w is fixed at a point in time, p is given by $w\lambda' = p$. Then r is given implicitly by $\frac{M}{pK} = m(r,y)$. Notice that under perfect foresight, surprise changes in M do not affect output at a point in time.

* * *

2. The introduction of $\alpha < 1$ into the Phillips curve does not change the dynamic analysis of the model under the "naive" adaptive expectations hypothesis $\beta = 0$ ($\pi = 0$ throughout, starting from "correctly" expected $\dot{p}/p = 0$ as in the text).

Under the general adaptive expectations assumption ($\beta > 0$), the analysis is much like that which appears near the end of Section V.1 of Macroeconomic Theory. However, with $0 < \alpha < 1$, the "overshooting" mentioned there will be muted: at the moment of the first intersection of the IS and LM curves at y^*, wages are rising more rapidly than they were with $\beta = 0$, but not as rapidly as they were with $\alpha = 1$. The dynamic path of the system could be very different from that associated with $\beta = 0$ or $\alpha = 1$, but assuming dynamic stability, the final resting place will not be different.

Under rational expectations and $\alpha = 1$, the Phillips curve could be treated like a labor supply curve; the model certainly has classical properties. But $\alpha \neq 1$ amounts to a suspension of the "natural rate:" agents respond to absolute, as well as relative price changes. One would suspect that the Keynesian properties of the model would be preserved in this case. Indeed, the labor demand and Phillips curves combine to yield

$$h\left(\frac{\lambda K}{N^S}\right) = \frac{f''(\lambda)}{f'(\lambda)}\dot{\lambda}(t) - (1 - \alpha)\frac{\dot{p}}{p},$$

a first-order non-homogeneous differential equation forced by the endogenous variable $\frac{\dot{p}}{p}$. Thus λ is not completely determined by past K and N^S and is therefore free to jump at a point in time; Keynesian properties are preserved. See also Chapter XVII, Exercise 1.

CHAPTER VIII

IMPLICIT LABOR CONTRACTS AND STICKY WAGES

EXERCISE

(Work sharing) In the setup above, each worker must work $L_1 - L_0$ in either state 1 or 2. So no shortening of hours per man was permitted, only layoffs in state 2. Suppose instead that the firm offers jobs to n(1) workers <u>all</u> of whom work $L_1 - L_0$ hours in state 1 but only $\alpha(L_1 - L_0)$ hours in state 2 where $\alpha < 1$.

A. Describe how α, w(1) and w(2) are determined.

B. Would this arrangement be better or worse than the setup in the text? Are there any incentives for the arrangement of this problem to emerge and replace the setup of the text? (Hint: given an exogenous, market-determined level of workers' expected utility, calculate the firm's expected profits under each kind of policy.)

SOLUTION

A. Given the $n(1)$ workers who are "tied" to the firm in state 1, the firm chooses an employment "contract" $(\alpha, w(\theta))$ to maximize its expected profits,

$$\pi(1)[p(1)f(n(1)) - w(1)n(1)] + \pi(2)[p(2)f(\alpha n(1)) - w(2)\alpha n(1)]$$

subject to a given, market-determined level of expected utility for workers. Notice that $n(1)$ and $\alpha n(1)$ represent worker "days," while $w(1)$ and $w(2)$ are "daily" wages.

Given $n(1)$, the "sharing factor" α and the state-contingent wages $w(1)$ and $w(2)$ are given by the solution to

$$\max_{\{\alpha, w(1), w(2)\}} \Big[\pi(1)\big(p(1)f[n(1)] - w(1)n(1)\big) + \pi(2)\big(p(2)f[\alpha n(1)] - w(2)\alpha n(1)\big) + \mu(\bar{v} - \pi(1)g[w(1), L_0] - \pi(2)g[\alpha w(2), (1 - \alpha)(L_1 - L_0) + L_0])\Big]$$

where $\bar{v}$ is the market-determined level of workers' expected utility and μ is a Lagrange multiplier. As in the text, $p(1) > p(2)$ gives rise to an interior solution for α, so the inequality constraint $\alpha < 1$ has been dropped. The first-order conditions for a maximum are

$$\alpha:\quad 0 = \pi(2)\big(p(2)f'[\alpha n(1)]n(1) - w(2)n(1)\big) - \mu\pi(2)\big(w(2)g_1[\alpha w(2), (1 - \alpha)(L_1 - L_0) + L_0] - (L_1 - L_0)g_2[\alpha w(2), (1 - \alpha)(L_1 - L_0) + L_0]\big)$$

$$w(1):\quad 0 = -\pi(1)n(1) - \mu\pi(1)g_1[w(1), L_0])$$

$$w(2):\quad 0 = -\pi(2)\alpha n(1) - \mu\pi(2)\alpha g_1[\alpha w(2), (1 - \alpha)(L_1 - L_0) + L_0]$$

$$\mu: \quad 0 = \bar{v} - \pi(1)g[w(1),L_0] - \pi(2)g[\alpha w(2),(1 - \alpha)(L_1 - L_0) + L_0].$$

The marginal conditions for w(1) and w(2) can be combined to yield

$$g_1[w(1), L_0] = g_1[\alpha w(2), (1 - \alpha)(L_1 - L_0) + L_0].$$

Given that $g_{12} > 0$ (a higher wage is more valuable the more leisure time one has)

$$g_1(w(1), L_0) > g_1(\alpha w(2), L_0).$$

Since $g_{11} < 0$, $w(1) < \alpha w(2) < w(2)$; wages are state-dependent. Moreover, wages are countercyclical, higher in state 2 ("bad times") than in state 1 ("good times"). Notice, however, that if $g_{12} < 0$ (consumption and leisure are direct substitutes in utility), wages will be procyclical.*

B. Both firms and workers could be better off under work sharing. To see the source of the possibility for improvement, suppose the firm contemplates a move from the layoff regime to the work sharing regime. Suppose further that the wage in state 1 is kept the same under the two regimes, and that $\alpha = \frac{n(2)}{n(1)}$, where n(1) and n(2) are the state-dependent employment levels from the layoff regime. Then in order that workers be indifferent between the two regimes,

$$\alpha g[w(2),L_0] + (1 - \alpha)g[0,L_1] = g[\alpha w^s(2),\alpha L_0 + (1 - \alpha)L_1]$$

where $w^s(2)$ is the state 2 work-sharing daily wage. Since g is concave, $w^s(2) < w(2)$. Thus, while expected revenues are the same under the two regimes, the expected wage bill is smaller under work sharing because

---

*For more on this point and an excellent survey and discussion of implicit contract models, see Sherwin Rosen, "Implicit Contracts: A Survey," Journal of Economic Literature 23, (September 1985): 1144-1175.

the wage in state 2 is smaller. Of course, the firm can in general do even better by moving along the other margins (for α, $w^s(1)$, and $n^s(1)$) as well.

Since any firm can keep its workers happy while at the same time improve its own lot by moving to work sharing, one would expect to see such a regime replace the layoff setup of the text. However, a number of factors might work against the emergence of work sharing. For example, workers' preferences might be such that smooth time paths for leisure are far inferior to "lumpy" ones (e.g., long weekends, seasonal vacations). Also, the firm might bear costs associated with the <u>size</u> of the workforce. These would make work sharing more costly relative to layoffs.

CHAPTER IX

DIFFERENCE EQUATIONS AND LAG OPERATORS

EXERCISES

1. Verify that the presence of both lagged employment and future values of w_t and a_t on the right-hand side of the employment decision rule (55) (demand schedule) depends on having the adjustment cost parameter d strictly positive. (Set d = 0 and rework the firm's optimum problem.)

2. Determine the effect of an increase in d on the speed of adjustment parameters λ_1 and λ_2. Does a firm facing a small d adjust its labor force more or less quickly in response to current conditions than a firm facing a larger value of d? (Hint: use Figure 4.)

3. (A Keynesian investment schedule) A firm chooses a sequence of capital $\{k_{t+j}\}_{j=0}^{\infty}$ to maximize

$$v_t = \sum_{j=0}^{\infty} b^j \{a_0 k_{t+j} - \frac{a_1}{2} k_{t+j}^2 - J_{t+j}(k_{t+j} - k_{t+j-1}) - \frac{d}{2}(k_{t+j} - k_{t+j-1})^2\},$$

given $k_{t-1} > 0$, where a_0, a_1, $d > 0$ and where $\{J_{t+j}\}_{j=0}^{\infty}$ is a known sequence of the price of capital relative to the price of the firm's output. The sequence $\{J_{t+j}\}_{j=0}^{\infty}$ is of exponential order less than 1/b, where $0 < b < 1$ is the discount factor (the reciprocal of one plus the real rate of interest).

A. Derive the Euler equations and the transversality condition.

B. Show that the optimum decision rule of the firm is of the form

$$k_{t+j+1} = \lambda_1 k_{t+j} + c_0 + \frac{c_1}{1 - \lambda_2^{-1}L^{-1}}(bJ_{t+j+2} - J_{t+j+1}),$$

where $0 < \lambda_1 < 1 < \lambda_2$, and c_0 and c_1 are constants. Find c_0 and c_1; show how to find λ_1 and λ_2; and prove that the λ's obey the inequalities just stated.

4. (Keynesian stabilization policy) The reduced form for GNP (Y) is

$$Y_t = \alpha + BS_t + cg_t, \qquad B > 0,\ c > 0,$$

where g is government purchases and S_t is exports, an exogenous variable outside the government's control. The sequence of exports $\{S_t\}_{t=0}^{\infty}$ is of exponential order less than $1/b$ where $0 < b < 1$. Suppose that the government sets g_t to minimize the loss function

$$T = \sum_{t=0}^{\infty} b^t\{(Y_t - Y_t^*)^2 + d(g_t - g_{t-1})^2\}, \qquad d \geq 0,$$

where $\{Y_t^*\}_{t=0}^{\infty}$ is a target sequence of GNPs that is of exponential order less than $1/b$, and d is non-negative and measures the cost of changing the setting of g from its previous value.

A. Derive an optimal rule for setting g_t under the assumption that $d = 0$.

B. Derive the optimal rule for setting g_t under the assumption that $d > 0$.

5. (Cass-Koopmans optimum growth problem) A planner wants to choose (consumption, capital) sequences that maximize

$$\sum_{t=0}^{\infty} \beta^t (u_0 c_t - \frac{u_1}{2} c_t^2), \qquad u_0, u_1 > 0$$

subject to $c_t + k_{t+1} \leq f_0 k_t$, where k_0 is given and satisfies $0 < k_0 < (u_0/u_1)[1/(f_0 - 1)]$. Here c_t is per capita consumption and k_t is per capita capital. Assume that $f_0 > 1/\beta > 1$, where β is the discount factor. The planner imposes the side condition that the $\{k_t\}$ sequence be bounded. (Actually, all we need is that k_t be required to be nonnegative, but boundedness does the job and is easier to handle technically.)

A. Find the Euler equation and the transversality condition. Interpret the transversality condition. (Hint: use the constraint to eliminate c_t from the objective function and differentiate with respect to successive k's.)

B. Solve the Euler equation for the steady state value of k, say $\bar{k}$. Find the steady-state value of $\bar{c}$. (Hint: you should get

$$\bar{k} = (\frac{1}{f_0 - 1})\frac{u_0}{u_1}, \qquad \bar{c} = \frac{u_0}{u_1}.)$$

Interpret the steady-state value of $\bar{c}$.

C. Show that the optimal feedback rule for setting k is

$$k_{t+1} = \frac{1}{f_0 \beta} k_t - (\frac{1}{f_0 - 1})(\frac{u_0}{u_1}(\frac{1}{\beta f_0} - 1)). \qquad (*)$$

(Hint: Solve the Euler equation.) Does this solution satisfy the transversality condition? If you had solved the "other" root backward, rather than forward, would the transversality condition be satisfied?

D. Prove that as $t \to \infty$ the solution for k_{t+1} in (*) converges to $\bar{k}$.

E. Prove that consumption increases as capital increases toward its steady-state value.

6. A consumer is assumed to face the sequence of budget constraints

$$A_{t+1} = (1 + r)A_t + (1 + r)(y_t - c_t), \qquad t = 0, 1, 2, \ldots \qquad (\dagger)$$

where A_t is his asset holdings at the beginning of period t, y_t is exogenous income, and c_t is consumption at t. Here $r > 0$ is the real rate of return on assets, assumed constant over time. The consumer earns (pays) each period $1 + r$ times his initial assets plus $1 + r$ times the addition (subtraction) to his assets made by consuming less (more) than his income. Assume that both c_t and y_t are of exponential order less than $1 + r$.

Suppose we impose upon the consumer the boundary condition

$$\lim_{t\to\infty} (1 + r)^{-t} A_t = 0.$$

Show that then the sequence of budget constraints (†) implies

$$A_t + \sum_{i=0}^{\infty} \frac{y_{t+i}}{(1 + r)^i} = \sum_{i=0}^{\infty} \frac{c_{t+i}}{(1 + r)^i}, \qquad t = 0, 1, 2, \ldots.$$

Interpret this result.

Assume that the consumer starts out with initial assets of A_0 at time 0. Show that the sequence of budget constraints (†) implies

$$A_t = \sum_{i=0}^{t-1} (1 + r)^{i+1}(y_{t-1-i} - c_{t-i-1}) + (1 + r)^t A_0.$$

Interpret this result.

7. Suppose that portfolio equilibrium is described by Cagan's equation:

$$m_t - p_t = -1(p_{t+1}^e - p_t), \qquad t = 0, 1, 2, \ldots$$

where m_t is the log of the money supply, p_t the log of the price level at t, and p_{t+1}^e the public's expectation of p_{t+1}, formed at time t. Suppose that expectations are "rational," so that

$$p_{t+1}^e = p_{t+1}.$$

A. Suppose that $\{m_t\}$, t = 0, 1, ..., is given by

$$m_t = 10\lambda^t, \qquad t = 0, 1, 2, \ldots.$$

Compute the equilibrium value of p_t for t = 0, 1, 2, and t = 5, 6 for the following values of λ:

(i) $\lambda = 1$;

(ii) $\lambda = 1.5$;

(iii) $\lambda = 2.0$.

B. Suppose that m_t follows the path

$$m_t = 10\lambda^t, \qquad t = 0, 1, 2, 3, 4$$

$$m_t = 11\lambda^t, \qquad t = 5, 6, 7, 8, \ldots.$$

Compute the equilibrium values of p_t for t = 0, 1, 2, 3, 4, 5, 6 assuming that $\lambda = 1.5$. How does this time path for $\{p_t\}$ compare with that computed in A(ii)? Graph the two paths.

8. (Advertising) A monopolist faces the following demand curve for his product,

$$p_t = A_0 - A_1 Q_t + g(L)a_t + u_t \qquad A_0, A_1 > 0$$

where p_t is price, Q_t is output, a_t is advertising, u_t is a sequence of shocks to demand, and $g(L) = g_0 + g_1 L + \dots + g_m L^m$, where $g_j > 0$ for $j = 0, \dots, m$. The firm maximizes

$$\sum_{t=0}^{\infty} \beta^t \{p_t Q_t - Q_t s_t - (1/2)[d(L)Q_t]^2 \tag{1}$$

$$- (\gamma/2)a_t^2 - a_t w_t\}, \qquad 0 < \beta < 1,$$

where $d(L) = \Sigma_{j=0}^n d_j L^j$. In (1), s_t is a shock to costs, $(1/2)[d(L)Q_t]^2$ represents costs of rapid adjustment, and the marginal costs of advertising at t are $(w_t + \gamma a_t)$, where w_t is a known sequence. We assume that (u_t, s_t, w_t) are known sequences of exponential order less than $1/\sqrt{\beta}$. The criterion (1) is to be maximized over sequences for $\{Q_s, a_s, s > 0\}$, taking as given $\{Q_s, a_s, s < 0\}$.

A. Find the Euler equations for this problem.

B. Argue that the solution will be linear laws of motion for (Q_t, a_t) in which each of (Q_t, a_t) depend on lagged values of both Q and a, and current and future values of all of (u, s, w).

9. (Time to build with two processes) Consider a monopolist whose output satisfies

$$Q_t = f(L)n_{1t} + g(L)n_{2t} \tag{1}$$

where

$$f(L) = \sum_{j=0}^{m} f_j L^j, \quad g(L) = \sum_{j=0}^{r} g_j L^j; \qquad f_j > 0,\ g_j > 0,$$

for all j. In (1), n_{1t} is the amount of labor at k that is assigned to process 1, while n_{2t} is the amount that is assigned to process 2. The idea is that output can be produced via two proceses, with different timing chararacteristics; e.g., to represent the notion that the first process is fast but wasteful, while the other is efficient but time consuming, we might set $f(L) = L$, $g(L) = (1/2)[L + L^2 + L^3 + L^4]$. The firm faces the demand curve

$$p_t = A_0 - A_1 Q_t + u_t, \qquad A_0, A_1 > 0 \tag{2}$$

where u_t is a known sequence of exponential order less than $1/\sqrt{\beta}$. The firm hires labor at the wage rate w_t, where w_t is a known sequence of exponential order less than $1/\sqrt{\beta}$. The firm's problem is to maximize

$$\sum_{t=0}^{\infty} \beta^t \{p_t Q_t - w_t(n_{1t} + n_{2t})\}, \qquad 0 < \beta < 1 \tag{3}$$

subject to (1) and (2), with $\{n_{1s}, s = 0\ 1, \ldots, -m\}$ $\{n_{2s}, s = -1, \ldots, -r\}$ given.

A. Find the Euler equations for this problem.

B. Indicate the form of the optimum decision rules for (n_{1t}, n_{2t}).

10. At time t, a farmer plants A_t units of land from which he produces $y_{t+1} = f_1 A_t$ units of output available to be sold at time (t+1) at price p_{t+1} where $f_1 > 0$. If A_t units of land are planted, the farmer's costs at time t are $c_0 A_t + (c_1/2) A_t^2 + c_2 A_t A_{t-1}$, where $c_0, c_1, c_2 > 0$. The term $c_2 A_t A_{t-1}$ reflects the wearing out of the land from two successive heavy plantings. The price of output p_t obeys the first order difference equation

$$p_{t+1} = \alpha p_t$$

with p_0 given and $|\alpha| < 1/\sqrt{\beta}$. The farmer faces the p_t sequence as a price-taker. The farmer chooses $A_0, A_1, \ldots$ to maximize

$$\sum_{t=0}^{\infty} \beta^{t+1} p_{t+1}(f_1 A_t) - \sum_{t=0}^{\infty} \beta^t [c_0 A_t + (c_1/2)A_t^2 + c_2 A_t A_{t-1}] \quad 0 < \beta < 1,$$

subject to A_{-1} given.

A. Obtain the first-order necessary conditions for optimization.

B. Assume that $c_1 = 5/2$, $c_2 = 10/9$, $\beta = 0.81$, $f_1 = 10$, and $c_0 = 1$.* Find an optimal acreage plan for the farmer of the form

$$A_t = L(A_{t-1}, p_t, \text{constant})$$

where L is a linear function. Compute actual numerical values for the linear coefficients under the alternative assumptions $\alpha = .5$, $\alpha = 0$, and $\alpha = -.5$.

C. Using your answer to B, describe how you would expect the farmer's supply of output next period, $y_{t+1} = f_1 A_t$, to vary with this period's price, p_t. When is supply y_{t+1} to vary inversely with p_t?

D. Use this example to illustrate the general observation that decision rules change whenever the economic environment changes.

11. A social planner wants to maximize the criterion

$$\sum_{t=0}^{\infty} b^t \{u_1(c_t - a) - (\tfrac{1}{2})u_2(c_t - a)^2 - u_3 n_t - (\tfrac{1}{2})u_4 n_t^2\} \tag{1}$$

$$0 < b < 1; \quad u_1, u_2, u_3, u_4 > 0; \quad a > 0,$$

*With $\beta = 1$ and $c_0 \neq 0$, the exercise suffers from convergence problems (the system is not "stabilizable").

subject to

$$\text{(a)} \quad c_t + n_{t+1} + g = fn_t, \qquad g > 0,\ f > 1,\ fb > 1, \qquad (2)$$

$$\text{(b)} \quad n_0 > 0, \text{ given.}$$

Here c_t is consumption, n_t is labor supplied, g is government purchases, which are fixed and outside the control of the planner, and a is a "bliss level" of consumption. (In the background in (1)-(2), it is understood that output at t equals $f \cdot \min(k_t, n_t)$ where k_t is capital at t. This fixed proportions technology makes it optimal to set $n_t = k_t$. We have substituted this into an original set of constraints to get (2).)

A. Show that the optimal path for $\{n_t\}$ converges as $t \to \infty$. Call the limit point the "stationary optimal value of n."

B. Give an explicit formula for the stationary optimal value of n, call it $\bar{n}$.

C. Stationary values of n_t must satisfy (2a) with $n_{t+1} = n_t = n$:

$$c + n + g = fn \qquad (3)$$

Consider the following "Golden rule" problem: to maximize

$$u_1(c - a) - (\tfrac{1}{2})u_2(c - a)^2 - u_3 n - (\tfrac{1}{2})u_4 n^2$$

subject to (3), by choice of c and n. (In words, find the utility maximizing sustainable levels of consumption and labor.) Solve this problem, finding an explicit formula for the "Golden rule" employment level, n_g.

D. Does $n_g = \bar{n}$, in general? If not, describe special settings of the parameter values for which $n_g = \bar{n}$. Interpret these special settings.

SOLUTIONS

1. When d = 0, the firm's problem becomes

$$\max_{\{n_t\}} \sum_{j=0}^{\infty} b^j\{(f_0 + a_{t+j})n_{t+j} - \frac{f_1}{2}n_{t+j}^2 - w_{t+j}n_{t+j}\}$$

subject to n_{t-1}, $\{a_{t+j}\}_{j=0}^{\infty}$, and $\{w_{t+j}\}_{j=0}^{\infty}$ given. Differentiating the summand with respect to n_{t+j}, j = 0, 1, 2,... , one obtains the first-order necessary conditions

$$f_0 + a_{t+j} - f_1 n_{t+j} - w_{t+j} = 0 \qquad j = 0, 1, \ldots.$$

Clearly, these conditions are also sufficient, for the matrix of second partial derivatives is diagonal, with diagonal elements equal to $-f_1$. Thus the firm's employment decision rule becomes

$$n_{t+j} = -\frac{1}{f_1}(w_{t+j} - a_{t+j} - f_0) \qquad j = 0, 1, 2, \ldots$$

in which neither lagged employment nor future values of a_t and w_t appear. Thus, when employment can be adjusted costlessly, the dynamics become trivial; the firm will maximize its present value by maximizing profits at each date.

* * *

2. Since $-\phi = \frac{f_1}{d} + 1 + b$, when d increases, $-\phi$ shrinks. Figure 4 indicates that as $-\phi$ shrinks, λ_1 increases and λ_2 decreases. Thus

$$\frac{\partial\lambda_2}{\partial d} < 0 < \frac{\partial\lambda_1}{\partial d} .$$

From equation (55) of the text,

$$\frac{\partial n_{t+j+1}}{\partial(w_{t+j+1} - a_{t+j+1})} = \frac{-\lambda_1}{d} < 0$$

measures the firm's (employment) response to a small change in the (effective) real wage. Since it is negative, an <u>increase</u> in this number means that the firm responds to current conditions <u>less rapidly</u>. Indeed, $\frac{\partial}{\partial d}(-\lambda_1/d) > 0$: a firm facing a small d adjusts its labor force more rapidly in response to current conditions than a firm facing a larger value of d.

To see that $\frac{\partial}{\partial d}(-\lambda_1/d) > 0$, notice that

$$\frac{\partial}{\partial d}\left(\frac{-\lambda_1}{d}\right) = \frac{-d\left(\frac{\partial\lambda_1}{\partial d}\right) - (-\lambda_1)}{d^2} = \frac{1}{d^2}\left(\lambda_1 - d\frac{\partial\lambda_1}{\partial d}\right).$$

Now

$$\lambda_1 = \frac{1}{2}[-\frac{\phi}{b} - (\phi^2/b^2 - 4/b)^{\frac{1}{2}}] = \frac{1}{2b}[-\phi - (\phi^2 - 4b)^{\frac{1}{2}}].$$

Thus

$$\frac{\partial\lambda_1}{\partial d} = -\frac{1}{2b}[\frac{\partial\phi}{\partial d} + \frac{1}{2}(\phi^2 - 4b)^{-\frac{1}{2}}(2\phi)\frac{\partial\phi}{\partial d}]$$

$$= -\frac{1}{2b}[-\frac{f_1}{d^2} - \frac{f_1}{d^2}\phi(\phi^2 - 4b)^{-\frac{1}{2}}]$$

$$= \frac{1}{2b}\frac{f_1}{d^2}[1 + \phi(\phi^2 - 4b)^{-\frac{1}{2}}].$$

Then

$$\lambda_1 - d[\frac{\partial\lambda_1}{\partial d}] = \frac{1}{2b}[-\phi - (\phi^2 - 4b)^{\frac{1}{2}} - \frac{f_1}{d}(1 + \phi(\phi^2 - 4b)^{-\frac{1}{2}})]$$

$$= \frac{1}{2b}\left[\frac{f_1}{d} + 1 + b - \frac{f_1}{d} - (\phi^2 - 4b)^{\frac{1}{2}} - \frac{f_1}{d}\phi(\phi^2 - 4b)^{-\frac{1}{2}}\right]$$

$$= \frac{1}{2b}\left[1 + b - \frac{\phi^2 - 4b + \frac{f_1}{d}\phi}{(\phi^2 - 4b)^{\frac{1}{2}}}\right]$$

$$= \frac{1}{2b}\left[\frac{(1 + b)(\phi^2 - 4b)^{\frac{1}{2}} - (\phi^2 - 4b + \frac{f_1}{d}\phi)}{(\phi^2 - 4b)^{\frac{1}{2}}}\right].$$

Thus the sign of $\lambda_1 - d[\frac{\partial\lambda_1}{\partial d}]$ is the same as the sign of

$$(1 + b)(\phi^2 - 4b)^{\frac{1}{2}} - (\phi^2 - 4b + \frac{f_1}{d}\phi).$$

But, using the definition of ϕ,

$$(1 + b)(\phi^2 - 4b)^{\frac{1}{2}} - (\phi^2 - 4b + \frac{f_1}{d}\phi)$$

$$= (1 + b)[(\frac{f_1}{d})^2 + (1 + b)^2 + 2\frac{f_1}{d}(1 + b) - 4b]^{\frac{1}{2}}$$

$$- [(\frac{f_1}{d})^2 + (1 + b)^2 + 2\frac{f_1}{d}(1 + b) - 4b - (\frac{f_1}{d})^2 - \frac{f_1}{d}(1 + b)]$$

$$= (1 + b)[(\frac{f_1}{d})^2 + (1 - b)^2 + 2\frac{f_1}{d}(1 + b)]^{\frac{1}{2}}$$

$$- [(1 - b)^2 + \frac{f_1}{d}(1 + b)]$$

$$> (1 + b)[(\frac{f_1}{d})^2 + (1 - b)^2 + 2\frac{f_1}{d}(1 - b)]^{\frac{1}{2}}$$

$$- (1 - b)^2 - \frac{f_1}{d}(1 + b)$$

$$= (1 + b)(\frac{f_1}{d} + 1 - b) - (1 - b)^2 - \frac{f_1}{d}(1 + b)$$

$$= (1 + b)(1 - b) - (1 - b)^2 > 0$$

since $0 < b < 1$. Thus

$$\frac{\partial}{\partial d}(\frac{-\lambda_1}{d}) > 0.$$

* * *

3. It will prove useful to begin by verifying versions of equation (60) and expression (99) of the text. Given

$$a(L) = \Sigma_{j=-\infty}^{\infty} a_j L^j, \qquad d(L) = \Sigma_{j=-\infty}^{\infty} d_j L^j,$$

the expressions

$$v_1 = \Sigma_{t=0}^{\infty} b^t a(L) y_t d(L) y_t$$

$$v_2 = \tfrac{1}{2}\Sigma_{t=0}^{\infty} b^t [d(L) y_t]^2$$

$$v_3 = \Sigma_{t=0}^{\infty} b^t a(L) z_t d(L) y_t$$

have derivatives

$$\partial v_1/\partial y_t = b^t[a(bL^{-1})d(L) + a(L)d(bL^{-1})]y_t$$

$$\partial v_2/\partial y_t = b^t d(bL^{-1})d(L)y_t$$

$$\partial v_3/\partial y_t = b^t d(bL^{-1})a(L)z_t.$$

To see the first of these, write out v_1 explicitly,

$$v_1 = \cdots + b^t(\cdots + a_{-1}y_{t+1} + a_0 y_t + a_1 y_{t-1} + \cdots)(\cdots + d_{-1}y_{t+1} + d_0 y_t + d_1 y_{t-1} + \cdots)$$
$$+ b^{t+1}(\cdots + a_{-1}y_{t+2} + a_0 y_{t+1} + a_1 y_t + \cdots)(\cdots + d_{-1}y_{t+2} + d_0 y_{t+1} + d_1 y_t + \cdots) + \cdots$$

and differentiate with respect to y_t to get

$$\partial v_1/\partial y_t = \cdots + b^{t-1}\{a_{-1}d(L)y_{t-1} + d_{-1}a(L)y_{t-1}\}$$
$$+ b^t\{a_0 d(L)y_t + d_0 a(L)y_t\}$$
$$+ b^{t+1}\{a_1 d(L)y_{t+1} + d_1 a(L)y_{t+1}\} + \cdots$$
$$= b^t\{[\cdots + a_{-1}b^{-1}L + a_0 b^0 L^0 + a_1 bL^{-1} + \cdots]d(L)y_t$$
$$+ [\cdots + d_{-1}b^{-1}L + d_0 b^0 L^0 + d_1 bL^{-1} + \cdots]a(L)y_t\}$$
$$= b^t[a(bL^{-1})d(L) + d(bL^{-1})a(L)]y_t.$$

The formula for $\partial v_2/\partial y_t$ is a special case of $\partial v_1/\partial y_t$.

Writing out v_3, one obtains

$$v_3 = \cdots + b^t a(L)z_t(\cdots + d_{-1}y_{t+1} + d_0 y_t + \cdots)$$
$$+ b^{t+1}a(L)z_{t+1}(\cdots + d_{-1}y_{t+2} + d_0 y_{t+1} + d_1 y_t + \cdots) + \cdots .$$

Then

$$\partial v_3/\partial y_t = \cdots + b^{t-1}a(L)z_{t-1}d_{-1} + b^t a(L)z_t d_0 + b^{t+1}a(L)z_{t+1}d_1 + \cdots$$
$$= b^t a(L)(\cdots + b^{-1}d_{-1}L + b^0 d_0 L^0 + bd_1 L^{-1} + \cdots)z_t$$
$$= b^t d(bL^{-1})a(L)z_t.$$

Now consider the finite horizon problem

$$\max_{\{k_{t+j}\}_{j=0}^{T}} v_t^T = \max_{\{k_{t+j}\}_0^T} \sum_{j=0}^{T} b^j\{a_0 k_{t+j} - \frac{a_1}{2}k_{t+j}^2 - J_{t+j}(k_{t+j} - k_{t+j-1})$$
$$- \frac{d}{2}(k_{t+j} - k_{t+j-1})^2\},$$

given $k_{t-1} > 0$; $a_0, a_1, d > 0$; $0 < b < 1$; and $\{J_{t+j}\}_{j=0}^{\infty}$ is a known sequence of exponential order less than 1/b. The first order necessary conditions for this problem are

$$\frac{\partial v_t^T}{\partial k_{t+j}} = 0 \quad j = 0, 1, \ldots, T-1, \qquad k_{t+T}\frac{\partial v_t^T}{\partial k_{t+T}} = 0.$$

Thus using the derivative formulas discussed above, the necessary conditions for j = 0, 1,..., T-1 are given by

$$\frac{\partial v_t^T}{\partial k_{t+j}} = 0 = b^j\{a_0 - a_1 k_{t+j} - (1 - bL^{-1})J_{t+j}$$
$$- d(1 - bL^{-1})(1 - L)k_{t+j}\}.$$

For j = T,

$$k_{t+T}\frac{\partial v_t^T}{\partial k_{t+T}} = 0 = b^T\{a_0 - a_1 k_{t+T} - J_{t+T} - d(k_{t+T} - k_{t+T-1})\}k_{t+T}.$$

A. The Euler equations for the infinite horizon problem of maximizing v_t are given by $\frac{\partial v_t^T}{\partial k_{t+j}} = 0$, j = 0, 1, 2, ...:

$$0 = a_0 - a_1 k_{t+j} - J_{t+j} + bJ_{t+j+1} - d(k_{t+j} - k_{t+j-1})$$
$$+ db(k_{t+j+1} - k_{t+j})$$

or

$$k_{t+j+1} - \frac{a_1 + d + db}{db}k_{t+j} + \frac{1}{b}k_{t+j-1} = \frac{1}{db}(J_{t+j} - bJ_{t+j+1} - a_0).$$

Let $\phi = -\frac{a_1 + d + db}{d}$. Thus the Euler equations can be written

$$(1 + \frac{\phi}{b}L + \frac{1}{b}L^2)k_{t+j+1} = \frac{1}{db}(J_{t+j} - bJ_{t+1+1} - a_0), \quad j = 0,1,2,\ldots . \quad (1)$$

The transversality condition is given by

$$\lim_{T\to\infty} k_{t+T} \frac{\partial v_t^T}{\partial k_{t+T}} = 0 = \lim_{T\to\infty} b^T[a_0 - J_{t+T} - (a_1 + d)k_{t+T} + dk_{t+T-1}]k_{t+T}.$$

B. Write

$$(1 - \lambda_1 L)(1 - \lambda_2 L) = 1 + \frac{\phi}{b}L + \frac{1}{b}L^2. \quad (2)$$

Thus $-(\lambda_1 + \lambda_2) = \frac{\phi}{b}$, $\lambda_1\lambda_2 = \frac{1}{b}$, and $-\phi = 1 + b + \frac{a_1}{d} > 1 + b$. This is the situation described in Section IX.8 of the text. By the argument given there, $0 < \lambda_1 < 1 < \frac{1}{b} < \lambda_2$. The optimum decision rule of the firm is the solution of the Euler equations which satisfies the transversality condition. (Actually, the appropriate side condition is $\Sigma_{t=0}^{\infty} b^t k_t^2 < \infty$ -- since $a_1 > 0$ -- but in this case the two conditions enforce the same exponential order restriction.)

Using (2) in the Euler equation, (1), and operating on both sides of the Euler equation with $(1 - \lambda_2 L)^{-1}$, obtain

$$(1 - \lambda_1 L)k_{t+j+1} = \frac{1}{db(1 - \lambda_2 L)}(J_{t+j} - bJ_{t+j+1} - a_0) + c_2\lambda_2^{t+j+1}$$

$$k_{t+j+1} = \lambda_1 k_{t+j} - \frac{a_0}{db(1 - \lambda_2 L)} + \frac{1}{db}(\frac{J_{t+j} - bJ_{t+j+1}}{1 - \lambda_2 L}) + c_2\lambda_2^{t+j+1}.$$

Unless $c_2 = 0$, $\{k_{t+j}\}$ will be of exponential order no smaller than $\lambda_2 > b^{-1} > 1/\sqrt{\beta}$, and the transversality condition will be violated (as will the condition analogous to (61), $\Sigma_{j=0}^{\infty} b^j k_{t+j}^2 < \infty$). Further, it is appropriate (see footnote 9 in the text) to operate on $\{J_{t+j}\}$ with the <u>forward</u> inverse of $(1 - \lambda_2 L)$. Thus set $c_2 = 0$, use the forward inverse, and write

$$k_{t+j+1} = \lambda_1 k_{t+j} - \frac{a_0}{db(1 - \lambda_2)} - \frac{L^{-1}}{db\lambda_2(1 - \lambda_2^{-1}L^{-1})}(J_{t+j} - bJ_{t+j+1})$$

or

$$k_{t+j+1} = \lambda_1 k_{t+j} + c_0 + \frac{c_1}{1 - \lambda_2^{-1}L^{-1}}(bJ_{t+j+2} - J_{t+j+1})$$

where

$$c_0 = \frac{-a_0}{db(1 - \lambda_2)} \quad \text{and} \quad c_1 = \frac{1}{db\lambda_2}.$$

* * *

4. A. When $d = 0$, the problem is

$$\min_{\{g_t\}_0^\infty} \sum_{t=0}^{\infty} b^t(\alpha + BS_t + cg_t - Y_t^*)^2.$$

Thus the minimand is

$$T = \ldots + b^t(\alpha + BS_t + cg_t - Y_t^*)^2$$
$$+ b^{t+1}(\alpha + BS_{t+1} + cg_{t+1} - Y_{t+1}^*)^2 + \ldots$$

where $B > 0$, $c > 0$, $0 < b < 1$, and $\{S_t\}_{t=0}^\infty$ and $\{Y_t^*\}_{t=0}^\infty$ are sequences of exponential order less than $1/b$. The first order conditions are obtained by differentiating T with respect to g_t, $t = 0, 1, \ldots$:

$$\frac{\partial T}{\partial g_t} = 0 = 2cb^t(\alpha + BS_t + cg_t - Y_t^*). \qquad t = 0, 1, \ldots .$$

(Notice that these conditions are also sufficient -- the second order partials are all positive: $\partial^2T/\partial g_t^2 = 2c^2b^t$.) The optimal rule for setting g_t is then

$$g_t = \frac{1}{c}(Y_t^* - \alpha - BS_t).$$

Notice that under this rule, T = 0.

B. The Euler equations for minimizing T when d > 0 are, using the derivative formulas given in the solution to Exercise 3,

$$\frac{\partial T}{\partial g_t} = 0 = b^t\{2(Y_t - Y_t^*)\frac{\partial Y_t}{\partial g_t} + 2d(1 - bL^{-1})(1 - L)g_t\}$$

$$= c\alpha + cBs_t - cY_t^* + [c^2 + d(1 - bL^{-1})(1 - L)]g_t$$

$$= c\alpha + cBs_t - cY_t^* + [-bd + (c^2 + d + db)L - dL^2]g_t$$

for $t = 0, 1, \ldots$. Let $-\phi = \dfrac{c^2 + d + db}{d} > 1 + b$. Then the Euler equations can be written as

$$(1 + \frac{\phi}{b} L + \frac{1}{b} L^2)g_{t+1} = \frac{1}{db}(c\alpha + cBS_t - cY_t^*) \qquad t = 0, 1, \ldots .$$

Write $(1 - \lambda_1L)(1 - \lambda_2L) = (1 + \frac{\phi}{b} L + \frac{1}{b} L^2)$. Thus $\lambda_1 + \lambda_2 = -\frac{\phi}{b}$, $\lambda_1\lambda_2 = 1/b$. Since $-\phi > 1 + b$, the arguments in Section IX.8 of the text can be used to show that $0 < \lambda_1 < 1 < \frac{1}{b} < \lambda_2$. Thus the Euler equations become

$$(1 - \lambda_1L)(1 - \lambda_2L)g_{t+1} = \frac{1}{db}(c\alpha + cBS_t - cY_t^*) \qquad t = 0, 1, \ldots .$$

Operating on both sides of this expression with $(1 - \lambda_2L)^{-1}$, one obtains

$$(1 - \lambda_1L)g_{t+1} = \frac{1}{db(1 - \lambda_2L)}(c\alpha + cBS_t - cY_t^*) + c\lambda_2^t$$

$$= \frac{c\alpha}{db(1 - \lambda_2)} + \frac{1}{db(1 - \lambda_2 L)}(cBS_t - cY_t^*) + c_2\lambda_2^t.$$

As in Exercise 3, unless $c_2 = 0$, $\{g_t\}$ will be of exponential order no smaller than $\lambda_2 > 1/b$. Thus the transversality condition requires $c_2 = 0$.

Because $\{S_t\}$ and $\{Y_t^*\}$ are of exponential order less than $\frac{1}{b} < \lambda_2$, the forward expansion of $(1 - \lambda_2 L)^{-1}(cBS_t - cY_t^*)$ is finite. Thus the optimal rule for setting g_t is

$$g_{t+1} = \lambda_1 g_t + \frac{c\alpha}{db(1 - \lambda_2)} - \frac{1}{db\lambda_2}\sum_{j=0}^{\infty} \lambda_2^{-j}(cBS_{t+1+j} - cY_{t+1+j}^*)$$

for $t = 0, 1, \ldots$.

* * *

5. When $c_t + k_{t+1} < f_0 k_t$, some consumption goods are being produced and then thrown away. Since the consumption good is valuable, it will not be discarded; the constraint will be binding. Thus use $f_0 k_t - k_{t+1}$ for c_t and write the problem as

$$\max_{\{k_t\}} \sum_{t=0}^{\infty} \beta^t \{u_0((f_0 - L^{-1})k_t) - \frac{u_1}{2}((f_0 - L^{-1})k_t)^2\}$$

subject to $0 < k_0 < \frac{u_0}{u_1}(\frac{1}{f_0 - 1})$ given, $f_0 > \frac{1}{\beta} > 1$, and $\{k_t\}$ bounded. The Euler equations are given by

$$u_0(f_0 - \beta^{-1}L) - u_1(f_0 - \beta^{-1}L)(f_0 - L^{-1})k_t = 0 \qquad t = 1, 2, \ldots,$$

(Notice that in applying the derivative formulas of Exercise 3, L^{-1} is replaced by $\beta^{-1}L$.)

To derive the transversality condition, consider the finite horizon problem of maximizing, by choice of c_0, c_1, ..., c_T, the expression

$$v_0^T = \Sigma_{t=0}^T \beta^t \{u_0 c_t - \frac{u_1}{2} c_t^2\}$$

subject to $c_t = (f_0 - L^{-1})k_t$. Upon using the constraint in v_0^T, the problem becomes one of maximizing v_0^T by choice of k_1, ..., k_{T+1}. The transversality condition is

$$\lim_{T\to\infty} \beta^T k_{T+1} \frac{\partial v_0^T}{\partial_{T+1}} = 0.$$

Notice that $-\partial v_0^T/\partial k_{T+1} = \partial\{u_0 c_T - \tfrac{1}{2}u_1 c_T^2\}/\partial c_T$, the marginal utility of consumption at time T. Thus $\partial v_0^T/\partial k_{T+1}$ is the (shadow) price of an extra unit of capital at the end of the planning horizon, measured in units of foregone utility (of consumption). Therefore the transversality condition requires that the discounted <u>value</u> of the terminal choice of capital approach zero as the horizon is indefinitely extended.

B. The Euler equations can be written

$$-f_0(1 - \beta^{-1}f_0^{-1}L)(1 - f_0 L)k_{t+1} = f_0(1 - \beta^{-1}f_0^{-1}L)u_0/u_1.$$

In a steady state, $k_t = \bar{k}$ for all t. Thus

$$\bar{k} = -\frac{(1 - \beta^{-1}f_0^{-1})}{(1 - \beta^{-1}f_0^{-1})(1 - f_0)} u_0/u_1$$

$$= \frac{1}{f_0 - 1}\frac{u_0}{u_1}.$$

Also, $\bar{c} = c_t = f_0\bar{k} - \bar{k}$ in steady state (for all t). Thus

$$\bar{c} = (f_0 - 1)\bar{k}$$
$$= u_0/u_1.$$

Notice that $\bar{c}$ sets the marginal utility of current period consumption to zero; i.e., $\bar{c}$ attains "bliss", and maximizes sustainable utility -- $\bar{c}$ is the "Golden rule" level of consumption.

C. The Euler equation is

$$(1 - f_0L)(1 - \frac{1}{\beta f_0}L)k_{t+1} = (\frac{1 - \beta f_0}{\beta f_0})(\frac{u_0}{u_1}) \qquad f_0 > 1,\ 0 < \frac{1}{\beta f_0} < 1,$$

which is an ordinary second order difference equation with solution

$$k_{t+1} = \frac{(1 - \beta f_0)u_0}{\beta f_0(1 - f_0)(1 - \frac{1}{\beta f_0})u_1} + \gamma_1(\frac{1}{\beta f_0})^{t+1} + \gamma_2(f_0)^{t+1}$$

$$= \frac{1}{f_0 - 1}\frac{u_0}{u_1} + \gamma_1(\frac{1}{\beta f_0})^{t+1} + \gamma_2(f_0)^{t+1}.$$

The transversality condition requires

$$\lim_{T\to\infty} \beta^T k_{t+1}[u_0 - u_1(f_0 - L^{-1})k_T] = 0.$$

Using the above candidate expression for k_{t+1} for $t = T - 1$, one finds

$$u_0 - u_1(f_0 - L^{-1})k_T = u_1\gamma_1(f_0 - L^{-1})(\beta f_0)^{-T}$$

$$= u_1\gamma_1(f_0 - \beta^{-1}f_0^{-1})(\beta f_0)^{-T}.$$

Thus

$$\beta^T[u_0 - u_1(f_0 - L^{-1})k_T] = u_1\gamma_1(f_0 - \beta^{-1}f_0^{-1})f_0^{-T}$$

and again using the candidate expression,

$$\lim_{T\to\infty} \beta^T k_{T+1}[u_0 - u_1(f_0 - L^{-1})k_T] = u_1(f_0 - \beta^{-1}f_0^{-1})f_0\gamma_1\gamma_2.$$

Thus the transversality condition requires $\gamma_1 = 0$ or $\gamma_2 = 0$.† Suppose first that $\gamma_1 = 0$. Then

$$k_0 = (u_0/u_1)(1/(f_0-1)) + \gamma_2$$

and

$$k_{t+1} = (u_0/u_1)(1/(f_0-1)) + [k_0 - (u_0/u_1)(1/(f_0-1))]f_0^{t+1},$$

indicating that $k_t \to -\infty$ as $t \to \infty$. Evidently, the side condition of boundedness forces one to choose $\gamma_2 = 0$. Then

$$k_{t+1} = \frac{(1 - \beta f_0)u_0}{\beta f_0(1 - f_0)(1 - \frac{1}{\beta f_0})u_1} + \gamma_1\left(\frac{1}{\beta f_0}\right)^{t+1}$$

or, equivalently,

$$k_{t+1} = \left(\frac{1}{\beta f_0}\right)k_t + \left(\frac{1 - \beta f_0}{\beta f_0}\right)\left(\frac{1}{1 - f_0}\right)\left(\frac{u_0}{u_1}\right)$$

or

$$k_{t+1} = \frac{1}{\beta f_0}k_t - \left[\frac{1}{\beta f_0} - 1\right]\left[\frac{1}{f_0 - 1}\right]\left[\frac{u_0}{u_1}\right]. \qquad (*)$$

---

†In this problem, the transversality condition is not sufficient to determine a unique optimum. In general, the transversality condition is not even necessary in infinite horizon problems. This point is made, e.g., by H. Halkin, "Necessary Conditions for Optimal Control Problems with Infinite Horizons," Econometrica 42, No. 2 (March 1974), pp. 267-272 and by K. Arrow and M. Kurz, Public Investment, The Rate of Return, and Optimal Fiscal Policy, 1970, Baltimore: The Johns Hopkins University Press (see especially Ch. II.6 and footnote 1 on p. 46).

D. Other ways to write (*) are

$$k_{t+1} = \bar{k} + \gamma_1\left(\frac{1}{\beta f_0}\right)^{t+1}$$

and

$$k_{t+1} = \bar{k} - \frac{1}{\beta f_0}[\bar{k} - k_t].$$

Since $\beta f_0 > 1$, k_t approaches $\bar{k}$ as $t \to \infty$.

E. By assumption, $k_0 < \bar{k}$. Further,

$$\bar{k} - k_{t+1} = \beta^{-1} f_0^{-1}[\bar{k} - k_t]$$

so that proportion $1/\beta f_0$ of the gap between $\bar{k}$ and the current value of k is closed each period; k increases to $\bar{k}$. Using the constraint,

$$c_t = (\beta^{-1} f_0^{-1} - 1)\bar{k} + (f_0 - \beta^{-1} f_0^{-1})k_t,$$

and since $f_0 > \beta^{-1} f_0^{-1}$ and k_t is increasing with t, c_t increases as time passes.

* * *

6. The budget constraints can be written

$$A_{t+1} = (1 + r)A_t + (1 + r)(y_t - c_t)$$

$$(1 - (1 + r)L)A_{t+1} = (1 + r)(y_t - c_t)$$

$$(1 - (1 + r)L)A_t = (1 + r)(y_{t-1} - c_{t-1})$$

or

$$A_t = \frac{1 + r}{1 - (1 + r)L}(y_{t-1} - c_{t-1}) + C_1(1 + r)^t.$$

Use the forward inverse since $(1 + r) > 1$:

$$A_t = \frac{(1 + r)\left(\frac{-1}{(1 + r)L}\right)}{1 - (1 + r)^{-1}L^{-1}}(y_{t-1} - c_{t-1}) + C_1(1 + r)^t$$

$$= \frac{c_t - y_t}{1 - (1 + r)^{-1}L^{-1}} + C_1(1 + r)^t$$

$$= \sum_{j=0}^{\infty} (1 + r)^{-j}(c_{t+j} - y_{t+j}) + C_1(1 + r)^t.$$

Now $\lim_{t\to\infty} (1 + r)^{-t}A_t = 0$ is imposed. Thus:

$$\lim_{t\to\infty} (1 + r)^{-t}A_t = \lim_{t\to\infty} \sum_{j=0}^{\infty} (1 + r)^{-t-j}(c_{t+j} - y_{t+j}) + C_1$$

so clearly $C_1 = 0$. Further, this is sufficient. The reason is that

$$|c_t| < K_c(X)^t, \quad |y_t| < K_y(X)^t, \quad \text{for some } X < (1 + r).$$

Then $|c_t - y_t| \leq |c_t| + |y_t| < (K_c + K_y)(X)^t$. Each term in the series is then characterized by

$$|(1 + r)^{-(t+j)}(c_{t+j} - y_{t+j})| < (K_c + K_y)\left(\frac{X}{1 + r}\right)^{t+j}.$$

But $X < (1 + r)$. Thus when $C_1 = 0$, $\lim_{t\to\infty} (1 + r)^{-t}A_t = 0$. Then

$$A_t = \sum_{j=0}^{\infty} (1 + r)^{-j}(c_{t+j} - y_{t+j})$$

or

$$A_t + \sum_{j=0}^{\infty} (1 + r)^{-j}y_{t+j} = \sum_{j=0}^{\infty} (1 + r)^{-j}c_{t+j}$$

which means that at date t, the present value of future consumption equals current assets plus the present value of future income.

Notice next that

$$A_1 = (1 + r)A_0 + (1 + r)(y_0 - c_0)$$

$$A_2 = (1 + r)^2 A_0 + (1 + r)^2(y_0 - c_0) + (1 + r)(y_1 - c_1)$$

$$A_3 = (1 + r)^3 A_0 + (1 + r)^3(y_0 - c_0) + (1 + r)^2(y_1 - c_1) + (1 + r)(y_2 - c_2)$$

$$\vdots$$

$$A_t = (1 + r)^t A_0 + \sum_{i=0}^{t+1} (1 + r)^{i+1}(y_{t-1-i} - c_{t-1-i})$$

which means that assets at date t equal the principal plus interest on initial assets plus interest (and principal) accumulated on any savings.

* * *

7. A. This problem is intended to illustrate the effects of anticipated regime changes on current economic activity. The solution is given by equation (44) in the text:

$$p_t = (\tfrac{1}{2}) \sum_{j=0}^{\infty} (\tfrac{1}{2})^i m_{t+i} + c2^t.$$

(i) $\lambda = 1$:

$$p_t = (\tfrac{1}{2}) \sum_{j=0}^{\infty} (\tfrac{1}{2})^i 10(1)^{t+i} + c2^t = \frac{5}{1 - \frac{1}{2}} + c2^t = 10 + c2^t$$

$$= m_t + c2^t.$$

(ii) $\lambda = 1.5$:

$$p_t = (\tfrac{1}{2}) \sum_{i=0}^{\infty} (\tfrac{1}{2})^i (10)(\tfrac{3}{2})^{t+i} + c2^t = 5(\tfrac{3}{2})^t (\frac{1}{1 - \frac{3}{4}}) + c2^t = 20(\tfrac{3}{2})^t + c2^t$$

$$= 2m_t + c2^t.$$

(iii) The infinite series in the forward solution does not converge, so another technique must be used. Cagan's equation can be written as

$$p_{t+1} - 2p_t = -10(2)^t$$

or

$$(1 - 2L)p_{t+1} = -10(2)^t.$$

Operating by $(1 - 2L)$ on both sides of this expression gives

$$(1 - 2L)(1 - 2L)p_{t+1} = (1 - 2L)(-10)(2)^t$$

$$(1 - 2L)^2 p_{t+1} = -(10)(2)^t - 2(-10)(2)^{t-1} = 0.$$

This implies

$$p_{t+1} = c_1 2^t + c_2 t(2)^t.$$

But then

$$(1 - 2L)p_{t+1} = (1 - 2L)c_1 2^t + (1 - 2L)c_2 t(2)^t = (1 - 2L)c_2 t2^t$$

$$= c_2[t2^t - 2(t - 1)2^{t-1}] = c_2 2^t = -10(2)^t$$

so that $c_2 = -10$. Thus $p_{t+1} = -10t(2)^t + c_1 2^t$. Notice that $p_{t+1} = (c_1 - 10t)2^t$, so the price level must eventually become negative. Evidently, if m_t behaves as x^t, there is no sensible solution for $\{p_t\}$ for $x \geq 2$.

Summarizing,

if $\lambda = 1$, $p_t = 10 + c(2)^t = m_t + c(2)^t$;

if $\lambda = 1.5$, $p_t = 20(\frac{3}{2})^t + c(2)^t = 2m_t + c(2)^t$;

if $\lambda = 2$, $p_t = -5t(2)^t + \tilde{c}(2)^t$.

These formulas illustrate how changes in the law of motion for the money supply (i.e., changes in λ) change the <u>mapping</u> from m_t to p_t. Equilibrium values for p_t can be found by evaluating these expressions at t = 0, 1, ...

B. Let $M_t = m_t^a + m_t^b$, where m_t^a denotes the sequence defined in part A, and

$$m_t^b = 0 \qquad t = 0, 1, \ldots, 4$$

$$m_t^b = \lambda^t \qquad t \geq 5,$$

so that $\{M_t\}$ is the money supply process for part B. Using the formula above,

$$p_t^B = \tfrac{1}{2} \sum_{i=0}^{\infty} (\tfrac{1}{2})^i M_{t+i} + c^*2^t$$

where c* is an as-yet-undetermined constant. Then

$$p_t^B = (\tfrac{1}{2}) \sum_{i=0}^{\infty} (\tfrac{1}{2})^i (m_{t+i}^a + m_{t+i}^b) + c^*2^t$$

$$= p_t^A + \tfrac{1}{2} \sum_{i=0}^{\infty} (\tfrac{1}{2})^i m_{t+i}^b$$

where $\{p_t^A\}$ denotes the price sequence from part A.ii, and it has been assumed that $c^* = c$. Since $m_t \geq 0$ for $t \geq 0$ and $m_s > 0$ for $s \geq 5$, $p_t^B > p_t^A$ for all t. Using the formula for m_t^b,

$$p_t^B = p_t^A + 2^t(\lambda/2)^5/(2 - \lambda) \qquad t = 0, 1, \ldots, 4$$

$$= p_t^A + \lambda^t/(2 - \lambda) \qquad t \geq 5.$$

The paths are graphed for $\lambda = 1.5$, $c = c^* = 0$, in Figure 5.

* * *

8. After substituting the demand curve into the objective function, the problem becomes: maximize

$$\sum_{t=0}^{\infty} \beta^t\{[A_0 - A_1Q_t + g(L)a_t + u_t]Q_t - Q_ts_t - (1/2)[d(L)Q_t]^2$$
$$- (\gamma/2)a_t^2 - a_tw_t\}$$

by choice of $\{Q_s, a_s; s \geq 0\}$.

A. Using the derivative formulas from Exercise 3, the Euler equations for a_t are given by

$$g(\beta L^{-1})Q_t - \gamma a_t + w_t = 0 \qquad t \geq 0$$

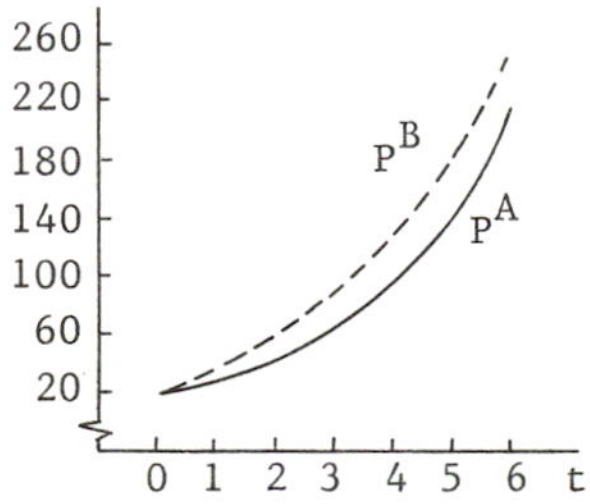

Figure 5

while those for Q_t are given by

$$A_0 - 2A_1Q_t + g(L)a_t + u_t - s_t - d(\beta L^{-1})d(L)Q_t = 0 \qquad t \geq 0.$$

These equations may be represented more compactly as

$$\begin{bmatrix} 2A_1 + d(\beta L^{-1})d(L) & -g(L) \\ -g(\beta L^{-1}) & \gamma \end{bmatrix} \begin{bmatrix} Q_t \\ a_t \end{bmatrix} = \begin{bmatrix} A_0 + u_t - s_t \\ w_t \end{bmatrix}.$$

B. The determinant of the polynomial matrix on the left hand side of the above expression is

$$2A_1\gamma + \gamma d(\beta L^{-1})d(L) - g(\beta L^{-1})g(L).$$

If z_0 is a zero of the determinant, then so is βz_0^{-1}. Also, the matrix is "β-symmetric:" transposition and replacement of L with βL^{-1} returns the original matrix. It then follows that the polynomial matrix has the factorization

$$\begin{bmatrix} 2A_1 + d(\beta L^{-1})d(L) & -g(L) \\ -g(\beta L^{-1}) & \gamma \end{bmatrix} = C(\beta L^{-1})'C(L)$$

where the zeros of det $C(z)$ exceed $\sqrt{\beta}$ in absolute value. Then (see equation (77) in the text) the optimal production-advertising policy is

$$C(L)[Q_t \quad a_t]' = C(\beta L^{-1})'^{-1}[A_0 + u_t - s_t \quad w_t]'$$

in which current settings for Q_t and a_t depend on lags of <u>both</u> Q and a and current and future values of <u>all</u> of u, s, and w (because C(L) is <u>not</u> diagonal).

* * *

9. After substituting the demand curve into the objective function, the problem becomes: maximize

$$\sum_{t=0}^{\infty} \beta^t \{[A_0 - A_1(f(L)n_{1t} + g(L)n_{2t}) + u_t][f(L)n_{1t} + g(L)n_{2t}]$$

$$- w_t[f(L)n_{1t} + g(L)n_{2t}]\}$$

by choice of $\{n_{1s}, n_{2s}, s \geq 0\}$.

A. Using the derivative formulas from Exercise 3, the Euler equations for n_{1t} are given by

$$f(\beta L^{-1})A_0 - 2A_1 f(\beta L^{-1})f(L)n_{1t} - A_1 f(\beta L^{-1})g(L)n_{2t}$$

$$+ f(\beta L^{-1})(u_t - w_t) = 0$$

for $t \geq 0$, while those for n_{2t} are given by

$$g(\beta L^{-1})A_0 - 2A_1 g(\beta L^{-1})g(L)n_{2t} - A_1 g(\beta L^{-1})f(L)n_{1t}$$

$$+ g(\beta L^{-1})(u_t - w_t) = 0$$

for $t \geq 0$. These equations may be written more compactly as

$$\begin{bmatrix} 2A_1 f(\beta L^{-1})f(L) & A_1 f(\beta L^{-1})g(L) \\ A_1 g(\beta L^{-1})f(L) & 2A_1 g(\beta L^{-1})g(L) \end{bmatrix} \begin{bmatrix} n_{1t} \\ n_{2t} \end{bmatrix}$$

$$= \begin{bmatrix} f(\beta)A_0 + f(\beta L^{-1})(u_t - w_t) \\ g(\beta)A_0 + g(\beta L^{-1})(u_t - w_t) \end{bmatrix}.$$

B. Note that the polynomial matrix on the left hand side of the above equation is β-symmetric; the determinant is

$$3A_1^2 f(\beta L^{-1})g(L)g(\beta L^{-1})g(L)$$

so if z_0 is a zero of the determinant, then so is βz_0^{-1}. Thus, the polynomial matrix has a factorization of the form $C(\beta L^{-1})'C(L)$ where the zeros of $\det[C(z)]$ exceed $\sqrt{\beta}$ in absolute value. Then the optimal employment policy for the firm is

$$C(L)[n_{1t} \quad n_{2t}]' = C(\beta L^{-1})'[f(\beta L^{-1}) \quad g(\beta L^{-1})]'(A_0 + u_t - w_t)$$

so that current settings for n_1 and n_2 depend on the history of employment of both types of labor as well as current and future values of u and w.

* * *

10. Write the objective function as

$$\sum_{t=0}^{\infty} \beta_t\{\beta p_{t+1}f_1A_t - c_0A_t - \frac{c_1}{2}A_t^2 - c_2A_tA_{t-1}\}.$$

A. Differentiating this expression with respect to A_0, A_1, ... using the derivative formulas of Exercise 3, one obtains the Euler equations

$$\beta f_1p_{t+1} - c_0 - c_1A_t - c_2[L + bL^{-1}]A_t = 0 \qquad t = 0, 1, \ldots,$$

which can be rearranged as

$$(bc_2 + c_1L + c_2L^2)A_{t+1} = c_0 - \beta f_1p_{t+1} \qquad t = 0, 1, \ldots .$$

(Adding the usual condition $\Sigma_{t=0}^{\infty} \beta^tA_t^2 < \infty$ completes the set of necessary and sufficient conditions for optimization. The optimal decision rule for the farmer is evidently the one which produces an $\{A_t\}$ sequence of exponential order less than $1/\sqrt{\beta}$.)

B. Under the stated conditions, the Euler equation becomes

$$\frac{9}{10}A_{t+1} + \frac{50}{20}A_t + \frac{10}{9}A_{t-1} = 10p_{t+1} - 1$$

or, substituting for p_{t+1}, and shifting the time period back one unit

$$\frac{9}{10}A_t + \frac{50}{20}A_{t-1} + \frac{10}{9}A_{t-2} = 10\alpha p_{t-1} - 1$$

which can be factored to

$$\frac{9}{10}[1 - (-\frac{5}{9})L][1 - (-\frac{20}{9})L]A_t = 10\alpha p_{t-1} - 1.$$

Let $\lambda_1 = -\frac{5}{9}$ and $\lambda_2 = -\frac{20}{9}$. Write

$$\frac{9}{10}(1 - \lambda_1 L)A_t = \frac{-\frac{1}{\lambda_2 L}}{1 - \frac{1}{\lambda_2 L}}10\alpha p_{t-1} - \frac{1}{1 - \lambda_2 L} + c_4\lambda_2^t$$

$$= \frac{-\frac{1}{\lambda_2 L}}{1 - \frac{1}{\lambda_2 L}}10\alpha p_{t-1} - \frac{1}{1 - \lambda_2} + c_4\lambda_2^t$$

$$= \frac{-10\alpha}{\lambda_2}\sum_{j=0}^{\infty}(\frac{1}{\lambda_2})^j p_{t+j} - \frac{1}{1 - \lambda_2} + c_4\lambda_2^t$$

or

$$(1 + \frac{5}{9}L)A_t = 5\alpha\sum_{j=0}^{\infty}(-\frac{9}{20})^j p_{t+j} - \frac{10}{29} + \tilde{c}_4\lambda_2^t.$$

As usual, the optimal $\{A_t\}$ sequence is of exponential order less than $1/\sqrt{\beta}$. But unless $\tilde{c}_4 = 0$, $\{A_t\}$ will be of exponential order no smaller than $\lambda_2 > 1/\sqrt{\beta}$. Thus set $\tilde{c}_4 = 0$ and obtain

$$A_t = -\frac{5}{9}A_{t-1} + 5\alpha\sum_{j=0}^{\infty}(-\frac{9}{20})^j\alpha^j p_t - \frac{10}{29}$$

$$= -\frac{5}{9}A_{t-1} + \frac{5\alpha}{1 - (\frac{-9\alpha}{20})}p_t - \frac{10}{29}$$

$$= -\frac{5}{9}A_{t-1} + \frac{100\alpha}{20 + 9\alpha}p_t - \frac{10}{29}$$

$$= L(A_{t-1}, p_t, \text{constant}),$$

a linear function with $\frac{\partial L}{\partial A_{t-1}} = -\frac{5}{9}$, $\frac{\partial L}{\partial p_t} = \frac{100\alpha}{20 + 9\alpha}$, and constant $= -\frac{10}{29}$. Denote $\frac{\partial L}{\partial A_{t-1}}$ by L_1, $\frac{\partial L}{\partial p_t}$ by L_2, and the constant by L_3. Then, for

$$\alpha = \frac{1}{2}: \quad L_2 = \frac{50}{24.5}$$

$$\alpha = 0: \quad L_2 = 0$$

$$\alpha = -\frac{1}{2}: \quad L_2 = -\frac{50}{15.5} .$$

C. We seek the derivative

$$\frac{\partial y_{t+1}}{\partial p_t} = f_1\left(\frac{\partial A_t}{\partial p_t}\right) = f_1 L_2 = \frac{f_1(100\alpha)}{20 + 9\alpha}.$$

Since $|\alpha| < \frac{1}{\sqrt{\beta}}$ and $\beta = 1$,

$$\frac{\partial y_{t+1}}{\partial p_t} \quad \begin{Bmatrix} > 0 \text{ for } 0 < \alpha < 1 \\ < 0 \text{ for } -1 < \alpha < 0 \end{Bmatrix}.$$

D. The general point is that an agent's decision rules (i.e., the <u>mappings</u> from environment to decisions) are not invariant to changes in the environment. In this case the farmer's current production (next period's output) increases with the current price (p_t) for $0 < \alpha < 1$ and varies inversely with p_t in an environment in which $-1 < \alpha < 0$.

* * *

11. After substituting the constraint into the objective function, the problem becomes: maximize

$$\sum_{t=0}^{\beta} b^t\{u_1[(f - L^{-1})n_t - a - g] - (\tfrac{1}{2})u_2[(f - L^{-1})n_t - a - g]^2 - u_3 n_t - (\tfrac{1}{2})u_4 n_t^2\}$$

by choice of $\{n_s, s > 0\}$, with n_0 given. Using the usual derivative formulas, the Euler equations are given by

$$u_1(f - b^{-1}L) - u_2(f - b^{-1}L)(f - L^{-1})n_t + u_2(a + g)(f - b^{-1}L) - u_3 - u_4 n_t = 0$$

for $t \geq 1$. This expression can be rearranged to get

$$[u_4 + u_2(f - b^{-1}L)(f - L^{-1})]n_t = u_1(f - b^{-1}) + u_2(a + g)(f - b^{-1}) - u_3 \equiv N$$

or

$$- u_2 f[1 - (u_2 f)^{-1}(u_4 + u_2(b^{-1} + f^2))L + b^{-1}L^2]n_{t+1} = N.$$

The polynomial in brackets has the factorization $(1 - \lambda_1 L)(1 - b\lambda_1^{-1}L)$, where $\lambda_1 + \lambda_2 = -\phi/b$; then $-\phi = bu_4/(u_2 f) + f^{-1} + fb > f^{-1} + fb = (bf - 1)(1 - f^{-1}) + 1 + b > 1 + b$. Thus, using Figure 4 in the text, $0 < \lambda_1 < 1 < 1/b < \lambda_2$.

A. The Euler equation is an ordinary second order difference equation with solution

$$n_{t+1} = N/[u_4 + u_2(f - b^{-1}L)(f - L^{-1})] + \gamma_1\lambda_1^t + \gamma_2(b\lambda_1)^{-t}.$$

The Euler equations together with the condition

$$\sum_{t=0}^{\infty} b^t n_t^2 < \infty$$

constitute necessary and sufficient conditions for an optimum. The latter condition requires that $\{n_t\}$ be of exponential order less than $1/\sqrt{\beta}$. But unless $\gamma_2 = 0$, $\{n_t\}$ will be of exponential order no smaller than $(b\lambda_1)^{-1} = \lambda_2 > 1/b$, so set $\gamma_2 = 0$. Then since $\lambda_1^t \to 0$ as $t \to \infty$, $\{n_t\}$ clearly converges as $t \to \infty$.

B. The stationary optimal value of n is, using the definition of N,

$$\bar{n} = \frac{u_1(f - b^{-1}) + u_2(a + g)(f - b^{-1}) - u_3}{u_4 + u_2(f - b^{-1})(f - 1)}$$

$$= \frac{u_1 + u_2(a + g) - u_3/(f - b^{-1})}{u_2(f - 1) + u_4/(f - b^{-1})}.$$

C. After using the constraint $c = (f - 1)n - g$ in the objective function, the problem becomes: maximize, by choice of n, the expression

$$u_1[(f - 1)n - a - g] - (\tfrac{1}{2})u_2[(f - 1)n - a - g]^2 - u_3 n - (\tfrac{1}{2})u_4 n^2.$$

Satisfaction of the first order condition

$$0 = u_1(f - 1) - u_2[(f - 1)n - a - g](f - 1) - u_3 - u_4 n$$

yields a maximum since the second derivative $(-u_2(f - 1) - u_4)$ is negative. Rearranging the first order condition and solving for n_g, one obtains

$$n_g = \frac{u_1(f - 1) + u_2(a + g)(f - 1) - u_3}{u_4 + u_2(f - 1)^2}$$

$$= \frac{u_1 + u_2(a + g) - u_3/(f - 1)}{u_2(f - 1) + u_4/(f - 1)}.$$

The Golden rule c is given by $c_g = (f - 1)n_g - g$.

D. It is straightforward to show that $\bar{n} < n_g$ in general. By inspection of the formulas, it is clear that $\bar{n} = n_g$ when $b = 1$ or $u_3 = u_4 = 0$. The more valuable is utility early in the program (the smaller is the discount factor b) and the more costly are capital and labor to accumulate (the larger are u_3 and u_4), the smaller are stationary n and c. The Golden rule represents "too much" capital accumulation unless there is no discounting or there are no direct costs of accumulating capital. [Notice that Exercise 5 is an example in which capital accumulation is <u>not</u> (directly) costly, and the optimal k_t and c_t therefore converged to their Golden rule values.]

CHAPTER X

LINEAR LEAST SQUARES PROJECTIONS (REGRESSIONS)

EXERCISES

1. Let the demand for money be governed by

$$m_t = p_t + ky + u_t$$

where $Eu_t = 0 = Eu_t m_t$. Here m_t is the log of the money supply, p_t the log of the price level, and y the constant level of the log of real income. Assume that Em_t^2 and Ep_t^2 exist.

Suppose that a researcher attempts to verify the absence of money illusion in this economy by estimating

$$m_t = \alpha p_t + \text{constant} + \text{residual}_t,$$

by least squares, and testing whether $\alpha = 1$. In arbitrarily large samples, will this procedure lead him to conclude the truth, namely that $\alpha = 1$? If this procedure is flawed provide a better one and defend it.

2. Suppose that the expectations theory of the term structure is correct and that

$$R_{2t} = \frac{1}{2}[R_{1t} + E_t R_{1t+1}]$$

where R_{nt} is the yield to maturity on an n-period bond and $E_t\{x\}$ is the mathematical expectation of x conditioned on information available at time t, assumed to include observations on past and present R_1 and R_2. Deduce the implications that the theory delivers for population values of α, β, and λ in the following least squares regression

$$R_{2t} - \frac{1}{2}[R_{1t} + R_{1t+1}] = \alpha + \beta R_{2t-1} + \lambda R_{1t-1} + u_t$$

where u_t is a least squares residual obeying $Eu_t = Eu_t R_{2t-1} = Eu_t R_{1t-1} = 0$.

Use the following information to solve problems 3-8. Let Y and $X \equiv (x_0, x_1, \ldots, x_n)$ be random variables with known means and variances, with $x_0 \equiv 1$.

3. Prove that if $Ex_1x_2 = 0$, then $P[Y|x_1, x_2] = P[Y|x_1] + P[Y|x_2]$.

4. Prove that if $E(x_1, x_2, \ldots, x_n) = (0, 0, \ldots, 0)$, then

$$P[Y|\ 1, x_1, x_2, \ldots, x_n] = P[Y|1] + P[Y|\ x_1, x_2, \ldots, x_n].$$

5. Prove that if $Ex_1x_2 = 0$, then $P[x_1|x_2] = 0$.

6. Let c, d be real numbers. Prove that $P[cY_1 + dY_2|X] = cP[Y_1|X] + dP[Y_2|X]$ where Y_1 and Y_2 are random variables.

7. Use 3, 5, and 6 to prove the Kalman filter (recursive projection) formula, (15'):

$$P[Y|\Omega,X] = P[Y|\Omega] + P\{(Y - P[Y|\Omega])|(X - P[X|\Omega])\}$$

where Ω and X are random variables.

8. Interpret Y, Ω, and X as sets, and $P[Y|\Omega,X]$ as $Y \cap (\Omega \cup X)$. Derive the Kalman filter formula using Venn diagrams. (Interpret Y - X as $Y \cap X^c$ where X^c is the complement of X.)

9. The labor supply schedule is given by

$$N_t = \gamma(w_t - \hat{E}p_t), \qquad \gamma > 0$$

where N_t is the logarithm of employment at time t, w_t is the logarithm of the money wage, and $\hat{E}p_t$ is the workers' perception of the average price of goods they will buy during period t. At the time that they see w_t and must make the decision to work or not, workers don't actually see the prices at which they will be able to buy goods. Instead, they must form their best guess about the average price at which they'll be able to buy things. Workers do know that the average price obeys

$$p_t = k + u_t$$

where k is a constant and u_t a serially uncorrelated random variable with mean zero and variance known by workers to be σ_u^2. The workers also know that w_t obeys

$$w_t = z_t + u_t$$

where z_t is a serially uncorrelated random variable with mean zero and variance σ_z^2. Assume also $Ez_tu_t = 0$. That is, u and z are uncorrelated. The variate z_t measures changes in actual real wages, while the variate u_t measures changes in w and p that actually leave the real wage unchanged. Workers know the value of w_t in each period and the parameters σ_u^2, σ_z^2, and k.

A. Derive an operational labor supply schedule of the form

$$N_t = \phi w_t + h$$

where h is a constant, and derive explicit formulas linking h and ϕ to the parameters γ, σ_u^2 and σ_z^2.

B. A researcher estimates the labor supply schedule, and finds $\phi > 0$ and a very high R^2. The researcher concludes that if the monetary authority wants to make N_t constant over time and equal to some high value N^*, it should follow a monetary policy that makes w constant over time at the value w that solves the equation

$$N^* = \phi w + h.$$

Is this a correct policy conclusion?

10. The consumption function is given by

$$C_t = c(Y_t - T_t^*)$$

where

C_t = consumption at time t

Y_t = income at time t

T_t^* = consumers' perception of the taxes they will pay at time t,

and c is the marginal propensity to consume out of (perceived) disposable income. At the time they make consumption decisions, agents do not know the taxes (T_t) they must pay at time t. Consumers do know that income is described by

$$Y_t = 3T_t + v_t$$

where v_t is a serially uncorrelated random variable with mean zero and variance σ_v^2. In addition, they know c, that $ET_t v_t = 0$ and the variance of T_t: $ET_t^2 = \sigma_T^2$.

A. Derive an operational consumption function of the form $C_t = \beta Y_t$ and give an explicit formula relating β to the parameters c, σ_v^2, and σ_T^2.

B. Suppose the Congress increases the volatility of taxes by an extraordinary amount. What happens to the consumption function?

SOLUTIONS

1. The researcher will incorrectly conclude $\alpha \neq 1$. To see this, notice that estimating

$$m_t = \alpha p_t + \text{constant} + \text{residual}_t$$

by least squares is equivalent to calculating the projection $P[m_t|1,p_t] = \alpha_0 + \alpha p_t$. The coefficients α_0 and α are determined by the normal equations

$$E(1 \quad p_t)'m_t = E(1 \quad p_t)'(1 \quad p_t)(\alpha_0 \quad \alpha)'$$

or

$$E\begin{bmatrix} 1 \\ p_t \end{bmatrix} m_t = E\begin{bmatrix} 1 & p_t \\ p_t & p_t^2 \end{bmatrix} \begin{bmatrix} \alpha_0 \\ \alpha \end{bmatrix}.$$

Since $m_t = p_t + ky + u_t$, the normal equations become

$$\begin{bmatrix} Ep_t + ky \\ Ep_t^2 + kyEp_t + Ep_tu_t \end{bmatrix} = \begin{bmatrix} 1 & Ep_t \\ Ep_t & Ep_t^2 \end{bmatrix} \begin{bmatrix} \alpha_0 \\ \alpha \end{bmatrix}.$$

Note that $Ep_t^2 - (Ep_t)^2 = \sigma_p^2$. Then

$$\begin{bmatrix} \alpha_0 \\ \alpha \end{bmatrix} = \frac{1}{\sigma_p^2} \begin{bmatrix} Ep_t^2 & -Ep_t \\ -Ep_t & 1 \end{bmatrix} \begin{bmatrix} Ep_t + ky \\ Ep_t^2 + kyEp_t + Ep_tu_t \end{bmatrix}.$$

Thus

$$\alpha = \frac{1}{\sigma_p^2} [-(Ep_t)^2 - kyEp_t + Ep_t^2 + kyEp_t + Ep_tu_t]$$

$$= \frac{\sigma_p^2 + Ep_tu_t}{\sigma_p^2}.$$

The estimate α differs from 1 because the least squares orthogonality conditions (which require $Ep_tu_t = 0$) are not satisfied:

$$Ep_tu_t = E(m_t - ky - u_t)u_t = Em_tu_t - kyEu_t - Eu_t^2$$
$$= -Eu_t^2 \neq 0.$$

A projection for which the orthogonality conditions are satisfied is $P[p_t|1, m_t] = \beta_0 + \beta m_t$. Money illusion is absent if and only if $\beta = 1$. The normal equations are

$$E\begin{bmatrix} 1 \\ m_t \end{bmatrix} p_t = E\begin{bmatrix} 1 & m_t \\ m_t & m_t^2 \end{bmatrix}\begin{bmatrix} \beta_0 \\ \beta \end{bmatrix}.$$

Then

$$\begin{bmatrix} \beta_0 \\ \beta \end{bmatrix} = \frac{1}{\sigma_m^2}\begin{bmatrix} Em_t^2 & -Em_t \\ -Em_t & 1 \end{bmatrix}\begin{bmatrix} Em_t - ky \\ Em_t^2 - kyEm_t \end{bmatrix}$$

which gives $\beta = 1$. A researcher employing this procedure will correctly conclude that the economy is not beset by money illusion.

* * *

2. Define ε_t by $R_{1t+1} = E_tR_{1t+1} + \varepsilon_{t+1}$ so that $E\varepsilon_{t+1} = 0 = E\varepsilon_{t+1}R_{1t-1} = E\varepsilon_{t+1}R_{2t-1}$. Then notice that

$$R_{2t} - \frac{1}{2}[R_{1t} + R_{1t+1}] = R_{2t} - \frac{1}{2}[R_{1t} + E_tR_{1t+1} + \varepsilon_t]$$
$$= \frac{1}{2}[R_{1t} + E_tR_{1t+1}] - \frac{1}{2}[R_{1t} + E_tR_{1t+1} + \varepsilon_t]$$
$$= -\frac{1}{2}\varepsilon_{t+1}.$$

The coefficients α, β, and λ in the regression:

$$R_{2t} - \frac{1}{2}[R_{1t} + R_{1t+1}] = \alpha + \beta R_{2t-1} + \lambda R_{1t-1} + u_t$$

are the same as those in the projection

$$P[-\frac{1}{2}\varepsilon_{t+1}|1, R_{2t-1}, R_{1t-1}] = \alpha + \beta R_{2t-1} + \lambda R_{1t-1}.$$

But ε_{t+1} has zero mean and is orthogonal to R_{2t-1} and R_{1t-1}. The normal equations then give $\alpha = \beta = \lambda = 0$. In fact, $u_t = -\frac{1}{2}\varepsilon_t$.

* * *

3. Let $P[Y|x_1, x_2] = a_1x_1 + a_2x_2$. The normal equations are

$$E\begin{bmatrix} x_1 \\ x_2 \end{bmatrix} Y = E\begin{bmatrix} x_1 \\ x_2 \end{bmatrix} [x_1 \; x_2] \begin{bmatrix} a_1 \\ a_2 \end{bmatrix}$$

or

$$\begin{bmatrix} Ex_1Y \\ Ex_2Y \end{bmatrix} = \begin{bmatrix} Ex_1^2 & Ex_1x_2 \\ Ex_2x_1 & Ex_2^2 \end{bmatrix} \begin{bmatrix} a_1 \\ a_2 \end{bmatrix}.$$

But then

$$\begin{bmatrix} a_1 \\ a_2 \end{bmatrix} = \begin{bmatrix} (Ex_1^2)^{-1} & 0 \\ 0 & (Ex_2^2)^{-1} \end{bmatrix} \begin{bmatrix} Ex_1Y \\ Ex_2Y \end{bmatrix}$$

which yields $a_1 = (Ex_1^2)^{-1}Ex_1Y$ and $a_2 = (Ex_2^2)^{-1}Ex_2Y$. Now let $P[Y|x_1] = \tilde{a}_1x_1$, $P[Y|x_2] = \tilde{a}_2x_2$. The parameter $\tilde{a}_1$ is determined by $Ex_1Y = Ex_1^2\tilde{a}_1$. The parameter $\tilde{a}_2$ is determined in a similar fashion. Clearly, $\tilde{a}_1 = a_1$ and $\tilde{a}_2 = a_2$. Thus when $Ex_1x_2 = 0$, $P[Y|x_1, x_2] = P[Y|x_1] + P[Y|x_2]$.

* * *

4. This is a simple consequence of the idea in Exercise 3. Let $P[Y|x_0, x_1, \ldots, x_n] = \Sigma_{j=0}^{n} a_j x_j$ with $x_0 = 1$. Define $x = (x_1, \ldots, x_n)$, $A = (a_0, a_1, \ldots, a_n)$, and $a = (a_1, \ldots, a_n)$. Then the normal equations are:

$$EX'Y = [EX'X]A'$$

$$= \begin{bmatrix} 1 & Ex \\ Ex' & Ex'x \end{bmatrix} [a_0 \; a]'.$$

Since $Ex = 0$, the matrix on the right is block diagonal. Then

$$A' = [a_0 \quad a]' = \begin{bmatrix} 1 & 0 \\ 0 & Ex'x \end{bmatrix}^{-1} EX'Y.$$

Thus $P[Y|X] = a_0 + xa'$. But $a_0 = Ex_0Y$ and a is clearly the solution to the normal equations for $P[Y|x]$; i.e., $P[Y|X] = P[Y|1] + P[Y|x]$.

* * *

5. Let $P[x_1|x_2] = ax_2$. The normal equation is

$$Ex_2x_1 = Ex_2^2a.$$

Thus $0 = Ex_2^2a$. The unique solution is $a = 0$. Thus $P[x_1|x_2] = 0 \cdot x_2 = 0$.

* * *

6. Let $P[cY_1 + dY_2|X] = Xa$ where a is an $(n+1 \times 1)$ vector. The normal equations are: $EX'(cY_1 + dY_2) = EX'Xa$. Thus

$$a = (EX'X)^{-1}(cEX'Y_1 + dEX'Y_2)$$

$$= c(EX'X)^{-1}EX'Y_1 + d(EX'X)^{-1}EX'Y_2.$$

Then $P[cY_1 + dY_2|X] = cX(EX'X)^{-1}EX'Y_1 + dX(EX'X)^{-1}EX'Y_2$. Now let $cP[Y_1|X] = cX\tilde{a}_1$ and $dP[Y_2|X] = dX\tilde{a}_2$. Then $\tilde{a}_1$ is determined from $EX'Y_1 = (EX'X)\tilde{a}_1$. Thus $\tilde{a}_1 = (EX'X)^{-1}EX'Y_1$. Similarly, $a_2 = (EX'X)^{-1}EX'Y_2$. Thus $cP[Y_1|X] + dP[Y_2|X] = cX\tilde{a}_1 + dX\tilde{a}_2 = cX(EX'X)^{-1}EX'Y_1 + dX(EX'X)^{-1}EX'Y_2 = P[cY_1 + dY_2|X]$.

* * *

7. First project X on Ω. Now $X - P[X|\Omega]$ is the resulting forecast error, representing the parts of X which cannot be expressed as linear combinations of the elements of Ω. Thus $X - P[X|\Omega]$ is orthogonal to Ω. But the span of (Ω, X) is the same as the span of $(\Omega, X - P[X|\Omega])$. Thus

$$\begin{aligned} P[Y|\Omega, X] &= P[Y|\Omega, X - P(X|\Omega)] \\ &= P[Y|\Omega] + P[Y|\{X - P(X|\Omega)\}] \end{aligned}$$

by Exercise 3. Now, $P[Y|\Omega]$ is in Ω and is thus orthogonal to $X - P[X|\Omega]$. Then

$$P[P(Y|\Omega)|\{X - P(X|\Omega)\}] = 0$$

by Exercise 5. But then

$$\begin{aligned} P[Y|\Omega, X] &= P[Y|\Omega, \{X - P(X|\Omega)\}] \\ &= P[Y|\Omega] + P[Y|\{X - P(X|\Omega)\}] - P[P(Y|\Omega)|\{X - P(X|\Omega)\}] \\ &= P[Y|\Omega] + P[\{Y - P(Y|\Omega)\}|\{X - P(X|\Omega)\}] \end{aligned}$$

by Exercise 6.

* * *

8. The Venn diagrams appear in Figure 1. In the figure, the set Ω comprises regions a, b, d, and e; the set X comprises regions b, c, e, and f; and the set Y comprises regions d, e, f, and g. Then

$$P[Y|X, \Omega] = \{d, e, f\}$$

$$P[Y|\Omega] = \{d, e\}$$

$$X - P[X|\Omega] = \{c, f\}$$

$$Y - P[Y|\Omega] = \{f, g\}$$

$$P[\{Y - P(Y|\Omega)\}|\{X - P(X|\Omega)\}] = \{f\}.$$

Thus

$$P[Y|X, \Omega] = \{d, e, f\}$$

$$P[Y|\Omega] + P[\{Y - P(Y|\Omega)\}|\{X - P(X|\Omega)\}] = \{d, e\} \cup \{f\} = \{d, e, f\}$$

$$= P[Y|X, \Omega].$$

* * *

9. A. The workers evaluate $\hat{E}p_t$ by projecting $p_t = k + u_t$ on a constant and $w_t = z_t + u_t$. Thus

$$\hat{E}p_t = P[p_t|1, w_t] = a_0 + a_1 w_t.$$

The coefficients a_0 and a_1 solve the normal equations

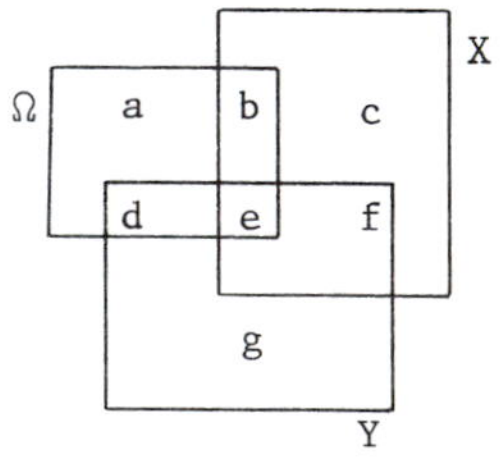

Figure 1

$$E(1 \quad w_t)'p_t = E[(1 \quad w_t)'(1 \quad w_t)](a_0 \quad a_1)'$$

or

$$E\begin{bmatrix} 1 \\ z_t + u_t \end{bmatrix}(k + u_t) = E\begin{bmatrix} 1 & z_t + u_t \\ z_t + u_t & z_t^2 + 2u_t z_t + u_t^2 \end{bmatrix}\begin{bmatrix} a_0 \\ a_1 \end{bmatrix}.$$

Thus

$$\begin{bmatrix} k \\ \sigma_u^2 \end{bmatrix} = \begin{bmatrix} 1 & 0 \\ 0 & \sigma_z^2 + \sigma_u^2 \end{bmatrix}\begin{bmatrix} a_0 \\ a_1 \end{bmatrix}$$

which gives $a_0 = k$, $a_1 = \sigma_u^2/(\sigma_z^2 + \sigma_u^2)$. Thus the labor supply function becomes

$$N_t = \gamma(w_t - a_0 - a_1 w_t)$$

$$= -\gamma k + \gamma[\sigma_z^2/(\sigma_z^2 + \sigma_u^2)]w_t.$$

Hence $h = -\gamma k$, $\phi = \gamma[\sigma_z^2/(\sigma_z^2 + \sigma_u^2)]$.

B. The policy conclusion is incorrect. The reason is that $N_t = h + \phi w_t$ describes behavior $[N_t = \gamma(w_t - \hat{E}p_t)]$ only when w_t is of the form $w_t = z_t + u_t$. When w_t is a constant, $N_t = h + \phi w_t$ is <u>not</u> the operational labor supply curve. To see this, suppose $w_t = \bar{w}$ for all t. Then $\hat{E}p_t = P[p_t|1,\bar{w}] = P[p_t|\bar{w}]$ (since 1 and $\bar{w}$ "span" the same space). Then $P[p_t|\bar{w}] = a\bar{w}$ where a is given by the normal equations

$$E[\bar{w}(k + u_t)] = E[\bar{w}^2 a]$$

which gives $a = k/\bar{w}$. Thus $\hat{E}p_t = a\bar{w} = k$. But then labor supply $N_t = \gamma(w_t - \hat{E}p_t)$ is given by $N_t = \gamma(\bar{w} - k)$ which is clearly constant.

If w is set according to $N^* = \phi w + h$ what labor supply actually occurs? First, solve for w:

$$w = (N^* - h)/\phi$$

$$= (N^* + \gamma k)(\sigma_z^2 + \sigma_u^2)/(\sigma_z^2\gamma).$$

Then actual labor supply is given by

$$N_t = \gamma\{\frac{(N^* + \gamma k)(\sigma_z^2 + \sigma_u^2)}{\gamma\sigma_z^2} - k\}$$

which is clearly <u>not</u> N^*. The correct policy in this context is to choose w to solve $N^* = \gamma(w - k)$.

* * *

10. Agents must solve a signal extraction problem: they know $Y_t = 3T_t + v_t$, $ET_t = Ev_t = ET_tv_t = 0$, $ET_t^2 = \sigma_T^2$, $Ev_t^2 = \sigma_v^2$, yet they want to know T_t. Using the projection formula,

$$T_t^* = P[T_t|3T_t + v_t]$$

$$= a(3T + v_t) = aY_t$$

where a is determined by the normal equation

$$E[3T_t + v_t][T_t] = E[3T_t + v_t]^2a,$$

$$E[3T_t^2 + v_tT_t] = E[9T_t^2 + 6T_tv_t + v_t^2]a,$$

or

$$3\sigma_T^2 = (9\sigma_T^2 + \sigma_v^2)a \qquad (ET_tv_t = 0).$$

Thus $a = 3\sigma_T^2/(9\sigma_T^2 + \sigma_v^2)$ and $T_t^* = (\frac{3\sigma_T^2}{9\sigma_T^2 + \sigma_v^2})Y_t$.

A. The consumption function is now given by

$$C_t = c\left(Y_t - \frac{3\sigma_T^2}{9\sigma_T^2 + \sigma_v^2}Y_t\right)$$

$$= c\left[1 - \frac{3\sigma_T^2}{9\sigma_T^2 + \sigma_v^2}\right]Y_t$$

$$C_t = c\left[\frac{6\sigma_T^2 + \sigma_v^2}{9\sigma_T^2 + \sigma_v^2}\right]Y_t \quad \left(= \beta Y_t \text{ with } \beta = c\left(\frac{6\sigma_T^2 + \sigma_v^2}{9\sigma_T^2 + \sigma_v^2}\right)\right)$$

which is an operational consumption function.

B. The volatility of taxes is measured by σ_T^2. Now as $\sigma_T^2 \to \infty$,

$$\frac{6\sigma_T^2 + \sigma_v^2}{9\sigma_T^2 + \sigma_v^2} \to \frac{6}{9} = \frac{2}{3}\ .$$

Thus as σ_T^2 is increased, the consumption function begins behaving like

$$C_t = \frac{2}{3}Y_t.$$

CHAPTER XI

LINEAR STOCHASTIC DIFFERENCE EQUATIONS

EXERCISES

1. (Sims's approximation error formula) Let (y_t, x_t) be jointly covariance stationary with means of zero. Let the projection of y_t on the x process be

$$\sum_{j=-\infty}^{\infty} b_j^0 x_{t-j}.$$

Suppose a researcher fits by least squares

$$y_t = \sum_{t=-\infty}^{\infty} b_j^1 x_{t-j} + u_t$$

where u_t is a disturbance and $\{b_j^1\}$ is a constrained parameterization so that b_j^1 cannot equal b_j^0 for all j. Some examples of commonly encountered constrained parametrizations are:

(i) truncation: $b_j^1 = 0$ for $|j| > m$, m a fixed positive integer;

(ii) polynomial approximation: $b_j^1 = \alpha_0 + \alpha_1 j + \ldots + \alpha_m j^m$, m a fixed positive integer, α_j free;

(iii) Pascal lag distributions (Solow)

$$b^1(L) = \frac{1}{(1 - \lambda L)^r}$$

where r is a fixed positive integer and $|\lambda| < 1$.

Derive Sims's formula, which asserts that in population, least squares picks b_j^1 to minimize

$$\int_{-\pi}^{\pi} |b^0(e^{-i\omega}) - b^1(e^{-i\omega})|^2 g_x(e^{-i\omega}) d\omega.$$

Hints: (a) Write y_t as

$$y_t = \sum_{j=-\infty}^{\infty} b_j^0 x_{t-j} + \varepsilon_t,$$

$E\varepsilon_t x_{t-j} = 0$ for all j. Then show that

$$E\Big(y_t - \sum_{j=-\infty}^{\infty} b_j^1 x_{t-j}\Big)^2 = E(z_t^2)$$

where

$$z_t = \sum_{j=-\infty}^{\infty} \big(b_j^0 - b_j^1\big) x_{t-j} + \varepsilon_t.$$

(b) Apply formula (33) to calculate the spectrum of z_t. (c) Apply formula (20) to calculate the variance of z_t (see Sims, 1972b).

2. ("Optimal" seasonal adjustment via signal extraction) Suppose that an analyst is interested in estimating x_t but only observes $X_t = x_t + u_t$ where $Ex_t u_s = 0$ for all t and s, and where x_t and u_t are both covariance stationary stochastic processes with means of zero and known (to the analyst) covariance generating functions $g_x(z)$ and $g_u(z)$ respectively; $g_u(e^{-i\omega}) > 0$ for all ω, but has most of its power concentrated at seasonal frequencies. The analyst estimates x_t by the projection

$$\hat{x}_t = \sum_{j=-\infty}^{\infty} h_j X_{t-j},$$

the projection of the unknown x_t on the X_t process.

A. Derive a formula for the h_j (use (45)).

B. Prove that $g_{\hat{x}}(e^{-i\omega}) < g_x(e^{-i\omega})$ for all ω.

C. Prove that if $g_x(e^{-i\omega})$ is relatively smooth across the seasonal and nonseasonal frequencies, then since $g_u(e^{-i\omega})$ has big peaks at the seasonal frequencies, it follows that $g_{\hat{x}}(e^{-i\omega})$ will have substantial dips at the seasonal frequencies.

3. Let x_t be any covariance stationary stochastic process with $Ex_t = 0$.

A. Prove that there exists a representation

$$x_t = \sum_{j=0}^{\infty} c_j u_{t+j} + \theta_t$$

where $c_0 = 1$, $\Sigma c_j^2 < \infty$, $Eu_t^2 \geq 0$, $Eu_t u_s = 0$ for $t \neq s$ and $E\theta_t u_s = 0$ for all t and s; θ_t is a process that can be predicted arbitrarily well by a linear function of only <u>future</u> values of x; and $u_t = x_t - P[x_t | x_{t+1}, x_{t+2}, \ldots]$.

B. Prove that $c_j = d_j$ where d_j is the object in Wold's theorem.

C. Does $u_t = \varepsilon_t$ where ε_t is the object in Wold's theorem? Does $Eu_t^2 = E\varepsilon_t^2$?

D. Does $\theta_t = \eta_t$ where η_t is the object in Wold's theorem?

4. Consider the "explosive" first-order Markov process $y_t = \lambda y_{t-1} + \varepsilon_t$, $t = 1, 2, \ldots$, $\lambda > 1$, where ε_t is white noise with mean zero and variance σ_ε^2, and y_0 is given.

A. Prove that for each realization $(\varepsilon_1, \varepsilon_2, \ldots,)$ the y_t process has the representation

$$y_t = \lambda^t \eta_0 + \frac{1}{1 - \lambda^{-1}L} u_t$$

where u_t is a white noise. Find formulas for η_0 and u_t in terms of the ε process, λ, and y_0. (Hint: solve the difference equation forward and impose the initial condition.)

B. Is the u_t process "fundamental" for y_t?

5. Consider the univariate first-order mixed moving average, autoregressive process $z_t = \lambda z_{t-1} + a_t - \beta a_{t-1}$ where a_t is a fundamental white noise for z, $0 < \beta < 1$ and $0 < \lambda < 1$.

A. Write the process in the form (104). (Hint: try $x_t = (z_t, a_t)'$ and $\varepsilon_t = (a_t, a_t)'$.)

B. Use formula (108) to derive a formula for $P[z_{t+2} | z_t, z_{t-1}, \ldots]$. Verify that this answer agrees with the result of applying the Wiener-Kolmogorov formula (62).

6. For the processes below, determine whether x Granger causes y and whether y Granger causes x.

A. $g_x(z) = \sigma_\varepsilon^2 [\frac{1}{1 - 0.9z}][\frac{1}{1 - 0.9z^{-1}}]$,

$g_y(z) = \sigma_u^2 (1 - 0.8z)(1 - 0.8z^{-1})$,

$g_{yx}(z) = \sigma_{u\varepsilon}(1 - 0.8z)(1 + 0.5z^{-1})$.

B. $g_x(z) = \sigma_\varepsilon^2 (1 + 0.99z)(1 + 0.99z^{-1})$,

$g_y(z) = \sigma_u^2 (\frac{1}{1 - 0.7z + 0.3z^2})(\frac{1}{1 - 0.7z^{-1} + 0.3z^{-2}})$,

$$g_{yx}(z) = \sigma_{u\varepsilon}(1 + 0.2z)(1 + 0.99z^{-1}).$$

C. $$g_x(z) = \sigma_\varepsilon^2\left(\frac{1}{1 - 0.7z}\right)\left(\frac{1}{1 - 0.7z^{-1}}\right),$$

$$g_y(z) = \sigma_u^2\left(\frac{1}{1 - 0.8z}\right)\left(\frac{1}{1 - 0.8z^{-1}}\right),$$

$$g_{yx}(z) = \sigma_{u\varepsilon}\left(\frac{1}{1 - 0.8z}\right)\left(\frac{1}{1 - 0.7z^{-1}}\right).$$

7. Consider the simple Keynesian macroeconomic model

$$c_t = \sum_{j=0}^{\infty} b_j Y_{t-j} + \varepsilon_t, \qquad \sum_{j=0}^{\infty} b_j^2 < \infty, \qquad c_t + I_t = Y_t \tag{*}$$

where c_t, Y_t, and I_t are consumption, GNP, and investment, respectively, all measured as deviations from their means. Here ε_t is a stationary disturbance process that satisfies $E\varepsilon_t I_s = E\varepsilon_t = 0$ for all t and s and I_s is a stationary stochastic process. Assume that $(1 - b(L))$ has a one-sided, square summable inverse in nonegative powers of L.

A. Determine whether Y Granger causes I.

B. Determine whether c Granger causes Y and whether Y Granger causes c. (Hint: solve for c_t and Y_t each as "reduced form" functions of I and ε, then apply formula (18) to calculate the cross spectrum and use formula (45) to investigate Granger causality.)

C. Is the consumption function (*) a projection (regression) equation?

8. Consider a (y,x) process that has a Wold moving average representation

$$y_t = a(L)\varepsilon_t + ka(L)u_t, \qquad x_t = c(L)\varepsilon_t$$

where k is a constant, a(L) and c(L) are each one-sided on the past and present and square summable, $Eu_t = E\varepsilon_t = Eu_t\varepsilon_s = 0$ for all t and s, and where ε_t and u_t are jointly fundamental for y and x. Finally, assume that both a(L) and c(L) are invertible, i.e., have square summable inverses that are one-sided in nonnegative powers of L.

A. Determine whether y Granger causes x and whether x Granger causes y.

B. Find the coefficient generating function for the projection of y on the entire x process.

C. Find the coefficient generating function for the projection of x on the entire y process.

D. Obtain a different Wold moving average representation for the (y,x) process. (Hint: choose one white noise process as $\eta_{1t} \equiv \varepsilon_t + ku_t$, and choose the other as η_{2t}, the error in the projection of ε_t on $\varepsilon_t + ku_t$, $\varepsilon_t = \rho(ku_t + \varepsilon_t) + \eta_{2t}$, where η_{2t} is a least squares disturbance.)

9. Consider Lucas's aggregate supply curve

$$y_t = \gamma(p_t - P[p_t|\Omega_{t-1}]) + \lambda y_{t-1} + u_t, \qquad 0 < |\lambda| < 1,\ \gamma > 0 \qquad (*)$$

where y is the log of real GNP, p the log of the price level, and u_t a stationary random disturbance process. Suppose that p_t follows the Markov process

$$p_t = \sum_{i=1}^{n} w_i p_{t-i} + \varepsilon_t \qquad (\dagger)$$

where $P[\varepsilon_t|\Omega_{t-1}] = 0$. Here Ω_{t-1} is an information set including at least lagged y's and lagged p's.

A. Suppose that $P[u_t|\Omega_{t-1}] = 0$, so that u_t is serially uncorrelated. Prove that p fails to Granger cause y. (In fact, this can be proved where p follows any arbitrary stationary stochastic process and is not dependent on p following (†).)

B. Now assume (†) and suppose that u_t is serially correlated, and in particular that

$$u_t = \rho u_{t-1} + \xi_t, \qquad 0 < |\rho| < 1$$

where $P[\xi_t|\Omega_{t-1}] = 0$. Prove that p Granger causes y by calculating

$$P[y_t|y_{t-1}, y_{t-2}, \ldots, p_{t-1}, p_{t-2}, \ldots].$$

10. Suppose that y_t fails to Granger cause x, where both y and x are seasonally unadjusted processes. Suppose that an investigator studies seasonally adjusted processes y_t^a and x_t^a (see Sims, 1974):

$$y_t^a = f(L)y_t, \qquad x_t^a = g(L)x_t$$

where f(L) and g(L) are each finite-order two-sided, symmetric ($f_j = f_{-j}$, $g_j = g_{-j}$) seasonal adjustment filters chosen so that y_t^a and x_t^a have less power at the seasonal frequencies than do y_t and x_t, respectively. Assume that y_t^a and x_t^a are strictly linearly indeterministic, as are y_t and x_t. Prove that if $f(L) \neq g(L)$, then y_t^a in general Granger causes x_t^a. (Hint: first calculate the coefficient generating function for the projection of y_t on the x process, then calculate the coefficient generating function for the projection of y_t^a on the x^a process.)

11. In a recent article, a macroeconomist reported a regression of the log of the price level (p_t) on current and past values of the log of the

money supply (m_t):

$$p_t = a + \sum_{j=0}^{\infty} h_j m_{t-j} + \varepsilon_t, \qquad E\varepsilon_t m_{t-j} = 0 \quad \text{for } j \geq 0 \qquad (*)$$
$$E\varepsilon_t = 0$$

where ε_t is a random disturbance. He found that the h_j were nonzero for many j's. He concluded that prices are "too sticky" to be explained by an equilibrium model. According to this economist, "classical" macroeconomics implies that $h_0 = 1$ and $h_j = 0$ for $j \neq 0$.

Now consider the following classical macroeconomic model:

$$m_t - p_t = \alpha(P_t p_{t+1} - p_t) + y_t + u_t \quad \text{(portfolio balance schedule)}$$

y_t = constant (extreme classical full-employment assumption). Here $\alpha < 0$, and u_t is a stationary random process obeying

$$Eu_t m_s = 0 \quad \text{for all } t,\ s, \qquad Eu_t = 0.$$

The money supply is exogenous and has moving average representation

$$m_t = d(L)e_t, \quad e_t = m_t - P[m_t | m_{t-1}, m_{t-2}, \ldots], \quad \text{and} \quad \sum_{j=0}^{\infty} d_j^2 < \infty.$$

Derive a formula giving the $h(L) = \Sigma_{j=0}^{\infty} h_j L^j$ in (*) as a function of α and $d(L)$. Is the macroeconomist correct in his interpretation of the implications of classical theory?

12. Let the portfolio balance schedule be Cagan's

$$\mu_t - x_t = \alpha(P_t x_{t+1} - P_{t-1} x_t) + \eta_t \qquad (*)$$

where μ_t is the rate of growth of the money supply, x_t is the rate of inflation, and η_t satisfies $P_{t-1}\eta_t = 0$, where $P_t[y] \equiv P[y | \mu_t, \mu_{t-1}, \ldots,$

$x_t, x_{t-1}, \ldots$) in which y is any random variable. (Equation (*) is just the first difference of Equation (93) in the text.)

A. Prove that a solution of (*) is

$$P_t x_{t+1} = \frac{1}{1-\alpha} \sum_{j=1}^{\infty} \left(\frac{-\alpha}{1-\alpha}\right)^{j-1} P_t \mu_{t+j}. \tag{†}$$

B. Suppose that (x_t, μ_t) has the bivariate vector moving average, autoregressive representation

$$\begin{bmatrix} x_t \\ \mu_t \end{bmatrix} = \begin{bmatrix} 1 & 0 \\ 1-\lambda & \lambda \end{bmatrix} \begin{bmatrix} x_{t-1} \\ \mu_{t-1} \end{bmatrix} + \begin{bmatrix} a_{1t} - \lambda a_{1t-1} \\ a_{2t} - \lambda a_{2t-1} \end{bmatrix}$$

where $a_{1t} = x_t - P_{t-1}x_t$, $a_{2t} = \mu_t - P_{t-1}\mu_t$, $|\lambda| < 1$, and a_{1t} and a_{2t} have finite variances and nonzero covariance. Prove that Cagan's formula for the expected rate of inflation π_t,

$$\pi_t = \frac{1-\lambda}{1-\lambda L} x_t$$

is implied by the hypothesis of rational expectations, i.e., by equation (†).

C. Prove that μ fails to Granger cause x.

D. Calculate the coefficients in the projection of $\mu_t - x_t$ on the x_t process. Is this projection equation the same as Cagan's equation

$$\mu_t - x_t = \frac{\alpha(1-\lambda)}{(1-\lambda L)}(1-L)x_t + \xi_t, \tag{§}$$

where ξ_t is random? If not, use your formula for the projection equation to determine the biases that would emerge from mistakenly regarding Cagan's (§) as a projection equation.

13. Depreciation, Gestation, and Delivery Lags. Consider a firm that is a perfect competitor in the market for its one output, and a

monopsonist in the market for additions to the stock of the single factor of production that it uses, capital. The firm sells its output at the price p, which is constant over time. Output in period t, q(t), is produced according to the production function

$$q(t) = A_0 + A_1 K(t) - \frac{A_2}{2} K(t)^2, \qquad A_0,\ A_1,\ A_2 > 0 \tag{1}$$

where K(t) is the firm's capital stock at the beginning of period t. The firm's capital stock is related to its investment decisions at t and earlier by

$$K(t) = g(L) I(t) \tag{2}$$

where I(t) is investment in period t, and

$$g(L) = g_0 + g_1 L + g_2 L^2 + \dots .$$

The polynomial g(L) reflects depreciation, delivery, and possible gestation lags. (A common example is the geometrical model $g(L) = L/(1 - (1 - \delta)L)$ where δ is "the" depreciation rate; (2) is designed to encompass this as well as all sorts of plausible alternative models of depreciation and gestation-delivery lags.) The firm faces a supply curve for investment of

$$J(t) = B_0 + \frac{B_1}{2} I(t) + \varepsilon(t) \qquad B_0,\ B_1 > 0$$

where J(t) is the price of investment goods, and where $\varepsilon(t)$ is a bounded sequence of shocks to supply. There is no uncertainty.

The firm's problem is to maximize undiscounted present value

$$\sum_{t=0}^{\infty} \{p[A_0 + A_1 g(L)I(t) - \frac{A_2}{2}[g(L)I(t)]^2] \tag{3}$$

$$- [B_0 + \frac{B_1}{2}I(t) + \varepsilon(t)]I(t)\}$$

with respect to $\{I(t): t \geq 0\}$ and taking as given $\{I(-s): s > 0\}$ and $\{\varepsilon(t): t \geq 0\}$. Answer the following questions:

A. Prove that the Euler equation for this problem is of the form

$$\{-B_0 - \varepsilon(t) + pA_1 g(1)\} = \{pA_2 g(L^{-1})g(L) + B_1\}I(t).$$

B. Prove that if $B_1 > 0$, then the optimal investment plan is obtained by solving the stable roots of the characteristic polynomial $\{pA_2 g(L^{-1})g(L) + B_1\}$ backwards, the unstable roots forwards.

C. Solve the special version of this problem that results when

$$g(L) = \frac{L}{1 - \mu L}$$

where $\mu = 1 - \delta$, δ = the depreciation rate, $0 < \mu < 1$.

D. Argue that the characteristic polynomial that must be factored in solving problem (C) is equivalent with the one encountered by John F. Muth in his signal extraction interpretation of the permanent income hypothesis. State a version of that signal extraction problem that leads to this same characteristic polynomial as encountered in (C).

14. Let (y_t, x_t) be a jointly covariance stationary process with means of zero. Consider the projection equations

$$x_t = \sum_{j=-\infty}^{\infty} b_j y_{t-j} + \varepsilon_t, \qquad E\varepsilon_t y_s = 0 \text{ for all } t, s \tag{i}$$

$$y_t = \sum_{j=-\infty}^{\infty} h_j x_{t-j} + u_t, \qquad Eu_t x_s = 0 \text{ for all } t, s. \tag{ii}$$

Let $g_y(\omega)$, $g_x(\omega)$, $g_u(\omega)$, $g_\varepsilon(\omega)$ be the spectral densities of y, x, u, and ε, respectively.

A. Prove that the coherence satisfies

$$\text{coh}(\omega) = 1 - \frac{g_u(\omega)}{g_y(\omega)}$$

$$\text{coh}(\omega) = 1 - \frac{g_\varepsilon(\omega)}{g_x(\omega)} .$$

B. Prove that the R^2 in equation (i) (i.e., $1 - (E\varepsilon^2/Ex^2)$) is given by

$$R^2_{xy} = \frac{\frac{1}{2\pi}\int_{-\pi}^{\pi} \text{coh}(\omega) g_x(\omega)\,d\omega}{\frac{1}{2\pi}\int_{-\pi}^{\pi} g_x(\omega)\,d\omega}.$$

C. Prove that the R^2 in equation (ii) is given by

$$R^2_{yx} = \frac{\frac{1}{2\pi}\int_{-\pi}^{\pi} \text{coh}(\omega) g_y(\omega)\,d\omega}{\frac{1}{2\pi}\int_{-\pi}^{\pi} g_y(\omega)\,d\omega} .$$

15. Let y_t be a mixed moving average, autoregressive process $y_t = (B(L)/A(L))\varepsilon_t$, where ε_t is a white noise with unit variance, $B(L) = \Pi_{j=1}^{m}(1 - \mu_j L)$, and $A(L) = \Pi_{j=1}^{n}(1 - \lambda_j L)$, $|\lambda_j| < 1$ for $j = 1, \ldots, n$ and where $\lambda_j \neq \lambda_i$ for $\substack{j=1 \\ i\neq j}$, $\lambda_j \neq \mu_k$ for all $j = 1, \ldots, n$, $k = 1, \ldots, m$, and $m < n$. The autocovariance generating function for y is $g_y(z) = [B(z)B(z^{-1})]/[A(z)A(z^{-1})]$. Use formula (25) to establish the formula

$$c_y(\tau) = \sum_{s=1}^{n} \frac{\lambda_s^{n+|\tau|-m-1} \prod_{j=1}^{m} (1 - \mu_j\lambda_s)(\lambda_s - \mu_j)}{\prod_{j=1}^{n} (1 - \lambda_j\lambda_s) \prod_{\substack{j=1 \\ j\neq s}}^{n} (\lambda_s - \lambda_j)} .$$

16. Let $b(L)$ be the polynomial in the lag operator $b(L) = (1 + \mu L)/(1 - \lambda L) = \Sigma_{j=-\infty}^{\infty} b_j L^j$ where $|\lambda| < 1$. Use formula (25) to establish that

$$b_j = \begin{cases} 0 & j < 0 \\ 1 & j = 0 \\ \lambda^j + \mu\lambda^{j-1} & j \geq 1. \end{cases}$$

17. Consider the generating function of the second-order Solow-Pascal lag distribution $w(z) = 1/(1 - \lambda z)^2$, $|\lambda| < 1$. Use formulas (23) and (25) to evaluate the coefficients of the lag distribution. Compare your results with equation (31) of Chapter IX.

18. Let x_t be a covariance stationary stochastic process with mean zero and covariogram

$$c(\tau) = \begin{cases} 1.25, & \tau = 0 \\ -.5, & \tau = 1 \\ 0, & |\tau| \geq 2. \end{cases}$$

A. Use a computer to calculate the projections

$$\hat{x}_t = P[x_t | x_{t-1}, \ldots, x_{t-n}] = \sum_{j=1}^{n} A_j^{(n)} x_{t-j}$$

for $n = 1, 2, 3, 4, 5$. As n increases, is A_j^n for fixed j seeming to approach a limit? What value seems to be approached?

B. Use the method of Section 15 to find a Wold (fundamental) moving average representation for x_t. Invert this moving average representation to obtain the autoregressive representation

$$\hat{x}_t = \sum_{j=1}^{\infty} A_j x_{t-j}.$$

Do the A_j^n calculated in part A seem to be approaching A_j as $n \to \infty$?

Three inverse optimal prediction problems.

19. Suppose that x_t is a stochastic process with Wold representation

$$x_t = c(L)\varepsilon_t, \qquad \varepsilon_t = x_t - P[x_t|x_{t-1},\ldots].$$

Suppose that x_t satisfies

$$P[x_{t+1}|x_t, x_{t-1},\ldots] = \rho x_t, \qquad |\rho| < 1.$$

Use the Wiener-Kolmogorov formula to prove that c(L) must be $1/(1 - \rho L)$.

20. Suppose that x_t is a stochastic process with Wold representation $x_t = c(L)\varepsilon_t$ where $\varepsilon_t = x_t - P[x_t|x_{t-1},\ldots]$. Suppose that x_t is such that

$$P[x_{t+2}|x_t, x_{t-1},\ldots] = \rho P[x_{t+1}|x_t, x_{t-1},\ldots]$$

where $|\rho| < 1$. Use the Wiener-Kolmogorov formula to prove that c(L) must be given by

$$c(L) = \frac{c_0 + (c_1 - \rho c_0)L}{1 - \rho L} .$$

21. Suppose that x_t is a stochastic process with Wold representation $x_t = c(L)\varepsilon_t$, where $\varepsilon_t = x_t - P[x_t]x_{t-1}, \ldots]$. Suppose that x_t is such that

$$P[x_{t+k}|x_t, x_{t-1}, \ldots] = \rho^{k-1}P[x_{t+1}|x_t, x_{t-1}, \ldots]$$

for all $k \geq 1$ where $|\rho| < 1$. Use the Wiener-Kolmogorov prediction formula to prove that $c(L) = (c_0 + (c_1 - \rho c_0)L)/(1 - \rho L)$.

22. (Seasonality) Consider a firm that faces the following optimum problem: to maximize

$$E_0 \sum_{t=0}^{\infty} \{f_0 n_t - \frac{f_1}{2} n_t^2 - \frac{d}{2}(n_t - n_{t-1})^2 - w_t n_t\} \tag{1}$$

subject to n_{-1} given, and where f_0, f_1, $d > 0$; E_t is the mathematical expectation conditioned on information known at time t. Here n_t is employment at t, and w_t is the real wage at t. The firm maximizes (1) over linear contingency plans for setting n_t as a function of information available at t, which includes n_{t-1} and $\{w_t, w_{t-1}, \ldots\}$. The real wage w_t is assumed to follow the Markov process

$$(1 - \delta L^4)w_t = \varepsilon_t, \qquad 0 < \delta < 1 \tag{2}$$

where ε_t is a fundamental white noise for w_t (we shall ignore constant terms in the w_t process). The data are <u>quarterly</u>.

A. Compute the <u>spectrum</u> of the w_t process, and plot it. Argue that w_t is characterized by a strong seasonal.

B. Compute the optimal linear decision rule of the form

$$n_t = \lambda n_{t-1} + \sum_{j=0}^{3} h_j w_{t-j}, \tag{3}$$

giving explicit closed-form formulas for the h_j's. Describe the cross-equation restrictions between the parameters of the Markov process (2) for w_t and the parameters of the decision rule (3).

C. Calculate the projection of n_t against $\{w_t, w_{t-1}, \ldots\}$. Then calculate the projection of n_t against the entire w process, $\{\ldots w_{t+2}, w_{t+1}, w_t, w_{t-1}, \ldots\}$. Argue that n fails to Granger cause w.

D. Because of the strong seasonal in real wages, an analyst forms the "seasonally adjusted" series

$$n_t^a = (1 - \delta L^4) n_t$$

$$w_t^a = (1 - \delta L^4) w_t.$$

Assuming that the economic agents look at the seasonally <u>un</u>adjusted series in forming their decisions, and so behave according to (3), calculate the projection of n_t^a on $\{w_t^a, w_{t-1}^a, \ldots\}$.

E. Suppose that economic agents care about the seasonally <u>un</u>adjusted data, and so behave according to (3). But, as often has been the practice, the econometrician uses the seasonally adjusted data. Let the econometrician construct his model by imagining that the agent is maximizing

$$E_0 \sum_{t=0}^{\infty} \{f_0 n_t^a - \frac{f_1}{2} n_t^{a^2} - \frac{d}{2}(n_t^a - n_{t-1}^a)^2 - w_t^a n_t^a\}$$

subject to n_{-1}^{a} given and the law of motion for w_t^a implied by (2) and the definition of w_t^a.

(i) Derive the decision rule of the form

$$n_t^a = \tilde{\lambda} n_{t-1}^a + \sum_{j=0}^{3} \tilde{h}_j w_{t-j}^a$$

that the econometrician attributes to the agent. Describe the cross-equation restrictions built into the econometrician's model.

(ii) Use the projection of n_t^a on w_t^a that you calculated earlier to argue that the econometrician's cross-equation restrictions will not describe the agents' behavior. Describe how the econometrician could mistakenly reject the "rational expectations hypothesis" because of his procedure of using seasonally adjusted data.

23. Consider a jointly covariance stationary, linearly indeterministic stochastic process (y_t, x_t, X_t) with means of zero. The processes y_t, x_t, X_t are connected as follows. The variable y_t is determined as

$$y_t = \alpha \sum_{j=0}^{\infty} \lambda^j P[x_{t+j} | \Omega_t], \qquad \alpha > 0, \ 0 < \lambda < 1 \tag{1}$$

where P is the linear least squares projection operator and $\Omega_t \supset \Omega_{t-1} \supset \Omega_{t-2}$ ... and $\Omega_t = (x_t, x_{t-1}, x_{t-2} \ldots)$. (In (1), y_t might be the log of the price level and x_t the log of the money supply, so that (1) becomes an implication of Cagan's portfolio balance condition.) There is available a noisy measure of x_t, namely X_t, which is governed by

$$X_t = x_t + u_t, \tag{2}$$

where u_t is a mean zero stochastic process satisfying $Eu_s x_t = 0$ for all t and s. The process u_t has covariance generating function

$$g_u(z) = \sum_{\tau=-\infty}^{\infty} z^{\tau} Eu_t u_{t-\tau}. \tag{3}$$

We suppose that $g_u(z)$ is known to an econometrician. We shall think of u_t as being a seasonal noise, so that $g_u(e^{-i\omega})$ has much of its power concentrated at the seasonal frequencies (although nothing in the analytics of this problem restricts us to this interpretation). The econometrician observes the processes for y_t, X_t, but not x_t. In preparation for estimation, the econometrician is interested in characterizing the restrictions which his knowledge (1), (2) and (3) places on the observables y_t, X_t. In answering the following questions, assume that the econometrician knows the covariance generating functions for all of the observables, $g_X(z)$, $g_y(z)$, $g_{yX}(z)$, as well as the covariance generating function (3).

A. Given the generating functions that are known, describe how to obtain a univariate Wold representation for X_t,

$$X_t = d(L)a_t \tag{4}$$

where $a_t = X_t - P[X_t | X_{t-1}, \ldots]$, $\Sigma_{j=0}^{\infty} d_j^2 < +\infty$.

B. Given the known generating functions, give a formula for $\theta(L)$ in the one-sided projection

$$x_t = \theta(L)X_t + \varepsilon_t \tag{5}$$

where $E\varepsilon_t X_{t-s} = 0$ for $s \geq 0$, $\theta(L) = \sum_{j=0}^{\infty} \theta_j L^j$. Define the "one-sided seasonally adjusted" series $\tilde{x}_t$ as

$$\tilde{x}_t = \theta(L)X_t. \tag{6}$$

How does $\tilde{x}_t$ compare with $\hat{x}_t$ associated with the two-sided seasonal adjustment procedure described in Problem 2?

C. Consider the projection of y_t on X_t, X_{t-1}, ...,

$$y_t = h(L)X_t + s_t \tag{7}$$

where $h(L) = \Sigma_{j=0}^{\infty} h_j L^j$ and $Es_t X_{t-j} = 0$ for $j \geq 0$. Prove that

$$h(L) = \alpha\left[\frac{\theta(L) - \lambda L^{-1}\theta(\lambda)d(\lambda)d(L)^{-1}}{1 - \lambda L^{-1}}\right] \tag{8}$$

(Hint: at this point it might help to be familiar with pages 266-277 of "Instrumental Variables Procedures for Estimating Linear Rational Expectations Models," by Lars Hansen & Thomas Sargent, Journal of Monetary Economics, 1982.)

D. Using long division on (8), derive explicit formulas for the h_j's in terms of λ, the θ_j's and the parameters of d(L). (Here it might help to consult Hansen & Sargent, "A Note on Wiener-Kolmogorov Formulas in Linear Rational Expectations Models," Economics Letters, 1982.)

E. Describe how to find a Wold representation for $\tilde{x}_t$ defined by (6). In the course of answering this question, describe special conditions on $\theta(L)$ which imply that

$$\tilde{x}_t = \theta(L)d(L)a_t$$

is a Wold representation for the one-sided seasonally adjusted series $\tilde{x}_t$.

F. Since the econometrician does not have data on x_t but has data on $\tilde{x}_t$, a friend recommends that he or she use the model

$$y_t = \alpha \sum_{j=0}^{\infty} \lambda^j P[\tilde{x}_{t+j} | \tilde{x}_t, \tilde{x}_{t-1}, \ldots] + \tilde{s}_t = f(L)\tilde{x}_t + \tilde{s}_t \tag{9}$$

where $E\tilde{s}_t\tilde{x}_{t-j} = 0$ for $j \geq 0$. (This model is derived by assuming that the agents in the model are acting on the basis of forecasts of the one-sided seasonally adjusted series $\tilde{x}_t$, when in fact they are setting y_t on the basis of forecasts of x_t.) Derive an explicit formula for f(L) in terms of the parameters of the Wold representation for $\tilde{x}_t$.

G. Under what circumstances is $f(L)\tilde{x}_t = h(L)X_t$, where $f(L)\tilde{x}_t$ is from (9) and $h(L)X_t$ is from (7)? Interpret these circumstances as describing conditions under which correct restrictions on the y_t, X_t process are derived by proceeding as if the agents set y_t as a function of forecasts of $\tilde{x}_t$.

H. Collect the restrictions on (y_t, x_t) as

$$X_t = d(L)a_t \tag{4}$$

$$x_t = \theta(L)X_t + \varepsilon_t \tag{5}$$

$$y_t = h(L)X_t + s_t \tag{7}$$

where $\theta(L)$, $d(L)$, $h(L)$ are given by the formulas that you have derived.

(i) Argue that in general y Granger causes X in (7). Prove that y <u>fails</u> to Granger cause x. (Hint: start by going back to equation (1).)

(ii) Argue informally (but precisely) that there is no reason to expect s_t to be serially uncorrelated.

(iii) Let s_t have a Wold representation $s_t = c(L)\eta_t$ where η_t is a fundamental white noise for s_t. Argue that in general $E\eta_t X_{t-j} \neq 0$ for $j \geq 0$. (Therefore, backward filtering in (5) designed to whiten the residual destroys the orthogonality with X_{t-j}.)

(iv) Prove that s_t has a representation $s_t = c(L^{-1})\tilde{\eta}_t$ where $\tilde{\eta}_t = s_t - P[s_t | s_{t+1}, s_{t+2}, \ldots]$. Prove that (5) implies that $E\tilde{\eta}_t X_{t-j} = 0$ for $j \geq 0$.

(v) Interpret the results in 3 and 4 in terms of the considerations motivating Hayashi and Sims.

I. Briefly describe an econometric strategy for estimating λ and α from the orthogonality conditions associated with (4), (5), and (7).

24. Let x_t have the Wold representation

$$x_t = c(L)\varepsilon_t, \qquad c(Z) = \sum_{j=0}^{\infty} c_j Z^j$$

where $\varepsilon_t = x_t - P[x_t | x_{t-1}, \ldots]$. Assume that x_t has an autoregressive representation so that $a(L)x_t = \varepsilon_t$ where $c(L)^{-1} = a(L)$.

Derive a formula for the h_j's in

$$\hat{E}_t\left[\sum_{j=0}^{\infty} \lambda^j x_{t+j+1} | x_t, x_{t-1}, \ldots\right] = \sum_{j=0}^{\infty} h_j x_{t-j}. \qquad |\lambda| < 1.$$

25. Assume that the first difference of a stochastic process z_t is covariance stationary, purely linearly indeterministic, and has Wold moving average representation

$$(1 - L)z_t = c(L)\varepsilon_t \tag{†}$$

where $c(L) = \Sigma_{j=0}^{\infty} c_j L^j$, $\Sigma_{j=0}^{\infty} c_j^2 < \infty$, and ε_t is a fundamental white noise for $(1 - L)z_t$. Beveridge and Nelson (1981) define the "permanent component" of z_t as

$$\bar{z}_t = z_t + \lim_{n \to \infty} E_t[\Delta z_{t+1} + \ldots + \Delta z_{t+n}]$$

where $\Delta \equiv (1 - L)$.

A. Prove that

$$\lim_{n\to\infty} E_t[\Delta z_{t+1} + \ldots + \Delta z_{t+n}] = [(c(L) - c(1))/(L - 1)]\varepsilon_t.$$

Hint: use the Hansen-Sargent formula (90) or the reasoning used to derive it.

B. Prove that $\bar{z}_t$ follows the "random walk" $(1 - L)\bar{z}_t = c(1)\varepsilon_t$.

C. Prove that $\bar{z}_t$ can be obtained from z_t by "filtering" according to the formula

$$\bar{z}_t = c(1)c(L)^{-1}z_t. \tag{*}$$

D. Beveridge and Nelson define the "cyclical" part of the series as $s_t = z_t - \bar{z}_t$. Show that s_t can be obtained from z_t via the formula

$$s_t = [1 - \frac{c(1)}{c(L)}]z_t.$$

E. Note that the preceding formula and the Wold representation (†) imply that

$$s_t = \frac{c(L) - c(1)}{1 - L}\,\varepsilon_t. \tag{**}$$

Is (**) a Wold representation for s_t?

Hints: at this point the reader might want to consult Hansen and Sargent (1980). Note that (**) is the version of formula (88) that is obtained by solving problem (24), then driving λ to unity from below. Does the assumption that $c(L)$ has a square summable inverse in nonnegative powers of L imply that $[c(L) - c(1)]$ has a square summable inverse in nonnegative powers of L?

F. In light of your answer to E, describe the effects of filtering a pair of time series (z_{1t}, z_{2t}), each with the univariate filter applied by Beveridge and Nelson, to obtain cyclical series (s_{1t}, s_{2t}). Suppose that z_2 fails to Granger cause z_1. Does it follow that s_2 fails to Granger cause s_1?

SOLUTIONS

1. Write y_t as

$$y_t = \sum_{j=-\infty}^{\infty} b_j^0 x_{t-j} + \varepsilon_t$$

where $E\varepsilon_t x_{t-j} = 0$ for all j by assumption. The researcher fits

$$y_t = \sum_{j=-\infty}^{\infty} b_j^1 x_{t-j} + u_t$$

by choosing the parameters b_j^1 to minimize Eu_t^2. But

$$Eu_t^2 = E\Big(y_t - \sum_{j=-\infty}^{\infty} b_j^1 x_{t-j}\Big)^2$$

$$= E\Big(\sum_{j=-\infty}^{\infty} b_j^0 x_{t-j} + \varepsilon_t - \sum_{j=-\infty}^{\infty} b_j^1 x_{t-j}\Big)^2$$

$$= E\varepsilon_t^2 + E\Big(\sum_{j=-\infty}^{\infty} (b_j^0 - b_j^1) x_{t-j}\Big)^2$$

because $\{\varepsilon_t\}$ and $\{x_t\}$ are orthogonal. The term $E\varepsilon_t^2$ is uncontrollable, and thus least squares chooses b_j^1 to minimize the variance of

$$\sum_{j=-\infty}^{\infty} (b_j^0 - b_j^1) x_{t-j}.$$

The spectrum of this process is, by (33),

$$|b^0(e^{-i\omega}) - b^1(e^{-i\omega})|^2 g_x(e^{-i\omega})$$

where $b^k(e^{-i\omega}) = \sum_{j=-\infty}^{\infty} b_j^k e^{-i\omega j}$ for k = 1, 2, and $g_x(e^{-i\omega})$ is the spectrum of $\{x_t\}$. The variance of a process is equal to the area under its spectrum divided by 2π, so

$$Eu_t^2 = E\varepsilon_t^2 + \frac{1}{2\pi}\int_{-\pi}^{\pi} |b^0(e^{-i\omega}) - b^1(e^{-i\omega})|^2 g_x(e^{-i\omega})d\omega.$$

Thus, the minimization of Eu_t^2 is equivalent to the minimization of Sims's approximation error formula.

* * *

2. A. From (45), the Fourier transform of the sequence $\{h_j\}_{-\infty}^{\infty}$ is given by

$$g_{xX}(e^{-i\omega}) = h(e^{-i\omega})g_X(e^{-i\omega}).$$

Because $\{x_t\}$ and $\{u_t\}$ are orthogonal,

$$g_X(e^{-i\omega}) = g_x(e^{-i\omega}) + g_u(e^{-i\omega}),$$

and

$$g_{xX}(e^{-i\omega}) = g_x(e^{-i\omega}).$$

Thus,

$$h(e^{-i\omega}) = g_{xX}(e^{-i\omega})/g_X(e^{-i\omega})$$

$$= g_x(e^{-i\omega})/[g_x(e^{-i\omega}) + g_u(e^{-i\omega})]$$

so that

$$h_j = \frac{1}{2\pi}\int_{-\pi}^{\pi} \frac{g_x(e^{-i\omega})e^{i\omega j}d\omega}{g_x(e^{-i\omega}) + g_u(e^{-i\omega})} .$$

B. From (33) $g_{\hat{x}}(e^{-i\omega})$ is given by

$$g_{\hat{x}}(e^{-i\omega}) = |h(e^{-i\omega})|^2 g_X(e^{-i\omega}).$$

By substituting for $h(e^{-i\omega})$ and $g_X(e^{-i\omega})$ from above, $g_{\hat{x}}(e^{-i\omega})$ can be written as

$$g_{\hat{x}}(e^{-i\omega}) = [\frac{g_x(e^{-i\omega})}{g_x(e^{-i\omega}) + g_u(e^{-i\omega})}][\frac{g_x(e^{i\omega})}{g_x(e^{i\omega}) + g_u(e^{i\omega})}]$$

$$\times [g_x(e^{-i\omega}) + g_u(e^{-i\omega})]$$

$$= [\frac{g_x(e^{i\omega})}{g_x(e^{i\omega}) + g_u(e^{i\omega})}]g_x(e^{-i\omega}) .$$

Because $g_x(\cdot) > 0$ and $g_u(\cdot) > 0$ for all ω, the term in braces is positive and less than unity for all ω. Thus, $g_{\hat{x}}(e^{-i\omega}) < g_x(e^{-i\omega})$ for all ω.

C. When $g_x(e^{-i\omega})$ is smooth across seasonal and nonseasonal frequencies and $g_u(e^{-i\omega})$ has peaks at the seasonal frequencies, $g_x(e^{i\omega})/[g_x(e^{i\omega}) + g_u(e^{i\omega})]$ clearly has dips at the seasonal frequencies, which translate, by the formula above, into seasonal dips in $g_{\hat{x}}(e^{-i\omega})$.

* * *

3. (The "Dlow" Decomposition Theorem)

A. The proof mimics the proof of the Wold theorem in the text. Consider projecting x_t on the n <u>future</u> values $x_{t+1}, x_{t+2}, \ldots, x_{t+n}$, and write

$$\tilde{x}_t^n = \sum_{i=1}^{n} \tilde{a}_i^n x_{t+i} = P[x_t | x_{t+1}, \ldots, x_{t+n}]$$

or

$$x_t = \tilde{x}_t^n + u_t^n$$

where $Eu_t^n x_{t+i} = 0$ for $i = 1, \ldots, n$ by the orthogonality principle. As in the text, the population covariogram $c_x(\tau)$ contains all of the information necessary to calculate the projection. Taking the limit as n is increased to infinity, we write

$$\tilde{x}_t = P[x_t | x_{t+1}, x_{t+2}, \ldots]$$

and decompose x_t as

$$x_t = P[x_t | x_{t+1}, \ldots] + u_t.$$

Notice that u_t is a linear combination* of current and future x's:

$$u_t = x_t - P[x_t | x_{t+1}, \ldots]$$

and can be interpreted as the one-step-behind backcast error made in backcasting x_t linearly from its own future. The backcast error is orthogonal to the information available when the backcast is made: $Eu_t x_{t+j} = 0$ for $j = 1, 2, \ldots$. But u_{t+s} is a linear combination of $x_{t+s}, x_{t+s+1}, \ldots$;

$$u_{t+s} = x_{t+s} - P[x_{t+s} | x_{t+s+1}, \ldots],$$

so $Eu_t u_{t+s} = 0$ for all t and $s \neq 0$. Thus $\{u_t\}$ is serially uncorrelated.

Project x_t on $\{u_t, u_{t+1}, \ldots, u_{t+m}\}$ to obtain

$$\tilde{x}_t^m = \sum_{j=0}^{m} c_j u_{t+j}$$

*Actually, since u_t is the mean square limit of u_t^n, it should be regarded as being representable as the limit of a sequence of linear combinations of current and future x's.

where the normal equations for c_j give

$$c_j = E(x_t u_{t+j})/\sigma_u^2 \qquad \sigma_u^2 = Eu_t^2$$

since the u_t's are orthogonal. Note that

$$c_0 = Ex_t u_t/\sigma_u^2 = (Eu_t^2 + Eu_t P[x_t | x_{t+1}, \ldots])/\sigma_u^2$$

$$= Eu_t^2/\sigma_u^2 = 1$$

since $Eu_t x_{t+s} = 0$ for $s \geq 1$. The prediction error variance is

$$E(x_t - \sum_{j=0}^{m} c_j u_{t+j})^2 = Ex_t^2 - 2Ex_t \Sigma c_j u_{t+j} + E(\Sigma c_j u_{t+j})^2$$

$$= Ex_t^2 - 2\Sigma c_j (Ex_t u_{t+j}) + \Sigma c_j^2 \sigma_u^2$$

$$= Ex_t^2 - 2\Sigma c_j^2 \sigma_u^2 + \Sigma c_j^2 \sigma_u^2$$

$$= Ex_t^2 - \sigma_u^2 \sum_{j=0}^{m} c_j^2 \geq 0.$$

Thus, since $Ex_t^2 < \infty$,

$$\sigma_u^2 \sum_{j=0}^{m} c_j^2 \leq Ex_t^2 < \infty$$

for all m, so that $\Sigma_{j=0}^{\infty} c_j^2 < \infty$.*

The deterministic component is given by

$$\theta_t = x_t - \sum_{j=0}^{\infty} c_j u_{t+j}.$$

---

*Notice that the regularity of the process (which in this case is equivalent to $E(x_t - P[x_t | x_{t+1}, \ldots])^2 > 0$) plays a role here, as it will in Part D. Here, if the variance of u is 0, the c_j coefficients are not determined, though the projection $c_0 u_t + c_1 u_{t-1} + \ldots$ is determined; it is, in fact, equal to zero in mean square.

Then for $s \geq 0$,

$$E\theta_t u_{t+s} = Ex_t u_{t+s} - Eu_{t+s}\Sigma c_j u_{t+j}$$

$$= \sigma_u^2 c_s - \sigma_u^2 c_s = 0.$$

For $s < 0$, $E\theta_t u_{t+s} = 0$ since u_{t+s} is uncorrelated with future x and future u. Thus $E\theta_t u_{t+s} = 0$ for all s.

Project θ_t on x_{t+1}, x_{t+2}, ... to get

$$P[\theta_t | x_{t+1}, \ldots] = P[x_t | x_{t+1}, \ldots] - P[\Sigma c_j u_{t+j} | x_{t+1}, \ldots]$$
$$= P[x_t | x_{t+1}, \ldots] - \Sigma_{j=1}^{\infty} c_j u_{t+j}$$

since $P[u_t | x_{t+1}, \ldots] = 0$ and u_{t+s} is a linear combination of $x_{t+1}, \ldots$ for $s > 0$ (so that $P[u_{t+s} | x_{t+1}, \ldots] = u_{t+s}$ for $s > 0$). Then

$$\theta_t - P[\theta_t | x_{t+1}, \ldots] = x_t - \Sigma_{j=0}^{\infty} c_j u_{t+j} - P[x_t | x_{t+1}, \ldots] + \Sigma_{j=1}^{\infty} c_j u_{t+j}$$
$$= x_t - P[x_t | x_{t+1}, \ldots] - c_0 u_t$$
$$= x_t - P[x_t | x_{t+1}, \ldots] - u_t = 0$$

from above. Thus $\theta_t = P[\theta_t | x_{t+1}, \ldots]$, so there is no (mean square) error in backcasting θ_t from future x's. Similarly,

$$\theta_t - P[\theta_t | x_{t+s}, \ldots] = x_t - \Sigma_{j=0}^{\infty} c_j u_{t+j} - P[x_t | x_{t+s}, \ldots] + \Sigma_{j=s}^{\infty} c_j u_{t+j}$$
$$= 0$$

so that θ_t can be backcast arbitrarily well from a semi-infinite record of x's which begins arbitrarily far into the future.

B. It simplifies matters somewhat to restrict attention in this part and part C to the purely indeterministic case. (Thus θ_t and η_t

are absent. The general case is discussed in part D.) The covariance generating function for $\{x_t\}$ can be represented in two ways:

$$g_x(z) = d(z)d(z^{-1})\sigma_\varepsilon^2 = c(z^{-1})c(z)\sigma_u^2,$$

where recall $d(0) = d_0 = c(0) = c_0 = 1$. Further, since ε_t must lie within the space spanned by $\{x_t, x_{t-1}, \ldots\}$, $d(z)$ must not be zero for any $|z| < 1$. (See Section XI.16 of the text.) Similarly, $c(z^{-1})$ must not be zero for any $|z^{-1}| < 1$ (or, $c(z) \neq 0$ for $|z| < 1$). Let z_j and z_j^{-1}, $j = 1, 2, \ldots$ be the zeros of $g_x(z)$, with $|z_j| < 1$ for $j = 1, 2, \ldots$. Then

$$g_x(z) = b \prod_{j\geq 1} (1 - z_j^{-1}z)(1 - z_j^{-1}z^{-1}) \qquad \text{(b constant)},$$

and $d(z)$ and $c(z)$ may each be identified with $\Pi(1 - z_j^{-1}z)$, as each is that 'square root' of $g_x(z)$ which has all zeros on or outside the unit circle. Evidently, the Wold decomposition (as well as the "Dlow" decomposition) amounts to finding a factorization of the covariance generating function in which the factors are symmetric in z and z^{-1}, and one of the factors can be taken to be nonzero on $|z| < 1$. The Wold decomposition is associated with this factor, the Dlow decomposition is associated with the other.

Additional insight into the result can be gained by considering how the factorization can be achieved. Let the Fourier series expansion of $\ln[g_x(e^{-i\omega})]$ be $\Sigma_{j=-\infty}^{\infty} a_j e^{-i\omega j}$, where

$$a_j = a_{-j} = \frac{1}{2\pi} \int_{-\pi}^{\pi} e^{i\omega j} \ln[g_x(e^{-i\omega})]d\omega.$$

Then

$$g_x(e^{-i\omega}) = \exp(\Sigma_{j=-\infty}^{\infty} a_j e^{-i\omega j})$$

$$= \exp(a_0)\exp(\Sigma_{j=1}^{\infty} a_j e^{-i\omega j})\exp(\Sigma_{j=-1}^{-\infty} a_j e^{-i\omega j})$$

$$= \exp(a_0)\exp(\Sigma_{j=1}^{\infty} a_j e^{-i\omega j})\exp(\Sigma_{j=1}^{\infty} a_j e^{i\omega j}).$$

Thus

$$d(e^{-i\omega}) = \exp(\Sigma_{j=1}^{\infty} a_j e^{-i\omega j})$$
$$c(e^{i\omega}) = \exp(\Sigma_{j=1}^{\infty} a_j e^{i\omega j})$$

or, using $z = e^{-i\omega}$,

$$d(z) = \exp(\Sigma_{j=1}^{\infty} a_j z^j)$$
$$c(z^{-1}) = \exp(\Sigma_{j=1}^{\infty} a_j z^{-j}).$$

Use $z = 0$ in the formula for $d(z)$ or $c(z)$ to determine $d_0 = d(0) = e^0 = 1 = c_0$. Further,

$$d_j = \frac{1}{2\pi}\int_{-\pi}^{\pi} e^{i\omega j}\exp(\Sigma_{k=1}^{\infty} a_k e^{-i\omega k})d\omega$$

$$= \frac{1}{2\pi i}\oint_U z^{-j}\exp(\Sigma_{k=1}^{\infty} a_k z^k)dz/z$$

$$c_j = \frac{1}{2\pi}\int_{-\pi}^{\pi} e^{i\omega j}c(e^{-i\omega})d\omega$$

$$= \frac{1}{2\pi i}\oint_U z^{-j}c(z)dz/z$$

$$= d_j.$$

C. The preceding discussion makes it clear that $u_t \neq \varepsilon_t$. In fact,

$$d(L)\varepsilon_t = c(L^{-1})u_t = d(L^{-1})u_t$$

so that

$$u_t = d(L^{-1})^{-1}d(L)\varepsilon_t.$$

To take an example, suppose $d(L) = 1 - DL$, $0 < |D| < 1$. Then

$$u_t = -D\varepsilon_{t-1} + (1 - D^2)\Sigma_{j=0}^{\infty} D^j \varepsilon_{t+j};$$

u_t is a function of past, present and <u>future</u> ε's.

For estimating x_t, one would be indifferent between knowing $\{x_{t-1}, x_{t-2}, \ldots\}$ and knowing $\{x_{t+1}, x_{t+2}, \ldots\}$; that is, $\sigma_\varepsilon^2 = \sigma_u^2$.* Computing Eu_t^2 from the formula above,

$$\sigma_u^2 = (2\pi i)^{-1} \oint [d(z^{-1})^{-1} d(z)][d(z)^{-1} d(z^{-1})] \sigma_\varepsilon^2 dz/z = \sigma_\varepsilon^2.$$

More formally, notice that $\sigma_\varepsilon^2 = \sigma_u^2$ must be equal to $\exp(a_0)$ (see part B above), so that

$$\sigma_\varepsilon^2 = \sigma_u^2 = \exp(a_0) = \exp\{\frac{1}{2\pi} \int_{-\pi}^{\pi} \ln g_x(e^{-i\omega}) d\omega\}$$
$$= \exp\{\frac{1}{2\pi i} \oint_U \ln[g_x(z)] dz/z\},$$

which is Kolmogorov's formula for the prediction error variance (see footnote 22 in the text).

D. It seems that η_t is equal to θ_t; the following arguments illustrate the issues involved in a rigorous answer to this question, but should not be regarded as proof.

The Wold theorem provides the decomposition of a process into the orthogonal components $\Sigma d_j \varepsilon_{t-j}$ and η_t, where η_t is deterministic. What is remarkable about the theorem is that this decomposition can be effected via linear operations involving only the past of the process (or, in the case of the Dlow theorem, operations involving only the future). To see this, note that in producing orthogonal components, the

---

*As will be seen below, this result hinges on the symmetry (in z) of the covariance generating function. Since cross covariance generating functions are not symmetric in general, one will generally <u>not</u> be indifferent in the vector case between knowing $\{x_s, s < t\}$ and knowing $\{x_s, s > t\}$, for purposes of estimating x_t.

decomposition partitions the spectrum of the x process.* But consider the following orthogonal decomposition of x_t:

$$x_t = A(L)x_t + B(L)x_t$$

where $B(L) = \Sigma B_j L^j$,

$$B(e^{-iw}) = \begin{cases} 1 \text{ for } \omega \in [\alpha - \tau/2, \alpha + \tau/2] \cup [-\alpha - \tau/2, -\alpha + \tau/2] \\ \qquad (0 < \tau/2 < \alpha < \pi - \tau/2) \\ 0 \text{ otherwise} \end{cases}$$

and $A(L) = 1 - B(L)$. Since $A(e^{-i\omega})B(e^{-i\omega}) = 0$ for all ω, $EA(L)x_tB(L)x_t = 0$. From formula (XI.36) of the text,

$$B_j = B_{-j} = (\pi j)^{-1}(\sin j(\alpha + \tau/2) - \sin j(\alpha - \tau/2))$$

and the filter which achieves the decomposition is two-sided, so that the decomposition requires future values of x. Moreover, B(z) does not have a factorization $B(z) = b(z)b(z^{-1})$ with $b(z) \neq 0$ for $|z| < 1$, since it is not true that $\int \ln B(e^{-i\omega})d\omega > -\infty$. (See again part B.) If this were true, we could use the fact that $|B(e^{-i\omega})|^2 = |b(e^{-i\omega})^2|^2$, write $x_t = [1 - (b(L))^2]x_t + (b(L))^2x_t$, and a one-sided orthogonal decomposition would have been achieved. The problem is that we are trying to partition the spectrum into two components, and we require the domain of each to be of positive length.

When the process is regular (the one-step-ahead linear forecast error is strictly positive, or, equivalently, $\int_{-\pi}^{\pi} \ln[g_x(e^{-i\omega})]d\omega > -\infty$), the deterministic component corresponds to (at most) a set of spectral

---

*Reference to Section XI.6 of the text might be useful at this point.

measure zero.* Then consider the problem of isolating the spectrum of x at the points $\pm\omega = \alpha$, where we imagine there is a "spike." Index $A(\cdot)$ and $B(\cdot)$ by the width τ of the interval about α, and write the decomposition as

$$x_t = A_\tau(L)x_t + B_\tau(L)x_t.$$

Now drive τ to zero. In the limit,

$$x_t = A_0(L)x_t + B_0(L)x_t,$$

and since $A_0(e^{-i\omega}) > 0$ except at the points $\pm\omega = \alpha$, $\int \ln A_0(e^{-i\omega})d\omega > -\infty$, and it is possible to factor $A_0(\cdot)$ as

$$A_0(z) = a(z)a(z^{-1})$$

where $a(z) \neq 0$ for $|z| < 1$. Then the decomposition can be achieved by

$$x_t = a(L)^2x_t + (1 - a(L)^2)x_t.$$

If α is the only frequency at which the spectrum of x is not well behaved, the deterministic component of the Wold decomposition is given by

---

*In fact, the spectral distribution function of any covariance stationary process (which is the primitive of the spectral density in the same way a probability distribution is the primitive of the probability density) can be written

$$F = F_c + F_j + F_r$$

where F_c is the smoothly varying (absolutely continuous) part, F_j is the "jump" function or discontinuous part of F, which increases only where F jumps, and F_r is "the rest" -- F_r is the set of points where F is continuous, but F' is infinite or does not exist, loosely, e.g., the "kinks" of F. (See J. Doob, Stochastic Processes, 1953, New York: Wiley, especially Chapter X, Section 5.)

$$\eta_t = (1 - a(L)^2)x_t,$$

and the indeterministic component is given by "the rest",

$$\sum_{j=0}^{\infty} d_j\varepsilon_{t-j} = a(L)^2x_t,$$

since the projections implicit in $\Sigma d_j\varepsilon_{t-j}$ are unique.* If there is a one-sided operator which isolates the frequency α, 1 - this operator must produce the indeterministic component of the Wold decomposition. Thus, for the process with the single spike at α,

$$x_t = a(L)^2x_t + (1 - a(L)^2)x_t$$

is the Wold decomposition, and

$$x_t = a(L^{-1})^2x_t + (1 - a(L^{-1})^2)x_t$$

is the Dlow decomposition. Then

$$\begin{aligned}\eta_t - \theta_t &= (1 - a(L)^2)x_t - (1 - a(L^{-1})^2)x_t \\ &= (a(L^{-1})^2 - a(L)^2)x_t\end{aligned}$$

and

$$E(\eta_t - \theta_t)^2 = \frac{1}{2\pi}\int_{-\pi}^{\pi}|a(e^{i\omega})^2 - a(e^{-i\omega})^2|^2dF(\omega)$$

where F' is the spectrum of x. Thus

$$E(\eta_t - \theta_t)^2 = \frac{1}{\pi}\int_{-\pi}^{\pi}\left(\mathrm{Im}(a(e^{-i\omega})^2)\right)^2dF(\omega)$$

---

*In fact, the sequences of moving average coefficients and moving average errors are unique. See Doob, op. cit., Theorem XII.4.2.

which is not zero unless $a(e^{-i\omega})^2$ can be taken to be unity or the Fourier transform of a two-sided symmetric sequence (i.e., $a_j = a_{-j}$). Yet notice that $a(e^{-i\omega})^2$ is unity except on a set of measure zero, and that it is the one-sided factorization of the limit (as the bandwidth approaches zero) of a bandpass filter which is symmetric. Thus it appears that $\eta_t = \theta_t$ in mean square.*

Making the above arguments rigorous, if it is possible to do so, will require much more careful treatment of limits and a substantial dose of measure theory. In addition to Doob, a useful reference is Y. Rosanov, Stationary Random Processes, 1967, San Francisco: Holden-Day. On the Wold-Dlow decompositions and time reversal, see G. Skoog, "Causality Characterizations: Bivariate, Trivariate, and Multivariate Propositions," 1976, Minneapolis: Federal Reserve Bank of Minneapolis Staff Report 14.

* * *

4. A. For $t \geq 1$, we have

$$y_t = \lambda y_{t-1} + \varepsilon_t,$$

with $\lambda > 1$ and y_0 given. Thus we seek a sequence $\{y_t\}$ such that

$$(1 - \lambda L)y_t = \varepsilon_t.$$

Recall (footnote 4 in Chapter IX of the text) that $f(t) = c\lambda^t$ is the only function for which $(1 - \lambda L)f(t) = 0$. Thus the solution for y_t must be of the form

---

*Proposed counterexamples are welcomed.

$$y_t = (1 - \lambda L)^{-1}\varepsilon_t + c\lambda^t.$$

Using the forward inverse of $(1 - \lambda L)$,

$$(1 - \lambda L)^{-1} = -(\lambda L)^{-1}(1 - \lambda^{-1}L^{-1})^{-1},$$

we have

$$y_t = -(\lambda L)^{-1}(1 - \lambda^{-1}L^{-1})^{-1}\varepsilon_t + c\lambda^t$$

$$= -\lambda^{-1} \Sigma_{j=0}^{\infty} \lambda^{-j}\varepsilon_{t+1+j} + c\lambda^t.$$

Now impose the initial condition,

$$y_0 = -\lambda^{-1} \Sigma_{j=0}^{\infty} \lambda^{-j}\varepsilon_{1+j} + c$$

which yields

$$c = y_0 + \lambda^{-1} \Sigma_{j=0}^{\infty} \lambda^{-j}\varepsilon_{1+j}.$$

Notice that each realization $(\varepsilon_1, \varepsilon_2, \ldots)$ determines a distinct constant c; this c is the required η_0.

Next, define u_t by

$$(1 - \lambda^{-1}L)^{-1}u_t = -(\lambda L)^{-1}(1 - \lambda^{-1}L^{-1})^{-1}\varepsilon_t,$$

i.e.,

$$u_t = -\lambda^{-1} \frac{1 - \lambda^{-1}L}{1 - \lambda^{-1}L^{-1}} \varepsilon_{t+1}$$

$$= -\lambda^{-1}(1 - \lambda^{-1}L) \Sigma_{j=0}^{\infty} \lambda^{-j}\varepsilon_{t+1+j},$$

so that u_t is a linear function of $\varepsilon_t, \varepsilon_{t+1}, \ldots$

B. The $\{u_t\}$ process is not fundamental for $\{y_t\}$ in the sense that u_t is not the error made in forecasting y_t linearly from its own past.

That error is ε_t, since $\varepsilon_t = y_t - \lambda y_{t-1}$. The process u_t, on the other hand, involves the entire future of $\{\varepsilon_t\}$, and thus $\{y_t\}$.

This problem, like Problem 3, illustrates some implications of the symmetry of covariance functions. Problem 3 explored some implications of the fact that zeros of covariance generating functions come in reciprocal pairs. Finding a fundamental process there involved choosing that factorization of the covariance generating function with all its zeros on or outside the unit circle. This problem explored some implications of the fact that poles of covariance generating functions come in reciprocal pairs. In stationary problems, finding a fundamental process involves choosing that factorization of the covariance generating function with all its poles outside the unit circle. Here, however, the fundamental process was associated with the explosive factorization. This illustrates the fact that "fundamentalness" does not always correspond to the factorization with no poles inside the unit circle: the "fundamental" characteristic of the process fundamental for y is that it is the sequence of one-step-ahead forecast errors made in predicting y linearly from its own past.

* * *

5. A. The (z_t, a_t) process can be written

$$\begin{bmatrix} z_t \\ a_t \end{bmatrix} = \begin{bmatrix} \lambda & -\beta \\ 0 & 0 \end{bmatrix} \begin{bmatrix} z_{t-1} \\ a_{t-1} \end{bmatrix} + \begin{bmatrix} a_t \\ a_t \end{bmatrix}.$$

B. From part A and formula (108),

$$p[z_{t+2} | z_t, \ldots] = \begin{bmatrix} \lambda & -\beta \\ 0 & 0 \end{bmatrix}^2 \begin{bmatrix} z_t \\ a_t \end{bmatrix}$$

$$= \begin{bmatrix} \lambda^2 & -\lambda\beta \\ 0 & 0 \end{bmatrix} \begin{bmatrix} z_t \\ a_t \end{bmatrix}$$

$$= \lambda^2 z_t - \lambda\beta a_t .$$

To apply the Wiener-Kolmogorov formula, note that

$$z_t = \frac{(1 - \beta L)a_t}{1 - \lambda L}$$

where a_t is fundamental for z_t. Then

$$P_t z_{t+2} = \left[\frac{(1 - \beta L)/(1-\lambda L)}{L^2}\right]_+ \frac{1 - \lambda L}{1 - \beta L} z_t$$

$$= \left[\frac{L^{-2}}{1 - \lambda L} - \frac{\beta L^{-1}}{1 - \lambda L}\right]_+ \frac{1 - \lambda L}{1 - \beta L} z_t$$

$$= \left[(1 + \lambda L + \lambda^2 L^2 + \ldots)L^{-2} - \beta L^{-1}(1 + \lambda L + \lambda^2 L^2 + \ldots)\right]_+$$

$$\times \frac{1 - \lambda L}{1 - \beta L} z_t$$

$$= \left(\frac{\lambda^2}{1 - \lambda L} - \frac{\beta\lambda}{1 - \lambda L}\right)\frac{1 - \lambda L}{1 - \beta L} z_t$$

$$= \frac{\lambda^2 - \beta\lambda}{1 - \beta L} z_t$$

$$= \frac{\lambda^2 - \lambda^2 \beta L + \lambda^2 \beta L - \lambda\beta}{1 - \beta L} z_t = \frac{\lambda^2(1 - \beta L) - \lambda\beta(1 - \lambda L)}{1 - \beta L} z_t$$

$$= \lambda^2 z_t - \lambda\beta a_t .$$

* * *

6. A. Let

$$y_t = \sum_{j=-\infty}^{\infty} h_j x_{t-j} + \varepsilon_t, \qquad E\varepsilon_t x_{t-j} = 0 \text{ for all } j.$$

By Sims's second theorem, y fails to Granger cause x if and only if $h_j = 0$, for all $j < 0$. But

$$h(z) = \frac{g_{yx}(z)}{g_x(z)} = \sum_{i=-\infty}^{\infty} h_i z^i$$

$$= \sigma_{u\varepsilon}(1 - .8z)(1 + .5z^{-1})/[\sigma_\varepsilon^2(1 - .9z)^{-1}(1 - .9z^{-1})^{-1}]$$

$$= \frac{\sigma_{u\varepsilon}}{\sigma_\varepsilon^2}(1 - .8z)(1 - .9z)(1 + .5z^{-1})(1 - .9z^{-1})$$

$$= \frac{\sigma_{u\varepsilon}}{\sigma_\varepsilon^2}[1 - .8z - .9z + .72z^2][1 + .5z^{-1} - .9z^{-1} - .45z^{-2}]$$

$$= \frac{\sigma_{u\varepsilon}}{\sigma_\varepsilon^2}[1 - 1.7z + .72z^2][1 - .4z^{-1} - .45z^{-2}]$$

$$= \frac{\sigma_{u\varepsilon}}{\sigma_\varepsilon^2}[1 - .4z^{-1} - .45z^{-2} - 1.7z + .4(1.7) + 1.7(.45)z^{-1}$$
$$+ .72z^2 - .72(.4)z - .72(.45)]$$

$$= \frac{\sigma_{u\varepsilon}}{\sigma_\varepsilon^2}([1 + .4(1.7) - .72(.45)]1 + [-1.7 - .72(.4)]z + .72z^2$$
$$+ [-.4 + 1.7(.45)]z^{-1} - .45z^{-2}).$$

Thus

$$h_{-1} = -.4 + 1.7(.45) \neq 0 \text{ and}$$
$$h_{-2} = -.45 \neq 0.$$

Hence, y Granger causes x. To check the converse, let

$$x_t = \sum_{j=-\infty}^{\infty} b_j y_{t-j} + \xi_t, \qquad E\xi_t y_{t-j} = 0 \text{ for all } j.$$

By Sims's second theorem, x fails to Granger cause y if and only if $b_j = 0$ for all $j < 0$. But

$$b(z) = \frac{g_{xy}(z)}{g_y(z)} = \frac{g_{yx}(z^{-1})}{g_y(z)}$$

$$= \frac{\sigma_{u\varepsilon}(1 - .8z^{-1})(1 + .5z)}{\sigma_u^2(1 - .8z)(1 - .8z^{-1})} = \left(\frac{\sigma_{u\varepsilon}}{\sigma_u^2}\right)\frac{1 + .5z}{1 - .8z}$$

$$= \frac{\sigma_{u\varepsilon}}{\sigma_u^2}(1 + .5z) \sum_{i=0}^{\infty} (.8)^i z^i$$

$$= \frac{\sigma_{u\varepsilon}}{\sigma_u^2} \sum_{i=0}^{\infty} (.8)^i z^i + 0.5\frac{\sigma_{u\varepsilon}}{\sigma_u^2} \sum_{i=0}^{\infty} (.8)^i z^{i+1}.$$

Therefore, $b_j = 0$ for all $j < 0$ because the coefficients on negative powers of z in this power series are all zero. Hence, x fails to Granger cause y.

B. Let

$$y_t = \sum_{j=-\infty}^{\infty} h_j x_{t-j} + \xi_t, \qquad E\xi_t x_{t-j} = 0 \text{ for all } j.$$

By Sims's second theorem, y fails to Granger cause x if and only if $h_j = 0$ for all $j < 0$. But

$$h(z) = \frac{g_{yx}(z)}{g_x(z)}$$

$$= \frac{\sigma_{u\varepsilon}}{\sigma_\varepsilon^2} \frac{(1 + .2z)(1 + .99z^{-1})}{(1 + .99z)(1 + .99z^{-1})}$$

$$= \frac{\sigma_{u\varepsilon}}{\sigma_\varepsilon^2} (1 + .2z) \sum_{i=0}^{\infty} (.99)^i z^i$$

$$= \frac{\sigma_{u\varepsilon}}{\sigma_\varepsilon^2} \sum_{i=0}^{\infty} (.99)^i z^i + .2\frac{\sigma_{u\varepsilon}}{\sigma_\varepsilon^2} \sum_{i=0}^{\infty} (.99)^i z^{i+1}.$$

Therefore, since $h_j = 0$ for all $j < 0$, y fails to Granger cause x. To check the converse, let

$$x_t = \sum_{j=-\infty}^{\infty} b_j y_{t-j} + u_t, \qquad Eu_t y_{t-j} = 0 \text{ for all } j.$$

By Sims's second theorem, x fails to Granger cause y if and only if $b_j = 0$ for all $j < 0$. But

$$b(z) = \frac{g_{xy}(z)}{g_y(z)} = \frac{g_{yx}(z^{-1})}{g_y(z)}$$

$$= \frac{\sigma_{u\varepsilon}}{\sigma_u^2}(1 + .2z^{-1})(1 + .99z)(1 - .7z + .3z^2)(1 - .7z^{-1} + .3z^{-2})$$

$$= \frac{\sigma_{u\varepsilon}}{\sigma_u^2}[1 + .2z^{-1} + .99z + 2(.99)][1 - .7z^{-1} + .3z^{-2} - .7z + .49$$
$$- .21z^{-1} + .3z^2 - .21z + .09]$$

$$= \frac{\sigma_{u\varepsilon}}{\sigma_u^2}[2.98 + .2z^{-1} + .99z][1.58 + (-.7 - .21)z + .3z^2$$
$$+ (-.7 - .21)z^{-1} + .3z^{-2}]$$

$$= \frac{\sigma_{u\varepsilon}}{\sigma_u^2}[2.98 + .2z^{-1} + .99z][1.58 - .91z + .3z^2 - .91z^{-1}$$
$$+ .3z^{-2}]$$

$$= \frac{\sigma_{u\varepsilon}}{\sigma_u^2}[2.98(1.58 - .91z + .3z^2 - .91z^{-1} + .3z^{-2})$$
$$+ .2(1.58z^{-1} - .91 + .3z - .91z^{-2} + .3z^{-3})$$
$$+ .99(1.58z - .91z^2 + .3z^3 - .91 + .3z^{-1})].$$

Notice that

$$b_{-3} = (.2)(.3) \neq 0.$$

Therefore, it is not true that $b_j = 0$ for all $j < 0$: x does Granger cause y.

C. Let

$$y_t = \sum_{j=-\infty}^{\infty} h_j x_{t-j} + \omega_t, \qquad E\omega_t x_{t-j} = 0 \text{ for all } j.$$

By Sims's second theorem y fails to Granger cause x if and only if $h_j = 0$ for all $j < 0$. But

$$h(z) = \frac{g_{yx}(z)}{g_x(z)} = \frac{\sigma_{u\varepsilon}}{\sigma_u^2} \frac{(1 - .7z)(1 - .7z^{-1})}{(1 - .8z)(1 - .7z^{-1})}$$

$$= \frac{\sigma_{u\varepsilon}}{\sigma_u^2}(1 - .7z) \sum_{i=0}^{\infty} (.8)^i z^i.$$

Therefore, $h_j = 0$ for all $j < 0$ so that y fails to Granger cause x. To check the converse, let

$$x_t = \sum_{j=-\infty}^{\infty} b_j y_{t-j} + v_t, \qquad Ev_t y_{t-j} = 0 \text{ for all } j.$$

By Sims's second theorem, x fails to Granger cause y if and only if $b_j = 0$ for all $j < 0$. Now

$$b(z) = \frac{g_{xy}(z)}{g_y(z)} = \frac{g_{yx}(z^{-1})}{g_y(z)}$$

$$= \frac{\sigma_{u\varepsilon}}{\sigma_u^2} \frac{(1 - .8z)(1 - .8z^{-1})}{(1 - .8z^{-1})(1 - .7z)}$$

$$= \frac{\sigma_{u\varepsilon}}{\sigma_u^2}(1 - .8z) \sum_{i=0}^{\infty} (.7)^i z^i.$$

Therefore $b_j = 0$ for all $j < 0$ so x fails to Granger cause y. In part C, note that x fails to Granger cause y <u>and</u> y fails to Granger cause x.

* * *

7. A. Write the model in the form

$$Y_t - I_t = \sum_{j=0}^{\infty} b_j Y_{t-j} + \varepsilon_t$$

or

$$[1 - b(L)]Y_t = I_t + \varepsilon_t$$

which gives

$$Y_t = [1 - b(L)]^{-1} I_t + [1 - b(L)]^{-1} \varepsilon_t.$$

Notice that since I_{t-j} is orthogonal to ε_t for all j, I_{t-j} is orthogonal to $[1 - b(L)]^{-1}\varepsilon_t$ for all j. Then the above expression is of the form $Y_t = \Sigma_{j=0}^{\infty} \tilde{b}_j I_{t-j} + V_t$ where V_t is orthogonal to I_{t-j} for all j. Hence by Sims's second theorem Y fails to Granger cause I.

B. From above,

$$\begin{aligned} c_t &= b(L)Y_t + \varepsilon_t \\ &= b(L)[(1 - b(L)]^{-1} I_t + b(L)[1 - b(L)]^{-1}\varepsilon_t + \varepsilon_t. \end{aligned}$$

Thus

$$\begin{bmatrix} c_t \\ Y_t \end{bmatrix} = \begin{bmatrix} b(L)[1 - b(L)]^{-1} & 1 + b(L)[1 - b(L)]^{-1} \\ [1 - b(L)]^{-1} & [1 - b(L)]^{-1} \end{bmatrix} \begin{bmatrix} I_t \\ \varepsilon_t \end{bmatrix}.$$

Notice that although I_t and ε_t have zero means and are pairwise orthogonal at all lags, they are arbitrarily serially correlated individually. Next form the univariate Wold decompositions

$$I_t = \sum_{j=0}^{\infty} h_j \omega_{t-j}$$

$$\varepsilon_t = \sum_{j=0}^{\infty} g_j \xi_{t-j}$$

where ω_t and ξ_t are mutually orthogonal white noises. Such a representation exists since I_t and ε_t are stationary, zero mean, indeterministic orthogonal processes. Now let

$$b(L)[1 - b(L)]^{-1} = \alpha(L)$$
$$[1 - b(L)]^{-1} = \beta(L).$$

and notice that $\alpha(L) = b(L)\beta(L)$ and $1 + \alpha(L) = \beta(L)$. Then

$$\begin{bmatrix} c_t \\ Y_t \end{bmatrix} = \begin{bmatrix} b(L)\beta(L) & \beta(L) \\ \beta(L) & \beta(L) \end{bmatrix} \begin{bmatrix} h(L) & 0 \\ 0 & g(L) \end{bmatrix} \begin{bmatrix} \omega_t \\ \xi_t \end{bmatrix}$$

which is the bivariate Wold moving average representation for the process (c_t, Y_t). Then

$$\begin{bmatrix} c_t \\ Y_t \end{bmatrix} = \begin{bmatrix} b(L)\beta(L)h(L) & \beta(L)g(L) \\ \beta(L)h(L) & \beta(L)g(L) \end{bmatrix} \begin{bmatrix} \omega_t \\ \xi_t \end{bmatrix}.$$

Consider the projection of Y_t on $\{c_t\}_{-\infty}^{\infty}$. The lag coefficient generating function is

$$\frac{g_{Yc}(z)}{g_c(z)} = \frac{b(z^{-1})h(z)h(z^{-1})\sigma_\omega^2 + g(z)g(z^{-1})\sigma_\xi^2}{b(z)b(z)^{-1}h(z)h(z^{-1})\sigma_\omega^2 + g(z)g(z^{-1})\sigma_\xi^2}$$

which will in general involve negative powers of z (note that $b(z) = 1$ is inadmissible) so that in general, Y Granger causes c. An exception occurs when investment and the disturbance are white noises ($g(z) = h(z) = 1$) and $b(z) = b_0$, in which case c_t and Y_t are contemporaneously correlated white noise processes, and of course $\{Y_t\}$ fails to help predict c_t.

Next consider the projection of c_t on $\{Y_t\}_{-\infty}^{\infty}$. The lag coefficient generating function is

$$\frac{g_{cY}(z)}{g_Y(z)} = \frac{b(z)h(z)h(z^{-1})\sigma_\omega^2 + g(z)g(z^{-1})\sigma_\xi^2}{h(z)h(z^{-1})\sigma_\omega^2 + g(z)g(z^{-1})\sigma_\xi^2}$$

which also generally involves negative powers of z, so that in general, c Granger causes Y. An exception occurs when $g(z) = h(z) = 1$, in which case the lag coefficient generating function,

$$\frac{b(z)\sigma_\omega^2 + \sigma_\xi^2}{\sigma_\omega^2 + \sigma_\xi^2}$$

does <u>not</u> involve negative powers of z, so that c fails to Granger cause Y. (Note that in this case $\{Y_t\}$ is a white noise process, but $\{c_t\}$ is serially correlated -- unless $b(z) = b_0$.)

C. To check this, compute $E\varepsilon_t Y_{t-j}$. Note first that

$$c_t = \sum_{j=0}^{\infty} b_j Y_{t-j} + \varepsilon_t = Y_t - I_t.$$

Then

$$\sum_{j=0}^{\infty} b_j Y_{t-j} - Y_t + \varepsilon_t + I_t = 0.$$

Now collect terms and multiply by ε_t:

$$(b_0 - 1)Y_t\varepsilon_t + \sum_{j=1}^{\infty} b_j Y_{t-j}\varepsilon_t + \varepsilon_t^2 + I_t\varepsilon_t = 0.$$

Taking expectations,

$$(b_0 - 1)EY_t\varepsilon_t + \sum_{j=1}^{\infty} b_j E\varepsilon_t Y_{t-j} = -\sigma_\varepsilon^2$$

since $EI_t\varepsilon_t = 0$. Hence, $E\varepsilon_t Y_{t-j} \neq 0$ for all j because at least one of the terms is nonzero. Therefore (*) is not a regression equation. This is the case even when h = g = I as in part B. There we found that there is an equation of the form

$$c_t = \sum_{j=0}^{\infty} B_j Y_{t-j} + V_t$$

with $B_0 = (\sigma_\omega^2 + \sigma_\xi^2)^{-1}(\sigma_\omega^2 b_0 + \sigma_\xi^2)$, $B_j = (\sigma_\omega^2 + \sigma_\xi^2)^{-1}\sigma_\omega^2 b_j$ for $j \geq 1$, and $EV_t Y_{t-s}$ for all s. This _is_ a regression equation. The point is that it is not (*).

* * *

8. The bivariate representation can be written

$$x_t = c(L)\varepsilon_t$$
$$y_t = a(L)\varepsilon_t + b(L)u_t,$$

where $b(L) = ka(L)$.

A. By Sims's theorem 1, y fails to Granger cause x. Now

$$g_x(e^{-i\omega}) = |c(e^{-i\omega})|^2\sigma_\varepsilon^2$$

$$g_y(e^{-i\omega}) = |a(e^{-i\omega})|^2\sigma_\varepsilon^2 + |b(e^{-i\omega})|^2\sigma_u^2$$

$$= |a(e^{-i\omega})|^2(\sigma_\varepsilon^2 + k^2\sigma_u^2)$$

$$g_{xy}(e^{-i\omega}) = c(e^{-i\omega})a(e^{i\omega})\sigma_\varepsilon^2.$$

Let

$$x_t = \sum_{j=-\infty}^{\infty} h_j y_{t-j} + \xi_j, \qquad E\xi_t y_{t-j} = 0 \text{ for all } j.$$

Then

$$h(e^{-i\omega}) = g_{xy}(e^{-i\omega})/g_y(e^{-i\omega})$$

$$= \frac{c(e^{-i\omega})a(e^{i\omega})\sigma_\varepsilon^2}{a(e^{-i\omega})a(e^{i\omega})(\sigma_\varepsilon^2 + k^2\sigma_u^2)}$$

and

$$h(z) = \frac{c(z)\sigma_\varepsilon^2}{a(z)(\sigma_\varepsilon^2 + k^2\sigma_u^2)}$$

which is one-sided in nonnegative powers of z since both c(z) and $[a(z)]^{-1}$ are. Hence x fails to Granger cause y. Notice that y fails to Granger cause x and x fails to Granger cause y.

B. The distributed lag weight generator is

$$b(z) = g_{yx}(z)/g_x(z)$$

$$= g_{xy}(z^{-1})/g_x(z)$$

$$= \frac{c(z^{-1})a(z)\sigma_\varepsilon^2}{c(z^{-1})c(z)\sigma_\varepsilon^2} = \frac{a(z)}{c(z)}$$

where b_i is the coefficient on z^i in $a(z)[c(z)]^{-1}$.

C. The distributed lag weight generator is

$$h(z) = g_{xy}(z)/g_y(z)$$

$$= \frac{c(z)\sigma_\varepsilon^2}{a(z)[\sigma_\varepsilon^2 + k^2\sigma_u^2]} .$$

Notice that b and h are both one-sided:

$$P[y_t | \{x_{t-j}\}_{-\infty}^{\infty}] = P[y_t | \{x_{t-j}\}_0^{\infty}]$$

so y fails to Granger cause x, and

$$P[x_t | \{y_{t-j}\}_{-\infty}^{\infty}] = P[x_t | \{y_{t-j}\}_0^{\infty}]$$

so x fails to Granger cause y.

D. When $\eta_{1t} = \varepsilon_t + ku_t$,

$$y_t = a(L)(\varepsilon_t + ku_t) = a(L)\eta_{1t}.$$

Now form η_{2t} by projecting ε_t on η_{1t}:

$$\varepsilon_t = \rho(\varepsilon_t + ku_t) + \eta_{2t}$$

where η_{2t} is a least squares disturbance and thus

$$E(\varepsilon_t + ku_t)\eta_{2t-j} = E\eta_{1t}\eta_{2t-j} = 0 \text{ for all j.}$$

Finally, write

$$x_t = c(L)\varepsilon_t \qquad = c(L)\rho\eta_{1t} + c(L)\eta_{2t}$$

$$y_t = a(L)\varepsilon_t + ka(L)u_t = a(L)\eta_{1t}.$$

Notice that the roles of x and y have been reversed, and by Sims's theorem 1, x fails to Granger cause y. This is not surprising given the results of part A.

* * *

9. From Granger's definition, p fails to Granger cause y if

$$P[y_t|y_{t-1}, y_{t-2}, \ldots; p_{t-1}, \ldots] = P[y_t|y_{t-1}, \ldots].$$

Suppose

$$\Omega_{t-1} = [y_{t-1}, y_{t-2}, \ldots; p_{t-1}, p_{t-2}, \ldots; \theta_{t-1}]$$

where θ_{t-1} contains information other than past values of y_t and p_t.

A. From (*),

$$\begin{aligned} P[y_t|\Omega_{t-1}] &= \gamma(P[p_t|\Omega_{t-1}] - P[p_t|\Omega_{t-1}]) + \lambda P[y_{t-1}|\Omega_{t-1}] \\ &\quad + P[u_t|\Omega_{t-1}] \\ &= \lambda P[y_{t-1}|\Omega_{t-1}] \\ &= \lambda y_{t-1}. \end{aligned}$$

By the law of iterated projections,

$$\begin{aligned} P[y_t|y_{t-1}, \ldots; p_{t-1}, \ldots] &= P[P[y_t|\Omega_{t-1}]|y_{t-1}, \ldots; p_{t-1}, \ldots] \\ &= P[\lambda y_{t-1}|y_{t-1}, \ldots] \\ &= \lambda y_{t-1}. \end{aligned}$$

Thus $P[y_t|y_{t-1}, y_{t-2}, \ldots; p_{t-1}, \ldots] = P[y_t|y_{t-1}, \ldots]$ so that p fails to Granger cause y.

B. Using (†) in (*),

$$\begin{aligned} y_t &= \gamma\varepsilon_t + \lambda y_{t-1} + u_t \\ &= \gamma\varepsilon_t + \lambda y_{t-1} + \rho u_{t-1} + \xi_t. \end{aligned}$$

Thus

$$P[y_t|\Omega_{t-1}] = \lambda y_{t-1} + \rho P[u_{t-1}|\Omega_{t-1}].$$

But

$$u_{t-1} = y_{t-1} - \gamma\varepsilon_{t-1} - \lambda y_{t-2}$$

$$= y_{t-1} - \lambda y_{t-2} - \gamma(p_{t-1} - \sum_{i=1}^{n} w_i p_{t-i-1})$$

so that

$$P[u_{t-1}|\Omega_{t-1}] = u_{t-1}$$

since $(y_{t-1}, y_{t-2}, p_{t-1}, p_{t-2}, \ldots, p_{t-n-1})$ is a subset of Ω_{t-1}. It is clear then, that

$$P[y_t|y_{t-1}, \ldots; p_{t-1}, \ldots] = \lambda y_{t-1} + \rho u_{t-1}.$$

But

$$\begin{aligned} P[y_t|y_{t-1}, \ldots] &= P\big[P[y_t|\Omega_{t-1}]|y_{t-1}, \ldots\big] \\ &= P[\lambda y_{t-1} + \rho u_{t-1}|y_{t-1}, \ldots] \\ &= \lambda y_{t-1} + \rho P[u_{t-1}|y_{t-1}, \ldots]. \end{aligned}$$

From above, u_{t-1} cannot be recovered without knowledge of p_{t-1}, p_{t-2}, $\ldots$, p_{t-n-1}. Thus $P[u_{t-1}|y_{t-1}, \ldots] \neq u_{t-1}$ and

$$P[y_t|y_{t-1}, \ldots; p_{t-1}, \ldots] \neq P[y_t|y_{t-1}, \ldots].$$

Hence p Granger causes y.

* * *

10. By Sims's theorem 1, when y fails to Granger cause x, the Wold representation for the bivariate process (x_t, y_t) is of the form

$$\begin{bmatrix} x_t \\ y_t \end{bmatrix} = \begin{bmatrix} a(L) & 0 \\ c(L) & d(L) \end{bmatrix} \begin{bmatrix} \varepsilon_t \\ u_t \end{bmatrix} .$$

Then (x_t^a, y_t^a) is given by

$$\begin{bmatrix} x_t^a \\ y_t^a \end{bmatrix} = \begin{bmatrix} g(L)\ a(L) & 0 \\ f(L)\ c(L) & f(L)\ d(L) \end{bmatrix} \begin{bmatrix} \varepsilon_t \\ u_t \end{bmatrix}.$$

This is not the Wold representation for (x_t^a, y_t^a) (because the determinant $g(z)a(z)f(z)d(z)$ has zeros inside the unit circle) and cannot be used with Sims's theorem 1 to assert that y^a fails to Granger cause x^a. However, the representation can be used to calculate the projection of y^a on x^a, since the coefficients in the projection are determined by the matrix covariance generating function and do not depend upon how one chooses to factor the function. Thus, the coefficient generating functions $h(z)$ and $h^a(z)$ for the projections

$$y_t = \sum_{j=-\infty}^{\infty} h_j x_{t-j} + v_t, \qquad Ev_t x_{t-j} = 0 \text{ for all } j$$

$$y_t^a = \sum_{j=-\infty}^{\infty} h_j^a x_{t-j}^a + v_t^a, \qquad Ev_t^a x_{t-j}^a = 0 \text{ for all } j$$

are given by

$$h(z) = \frac{g_{yx}(z)}{g_x(z)} = \frac{c(z)a(z^{-1})\sigma_\varepsilon^2}{a(z)a(z^{-1})\sigma_\varepsilon^2} = \frac{c(z)}{a(z)}$$

$$h^a(z) = \frac{g_{y^a x^a}(z)}{g_{x^a}(z)} = \frac{f(z)c(z)g(z^{-1})a(z^{-1})\sigma_\varepsilon^2}{g(z)a(z)g(z^{-1})a(z^{-1})\sigma_\varepsilon^2} = \frac{f(z)c(z)}{g(z)a(z)} .$$

Now $h(z)$ is one-sided in nonnegative powers of z by construction, but since $f(z)$ and $g(z)$ are both two-sided, $h^a(z)$ is also two-sided unless $f(z) = g(z)$. Thus, by Sims's second theorem, under asymmetric seasonal adjustment, y^a generally Granger causes x^a even if y fails to Granger cause x.

* * *

11. Let $y_t \equiv y$ and note that $Em_t = 0$. Then $Ep_t = -y$, so that in the projection (*), $a = -y$. Since we are interested only in $h(L)$, assume without loss of generality that $y = 0$. Let u_t have the moving average representation

$$u_t = f(L)v_t \qquad v_t = u_t - P[u_t|u_{t-1},\ldots]$$

and note that $Eu_t m_s = 0$ for all t,s implies $Ev_t e_s = 0$ for all t,s. Write the moving average representation for the joint (p_t, m_t) process as

$$\begin{bmatrix} p_t \\ m_t \end{bmatrix} = \begin{bmatrix} a(L) & c(L) \\ 0 & d(L) \end{bmatrix} \begin{bmatrix} v_t \\ e_t \end{bmatrix} \qquad (\dagger)$$

where $a(L)$ and $c(L)$ are as-yet undetermined polynomials in the lag operator. Note that p fails to Granger cause m. Thus, even without knowing what $a(L)$ and $c(L)$ are, one can be certain, using Sims's theorem 1, that the one-sided projection in (*) is actually also the projection of p_t on the <u>entire</u> $\{m_t\}$ process. The lag coefficient generating function is

$$h(z) = \frac{g_{pm}(z)}{g_m(z)} = \frac{c(z)d(z^{-1})\sigma_e^2}{d(z)d(z^{-1})\sigma_e^2} = c(z)/d(z).$$

Thus to determine the nature of $h(z)$, it is necessary to determine what restrictions the portfolio balance equation places on $c(z)$.

Using the moving average representation (†), the portfolio balance equation can be written

$$d(L)e_t - a(L)v_t - c(L)e_t = \alpha([L^{-1}a(L)]_+v_t + [L^{-1}c(L)]_+e_t - a(L)v_t - c(L)e_t) + f(L)v_t.$$

Since $\{e_t\}$ and $\{v_t\}$ are orthogonal and the portfolio balance equation holds for all realizations of $\{e_t\}$ and $\{v_t\}$,

$$d(L) - c(L) = \alpha([L^{-1}c(L)]_+ - c(L))$$
$$- a(L) = \alpha([L^{-1}a(L)]_+ - a(L)) + f(L).$$

The equation involving $c(L)$ can be written

$$d(L) + \alpha L^{-1}c_0 = (\alpha L^{-1} - (\alpha - 1))c(L).$$

The value of c_0 is found by evaluating this expression at $L = \alpha/(\alpha - 1)$: $c_0 = -(\alpha - 1)^{-1}d(\alpha/(\alpha - 1))$.* Then

$$c(L) = (1 - \alpha)^{-1}\left[\frac{d(L) - \lambda d(\lambda)L^{-1}}{1 - \lambda L^{-1}}\right]$$

where $\lambda = \alpha/(\alpha - 1)$. Then

$$h(z) = (1 - \alpha)^{-1}\,\frac{1 - \lambda d(\lambda)d(z)^{-1}z^{-1}}{1 - \lambda z^{-1}}\,.$$

---

*Further discussion of calculations like this one and the ones in Sections 18, 19, and 21 in the text can be found in C.H. Whiteman, Linear Rational Expectations Models: A User's Guide, 1983, Minneapolis: University of Minnesota Press.

Note that $h_0 = (1 - \alpha)^{-1}d(\lambda)/d_0$, which is not generally unity, and h_j will not generally be zero for $j \geq 1$. Suppose that $\{m_t\}$ has the rth order autoregressive representation

$$A(L)m_t = d(L)^{-1}m_t = e_t, \qquad A(L) = 1 - \sum_{j=1}^{r} A_j L^j.$$

Then, using formula (90) from the text,

$$h(z) = (1 - \alpha)^{-1}d(\lambda)[1 + \sum_{j=1}^{r-1} (\sum_{k=j+1}^{r} \lambda^{k-j}A_k)z^j]$$

so that

$$h(z) = \sum_{j=0}^{r-1} h_j z^j$$

with

$$h_0 = (1 - \alpha)^{-1}d(\lambda),$$

$$h_j = (1 - \alpha)^{-1}d(\lambda) \sum_{k=j+1}^{r} \lambda^{k-j}A_k \qquad j = 1, \ldots, r-1.$$

Clearly, "classical" macroeconomics does not imply $h_0 = 1$, $h_j = 0$ for $j \geq 1$; the economist misinterpreted the theory.

* * *

12. A. First, lead (*) one period:

$$\mu_{t+1} - x_{t+1} = \alpha(P_{t+1}x_{t+2} - P_t x_{t+1}) + \eta_{t+1}.$$

Then apply the projection operator to get

$$P_t\mu_{t+1} - P_t x_{t+1} = \alpha(P_t x_{t+2} - P_t x_{t+1}) \qquad (**)$$

since $P_t(P_{t+1}x_{t+2}) = P_t x_{t+2}$ by the law of iterated projections, and $P_t\eta_{t+1} = 0$ by assumption. Now (†) can be used to evaluate $P_t x_{t+1}$ and $P_t x_{t+2}$, and the result substituted into (**) to get

$$\begin{aligned}
P_t\mu_{t+1} &= (1 - \alpha)\frac{1}{1 - \alpha}\sum_{j=1}^{\infty}\left(\frac{-\alpha}{1 - \alpha}\right)^{j-1}P_t\mu_{t+j} \\
&\quad + \alpha\frac{1}{1 - \alpha}\sum_{j=1}^{\infty}\left(\frac{-\alpha}{1 - \alpha}\right)^{j-1}P_t\mu_{t+j+1} \\
&= \frac{1 - \alpha}{1 - \alpha}P_t\mu_{t+1} + \frac{1 - \alpha}{1 - \alpha}\sum_{j=2}^{\infty}\left(\frac{-\alpha}{1 - \alpha}\right)^{j-1}P_t\mu_{t+j} \\
&\quad - \frac{-\alpha}{1 - \alpha}\sum_{j=1}^{\infty}\left(\frac{-\alpha}{1 - \alpha}\right)^{j-1}P_t\mu_{t+j+1} \\
&= P_t\mu_{t+1},
\end{aligned}$$

which is an identity for all t. Thus (†) solves (*).

B. By assumption,

$$\mu_t = (1 - \lambda)x_{t-1} + \lambda\mu_{t-1} + a_{2t} - \lambda a_{2t-1}.$$

Thus, since $|\lambda| < 1$,

$$\mu_t = \frac{(1 - \lambda)}{1 - \lambda L}x_{t-1} + a_{2t}.$$

Leading the above expression once and taking projections,

$$P_t\mu_{t+1} = \frac{1 - \lambda}{1 - \lambda L}x_t = \frac{1 - \lambda}{1 - \lambda L}\,\frac{1 - \lambda L}{1 - L}\,a_{1t} = \frac{1 - \lambda}{1 - L}\,a_{1t}.$$

Now define the stochastic process $Y_t = P_t\mu_{t+1} = (1 - \lambda)(1 - L)^{-1}a_{1t}$. From Section XI.14 of the text, $P_tY_{t+j} = P_tY_{t+1} = Y_t$. Thus $P_t\mu_{t+j} = \frac{1 - \lambda}{1 - \lambda L}x_t$ for all $j \geq 1$. Using this in (†),

$$P_tx_{t+1} = \frac{1}{1 - \alpha}\sum_{j=1}^{\infty}(\frac{-\alpha}{1 - \alpha})^{j-1}[\frac{1 - \lambda}{1 - \lambda L}]x_t$$

$$= \frac{1}{1 - \alpha}[\frac{1}{1 + \frac{\alpha}{1 - \alpha}}][\frac{1 - \lambda}{1 - \lambda L}]x_t$$

$$= [\frac{1 - \lambda}{1 - \lambda L}]x_t.$$

Thus $\pi_t = P_tx_{t+1}$, and Cagan's scheme is rational.

C. From above,

$$P[x_{t+1}|x_t, \mu_t, x_{t-1}, \mu_{t-1},\ldots] = P[P_tx_{t+1}|x_t, \mu_t, x_{t-1}, \mu_{t-1}, \ldots]$$

$$= P[\frac{1 - \lambda}{1 - \lambda L}x_t|x_t, \mu_t, x_{t-1}, \mu_{t-1}, \ldots]$$

$$= \frac{1 - \lambda}{1 - \lambda L}x_t$$

$$= P[x_{t+1}|x_t, x_{t-1}, \ldots].$$

Thus μ fails to Granger cause x.

D. To calculate $P[\mu_t - x_t|\{x_t\}]$, it will be necessary to derive a Wold representation for $[(1 - L)x_t, (1 - L)\mu_t]$. First, from (*) and (†),

$$\mu_t - x_t = \alpha(\frac{1 - \lambda}{1 - \lambda L}x_t - \frac{1 - \lambda}{1 - \lambda L}x_{t-1}) + \eta_t$$

$$= \alpha(1 - L)\frac{1 - \lambda}{1 - \lambda L}x_t + \eta_t.$$

Next, since $P_t\mu_{t+1} = (1 - \lambda)(1 - \lambda L)^{-1}x_t = P_t(1 - \lambda)(1 - \lambda L)^{-1}x_{t+1}$, μ_{t+1} can be written as

$$\mu_{t+1} = P_t\mu_{t+1} + \varepsilon_{t+1} = (1 - \lambda)(1 - \lambda L)^{-1}x_{t+1} + \varepsilon_{t+1}$$

where $\varepsilon_{t+1} = \mu_{t+1} - P_t\mu_{t+1}$, and of course $P_t\varepsilon_{t+1} = 0$. Thus

$$\mu_t - x_t = (1 - \lambda)(1 - \lambda L)^{-1}x_t + \varepsilon_t - x_t$$

$$= \alpha(1 - \lambda)(1 - \lambda L)^{-1}x_t + \eta_t.$$

After collecting terms involving x_t and rearranging, one obtains

$$(1 - L)x_t = \phi^{-1}(1 - \lambda L)(\varepsilon_t - \eta_t)$$

where $\phi \equiv \lambda + \alpha(1 - \lambda)$. Then

$$(1 - L)\mu_t = (1 - L)(1 - \lambda)(1 - \lambda L)^{-1}x_t + (1 - L)\varepsilon_t$$

$$= (1 - \lambda)\phi^{-1}(\varepsilon_t - \eta_t) + (1 - L)\varepsilon_t.$$

Choose $\varepsilon_t - \eta_t$ to be one of the noises in the Wold representation. Then project ε_t on $(\varepsilon_t - \eta_t)$ to find a ρ such that $\varepsilon_t = \rho(\varepsilon_t - \eta_t) + V_t$ where V_t is orthogonal to $\varepsilon_t - \eta_t$. Then

$$(1 - L)\mu_t = \frac{1 - \lambda}{\phi}(\varepsilon_t - \eta_t) + \rho(\varepsilon_t - \eta_t) + V_t - \rho(\varepsilon_{t-1} - \eta_{t-1}) - V_{t-1}$$

$$(1 - L)\mu_t = \left[\frac{1 - \lambda}{\phi} + \rho(1 - L)\right](\varepsilon_t - \eta_t) + (1 - L)V_t.$$

Thus

$$(1 - L)x_t = \frac{1 - \lambda L}{\phi}(\varepsilon_t - \eta_t) \tag{a}$$

$$(1 - L)\mu_t = \left[\frac{1 - \lambda}{\phi} + \rho(1 - L)\right](\varepsilon_t - \eta_t) + (1 - L)V_t \tag{b}$$

which is the Wold moving average representation with orthogonal innovations. Now invert (a) to get

$$\phi\frac{(1 - L)}{1 - \lambda L}x_t = \varepsilon_t - \eta_t,$$

and substitute into (b):

$$(1 - L)\mu_t = [\frac{1 - \lambda}{\phi} + \rho(1 - L)]\phi\frac{(1 - L)}{1 - \lambda L}x_t + (1 - L)V_t$$

or simplifying,

$$\mu_t = [\frac{1 - \lambda}{\phi} + \rho(1 - L)]\phi\frac{x_t}{1 - \lambda L} + V_t.$$

This is a regression equation since $EV_t x_{t-j} = 0$ for all j by construction. Thus

$$\mu_t = \frac{1 - \lambda + \phi\rho(1 - L)}{1 - \lambda L}x_t + V_t$$

giving

$$\mu_t - x_t = \frac{1 - \lambda + \phi\rho(1 - L) - (1 - \lambda L)}{1 - \lambda L}x_t + V_t$$

$$= \frac{-\lambda + \lambda L + \phi\rho(1 - L)}{1 - \lambda L}x_t + V_t$$

$$= \frac{-\lambda + \phi\rho}{1 - \lambda L}(1 - L)x_t + V_t$$

which is <u>not</u> the same as (§). Thus, Cagan's estimate of $\alpha(1 - \lambda)$ would, in population, be $-\lambda + \rho[\lambda + \alpha(1 - \lambda)]$. Notice that if the portfolio balance equation holds without error ($\eta_t = 0$), then $\rho = 1$, Cagan's equation is a projection equation, and Cagan's estimate of $\alpha(1 - \lambda)$ would be correct in population.*

* * *

---

*Further discussion of the issues involved in estimating Cagan's demand for money schedule can be found in, e.g., T. J. Sargent, "The Demand for Money during Hyperinflations under Rational Expectations," International Economic Review 18 (February 1977), pp. 59-82.

13. A. A straightforward application of the derivative formulas of Problem IX.3 yields

$$0 = pA_1 g(L) - A_2 g(L^{-1}) g(L) - B_0 - B_1 - \varepsilon(t)$$

or

$$\{B_1 + pA_2 g(L^{-1}) g(L)\} I(t) = -B_0 + pA_1 g(1) - \varepsilon(t).$$

B. Make the reasonable assumptions that $K(-1) \geq 0$ and $g_j \to 0$ as $j \to \infty$. Under these assumptions, the firm can assure itself of a finite (though perhaps negative) present value by following the feasible strategy $I(t) = 0$ for $t \geq 0$. It follows that the optimal strategy produces a present value no smaller than this, and thus that

$$B_1 \Sigma_{t=0}^{\infty} I(t)^2 < \infty$$

whenever $B_1 > 0$. (If $B_1 = 0$, the firm might be able to drive $I(t)$ to $\pm\infty$ without adversely affecting present value. See Problem IX.5.) Therefore, the investment sequence must be of exponential order less than unity.

Suppose $B_1 > 0$ and that $g(L)$ is of finite order, $g(L) = \Sigma_{j=0}^{m} g_j L^j$, for finite m. Then the characteristic polynomial has factorization

$$B_1 + pA_2 g(L) g(L^{-1}) = c_0^2 \Pi_{j=1}^{m} (1 - \lambda_j L)(1 - \lambda_j L^{-1}), \qquad (c_0 \text{ constant})$$

since the 2m roots come in reciprocal pairs. Take $|\lambda_j| \leq 1$ and note that $B_1 > 0$ insures that in fact $|\lambda_j| < 1$ for all j. (Unity is not a root since $B_1 + pA_2 g(1)^2 \geq B_1 > 0$.) Now the arguments in Section IX.9 can be applied to show that optimal investment is produced by

$$\Pi_{j=1}^{m} (1 - \lambda_j L) I(t) = \{pA_1 g(1) - B_0\} / \{c_0^2\, \Pi_{j=1}^{m} (1 - \lambda_j)\}$$
$$- c_0^{-2} (\Pi_{j=1}^{m} (1 - \lambda_j L^{-1}))^{-1} \varepsilon(t);$$

i.e., by solving the "stable" roots (λ_j) backward and the "unstable" roots (λ_j^{-1}) forward.

While the analysis of Section IX.9 covers the case of a finite order g(L), some modifications are necessary to deal with the situation (e.g., the "common example" of the problem statement) in which g(L) is given by the ratio of two finite order polynomials. Thus suppose that

$$g(L) = \Sigma_{j=0}^{m} g_j^n L^j / \Sigma_{j=0}^{q} g_j^d L^j = g^n(L)/g^d(L),$$

where the numerator polynomial $g^n(L)$ and the denominator polynomial $g^d(L)$ have no common factors, and write the characteristic polynomial as

$$\frac{B_1 g^d(L) g^d(L^{-1}) + pA_2 g^n(L) g^n(L^{-1})}{g^d(L) g^d(L^{-1})} = \frac{\gamma_0^2 \Pi_{j=1}^{r} (1 - \gamma_j L)(1 - \gamma_j L^{-1})}{g^d(L) g^d(L^{-1})}$$

where r = max(m,q). The no common factor assumption -- that g(L) is "minimal" -- ensures that there are no common roots in $\Pi_1^r(1 - \gamma_j L)$ and $g^d(L)$. Next, define

$$x(t) = [g^d(L) g^d(L^{-1})]^{-1} I(t)$$

and note that

$$I(t) = g^d(L) g^d(L^{-1}) x(t),$$

being a linear combination of a finite numer of leads and lags of x_t, will be of exponential order less than unity whenever x_t is. In terms of x_t, the Euler equation is

$$\gamma_0^2 \Pi_{j=1}^{r} (1 - \gamma_j L)(1 - \gamma_j L^{-1}) x(t) = -B_0 + pA_1 g(1) - \varepsilon(t).$$

From above, the solution to this difference equation which produces an {x(t)} sequence of exponential order less than unity is

$$\Pi_{j=1}^{r}(1 - \gamma_j L)x(t) = \{pA_1 g(1) - B_0\}/\{\gamma_0^2 \Pi_{j=1}^{r}(1 - \gamma_j)\}$$
$$- \gamma_0^{-2}(\Pi_{j=1}^{r}(1 - \gamma_j L^{-1}))^{-1}\varepsilon(t),$$

where the stable roots have been solved backward and the unstable roots forward. Define y_t as the right-hand-side of the above equation. Then the investment decision rule can be written

$$\frac{\Pi_{j=1}^{m}(1 - \gamma_j L)}{g^d(L)} I(t) = g^d(L^{-1})y_t,$$

which emphasizes how the entire history of investment decisions impinges on current investment, or

$$\Pi_{j=1}^{m}(1 - \gamma_j L)I(t) = g^d(L)g^d(L^{-1})y_t.$$

The point of this problem is that the roots which "matter" are the roots of $B_1 + pA_2 g(z)g(z^{-1})$; the poles of $g(z)$ play a lesser role.

C. If $g(L) = L/(1 - \mu L)$,

we have

$$\frac{B_1(1 - \mu L)(1 - \mu L^{-1}) + pA_2}{(1 - \mu L)(1 - \mu L^{-1})} I(t) = -B_0 + pA_1 g(1) - \varepsilon(t).$$

Define ρ_0 and ρ (with $0 < \rho < 1$) by

$$\rho_0(1 - \rho L)(1 - \rho L^{-1}) = pA_2 + B_1(1 - \mu L)(1 - \mu L^{-1}).$$

Then optimal investment is given by

$$\frac{1 - \rho L}{1 - \mu L} I(t) = \rho_0^{-1} \frac{1 - \mu L^{-1}}{1 - \rho L^{-1}} \{-B_0 + pA_1 g(1) - \varepsilon(t)\}$$
$$= \rho_0^{-1} \frac{1 - \mu}{1 - \rho} \{-B_0 + pA_2 g(1)\} - \rho_0^{-1}(1 - \mu L^{-1})\Sigma_{j=0}^{\infty}\rho^j \varepsilon(t+j).$$

(Compare this to the "learning by doing" example in Section IX.11 of the text.)

D. Muth's problem was to forecast future income Y_{t+1} from current and past income Y_t, Y_{t-1}, ..., where income evolves according to

$$Y_t = Y_t^p + \eta_t,$$

with "permanent" income Y_t^p governed by the first order autoregression

$$Y_t^p = rY_{t-1}^p + \varepsilon_t \qquad (E\varepsilon_t\varepsilon_s = 0 \text{ for } t \neq s)$$

and transitory income η_t given by a white noise. Muth further assumed $E\varepsilon_t\eta_t = 0$. The covariance generating function for Y_t is

$$\frac{\sigma_\varepsilon^2}{(1 - rz)(1 - rz^{-1})} + \sigma_\eta^2.$$

Given a factorization

$$\sigma^2 d(z)d(z^{-1}) = \sigma_\eta^2 + \sigma_\varepsilon^2/[(1 - rz)(1 - rz^{-1})]$$

the Wiener-Kolmogorov formula gives

$$P[Y_{t+1}|Y_t, \ldots] = \left[\frac{d(L)}{L}\right]_+ \frac{1}{d(L)}Y_t.$$

Making this optimal forecast requires the factorization of the covariance generating function of Y_t. Putting

$$r = \mu, \quad \sigma_\varepsilon^2 = pA_2, \quad \sigma_\eta^2 = B_1,$$

the covariance-generating-function-factorization problem and the Euler equation factorization problem coincide.

* * *

14. The following identities will prove useful:

$$g_x(\omega) = |b(\omega)|^2 g_y(\omega) + g_\varepsilon(\omega)$$

$$b(\omega) = \sum_{j=-\infty}^{\infty} b_j e^{-i\omega j} = g_{xy}(\omega)/g_y(\omega)$$

$$g_y(\omega) = |h(\omega)|^2 g_x(\omega) + g_u(\omega)$$

$$h(\omega) = \sum_{j=-\infty}^{\infty} h_j e^{-i\omega j} = g_{yx}(\omega)/g_x(\omega)$$

where $g_{yx}(\omega)$ denotes the cross spectral density of y and x, and $g_{xy}(\omega) = g_{yx}(-\omega)$.

A. The coherence is defined by

$$\text{coh}(\omega) = \frac{|g_{yx}(\omega)|^2}{g_y(\omega)g_x(\omega)} = \frac{|g_{xy}(\omega)|^2}{g_y(\omega)g_x(\omega)}.$$

Substitute $h(\omega)g_x(\omega)$ for $g_{yx}(\omega)$ to get

$$\text{coh}(\omega) = \frac{|h(\omega)g_x(\omega)|^2}{g_y(\omega)g_x(\omega)} = \frac{|h(\omega)|^2 g_x}{g_y(\omega)},$$

and then substitute for $|h(\omega)|^2$ using the third identity above to get

$$\text{coh}(\omega) = \frac{(g_y(\omega) - g_u(\omega))g_x(\omega)}{g_x(\omega)g_y(\omega)}$$

$$= 1 - \frac{g_u(\omega)}{g_y(\omega)}.$$

Identical algebra using the other pair of identities yields

$$\text{coh}(\omega) = 1 - \frac{g_\varepsilon(\omega)}{g_x(\omega)}.$$

B. Write

$$
\begin{aligned}
R^2_{xy} &= 1 - 2\pi E\varepsilon^2/2\pi Ex^2 \\
&= 1 - \left[\int_{-\pi}^{\pi} g_\varepsilon(\omega)d\omega / \int_{-\pi}^{\pi} g_x(\omega)d\omega \right] \\
&= \left[\int_{-\pi}^{\pi} (g_x(\omega) - g_\varepsilon(\omega))d\omega \right] / \int_{-\pi}^{\pi} g_x(\omega)d\omega \\
&= \left[\int_{-\pi}^{\pi} |b(\omega)|^2 g_y(\omega)d\omega \right] / \int_{-\pi}^{\pi} g_x(\omega)d\omega \\
&= \left[\int_{-\pi}^{\pi} \frac{|g_{xy}(\omega)|^2}{g_y(\omega)} d\omega \right] / \int_{-\pi}^{\pi} g_x(\omega)d\omega \\
&= \left[\int_{-\pi}^{\pi} \text{coh}(\omega) g_x(\omega)d\omega \right] / \int_{-\pi}^{\pi} g_x(\omega)d\omega
\end{aligned}
$$

as desired.

C. Use the identity

$$R^2_{yx} = 1 - 2\pi Eu^2/2\pi Ey^2;$$

the relation between $g_y(\omega)$, $h(\omega)$, $g_x(\omega)$, and $g_u(\omega)$; and the procedure used in part B to get

$$R^2_{yx}(\omega) = \left[\int_{-\pi}^{\pi} \text{coh}(\omega) g_y(\omega)d\omega \right] / \int_{-\pi}^{\pi} g_y(\omega)d\omega.$$

* * *

15. It is most convenient to use the formula "$c_y(\tau)$ = sum of residues of $g_y(z^{-1})z^{\tau-1}$ at poles inside the unit circle" for $\tau \geq 0$, along with $c_y(-\tau) = c_y(\tau)$. Thus, for $\tau \geq 0$

$$c_y(\tau) = (2\pi i)^{-1}\oint_\Gamma\Big[\prod_{j=1}^{m}(1-\mu_j z)(1-\mu_j z^{-1})z^{\tau-1}\Big/\prod_{j=1}^{n}(1-\lambda_j z)(1-\lambda_j z^{-1})\Big]dz$$

$$= (2\pi i)^{-1}\oint_\Gamma\Big[\prod_{j=1}^{m}(1-\mu_j z)(z-\mu_j)z^{-m+\tau-1+n}\Big/\prod_{j=1}^{n}(1-\lambda_j z)(z-\lambda_j)\Big]dz.$$

Since $n + \tau - m - 1 \geq 0$, the integrand has n poles at $\lambda_1, \ldots, \lambda_n$. The residue at λ_s is given by

$$\lambda_s^{n+\tau-m-1}\prod_{j=1}^{m}(1-\mu_j\lambda_s)(\lambda_s-\mu_j)\Big/\prod_{j=1}^{n}(1-\lambda_j\lambda_s)\prod_{\substack{j=1\\ j\neq s}}^{n}(\lambda_s-\lambda_j).$$

The required formula is obtained by summing over s and noting that $c_y(\tau) = c_y(-\tau)$.

* * *

16. For $j < 0$,

$$b_j = (2\pi i)^{-1}\oint_\Gamma[(1+\mu z)z^{-j-1}/(1-\lambda z)]dz.$$

The integrand is analytic on and inside the unit circle, so $b_j = 0$, $j < 0$. For $j = 0$,

$$b_0 = (2\pi i)^{-1}\oint_\Gamma[(1+\mu z)/(1-\lambda z)]z^{-1}dz = 1.$$

When $j > 0$,

$$b_j = (2\pi i)^{-1}\oint_\Gamma[(1+\mu z)/z^{j+1}(1-\lambda z)]dz.$$

Thus

$$b_j = \text{sum of residues of } (1 + \mu z)/z^{j+1}(1 - \lambda z) \text{ inside the unit circle}$$

or

$$b_j = \text{sum of residues of } (1 + \mu z^{-1})z^j/z(1 - \lambda z^{-1}) \text{ inside the unit circle.}$$

The latter formula is clearly more convenient, as it involves only a simple pole rather than one of order j+1. Thus

$$b_j = \lim_{z \to \lambda} (1 + \mu z^{-1})z^j = \lambda^j + \mu\lambda^{j-1}$$

as required.

* * *

17. Here,

$$w_j = (2\pi i)^{-1}\oint_\Gamma [(1 - \lambda z)^2 z^{j+1}]^{-1} dz.$$

Thus,

$$w_j = \text{sum of residues of } z^{-j-1}/(1 - \lambda z)^2 \text{ inside the unit circle}$$
$$= \text{sum of residues of } z^{j-1}/(1 - \lambda z^{-1})^2 \text{ inside the unit circle.}$$

Again, the latter formula is more useful. Notice that

$$z^{j-1}/(1 - \lambda z^{-1})^2 = z^{j+1}/(z - \lambda)^2.$$

Thus, using formula (23),

$$w_j = (j + 1)\lambda^j$$

which is a special case of formula (39) of Chapter IX; the lag weights correspond to those which appear in equation (31) of Chapter IX.

* * *

18. A. Define

$$A^{(n)} = [A_1^{(n)}, A_2^{(n)}, \ldots, A_n^{(n)}]'$$

$$x^{(n)} = [x_{t-1}, \ldots, x_{t-n}].$$

Then the normal equations for $A^{(n)}$ can be written

$$Ex^{(n)'}x_t = [Ex^{(n)'}x^{(n)}]A^{(n)},$$

where $Ex^{(n)'}x_t$ is an (n x 1) column vector with c(1) in the first row and zeros elsewhere, and $Ex^{(n)'}x^{(n)}$ is an (n x n) matrix with c(0) on the diagonal, c(1) on the first super- and sub-diagonals, and zeros elsewhere. The coefficients are:

$A^{(1)}$ =	-0.4				
$A^{(2)}$ =	-0.476	-0.190			
$A^{(3)}$ =	-0.494	-0.235	-0.094		
$A^{(4)}$ =	-0.499	-0.246	-0.117	-0.047	
$A^{(5)}$ =	-0.500	-0.249	-0.123	-0.059	-0.023.

The $A_j^{(n)}$ seem to approach $-(\frac{1}{2})^j$ as n increases. That this apparent limit is appropriate is established below.

B. The covariance generating function for the $\{x_t\}$ process is

$$g(z) = -0.5z^{-1} + 1.25 - 0.5z,$$

and we seek a factorization $d(z)d(z^{-1})\sigma^2 = g(z)$, with $d(z) \neq 0$ for $|z| < 1$ and $d_0 = 1$. Notice that $g(2) = g(\frac{1}{2}) = 0$. Thus $d(z) = 1 - \frac{1}{2}z$. From the Wiener-Kolmogorov formula,

$$P[x_t | x_{t-1}, \ldots] = [L^{-1}d(L)]_+ \, d(L)^{-1}x_{t-1}$$

$$= -\tfrac{1}{2}\Sigma_{k=0}^{\infty}(\tfrac{1}{2})^k x_{t-k-1} = -\Sigma_{k=0}^{\infty}(\tfrac{1}{2})^{k+1} x_{t-k-1}.$$

That is, $A_j^{(\infty)} = -(\frac{1}{2})^j$ for $j = 1, 2, \ldots$, as expected.

* * *

19. Use the Wiener-Kolmogorov formula to calculate $P[x_{t+1}|x_t, \ldots]$:

$$P[x_{t+1}|x_t, \ldots] = [L^{-1}c(L)]_+ \, c(L)^{-1}x_t.$$

But this equals ρx_t:

$$[L^{-1}c(L)]_+ c(L)^{-1}x_t = \rho x_t,$$

so that

$$[L^{-1}c(L)]_+ c(L)^{-1} = \rho$$

or

$$L^{-1}[c(L) - c_0]c(L)^{-1} = \rho.$$

Thus

$$c(L) = \rho L c(L) + c_0$$

or

$$c(L) = c_0/(1 - \rho L).$$

By appropriately scaling the variance of $\{\varepsilon_t\}$, we are free to choose $c_0 = 1$. Thus $c(L) = 1/(1 - \rho L)$.

* * *

20. Use the Wiener-Kolmogorov formula to write the given identity in projections as

$$[L^{-2}c(L)]_+ c(L)^{-1}x_t = \rho[L^{-1}c(L)]_+ c(L)^{-1}x_t.$$

Thus

$$[L^{-2}c(L)]_+ = \rho[L^{-1}c(L)]_+$$

or

$$L^{-2}[c(L) - c_0 - c_1L] = \rho L^{-1}[c(L) - c_0]$$

whence

$$(1 - \rho L)c(L) = c_0 + (c_1 - \rho c_0)L,$$

or

$$c(L) = (1 - \rho L)^{-1}(c_0 + (c_1 - \rho c_0)L).$$

* * *

21. Use the Wiener-Kolmogorov formula to write the given identity in projections as

$$[L^{-k}c(L)]_+ c(L)^{-1}x_t = \rho^{k-1}[L^{-1}c(L)]_+ c(L)^{-1}x_t.$$

Thus

$$[z^{-k}c(z)]_+ = \rho^{k-1}[z^{-1}c(z)]_+$$

or

$$\Sigma_{j=k}^{\infty} c_j z^{j-k} = \rho^{k-1}\Sigma_{j=1}^{\infty} c_j z^{j-1}.$$

Now multiply each side of the above equation by z^{-1}, and integrate with respect to z,

$$(2\pi i)^{-1}\oint z^{-1}\Sigma_{j=k}^{\infty} c_j z^{j-k}dz = (2\pi i)^{-1}\oint z^{-1}\rho^{k-1}\Sigma_{j=1}^{\infty} c_j z^{j-1}dz$$

to obtain

$$c_k = \rho^{k-1}c_1$$

for $k \geq 1$. Now multiply by z^k and sum over $k \geq 1$ to get

$$\Sigma_{k=1}^{\infty} c_k z^k = c_1\Sigma_{k=1}^{\infty}\rho^{k-1}z^k$$

or

$$c(z) - c_0 = c_1 z/(1 - \rho z).$$

Then

$$c(L) = [c_0 + (c_1 - \rho c_0)L]/(1 - \rho L).$$

* * *

22. A. The spectrum of the wage process is given by

$$g_w(e^{-i\omega}) = \sigma_\varepsilon^2/[(1 - \delta e^{-i4\omega})(1 - \delta e^{i4\omega})]$$

$$= \sigma_\varepsilon^2/[1 + \delta^2 - 2\delta\cos 4\omega]$$

which has three peaks on $[0, \pi]$ at the frequencies 0, $\pi/2$, and π. The value of $g_w(\cdot)$ at the peaks is $\sigma_\varepsilon^2/(1 - \delta)^2$. There are two troughs on $[0, \pi]$, at $\omega = \pi/4$ and $3\pi/4$, where the spectrum takes the value $\sigma_\varepsilon^2/(1 + \delta)^2$. (Qualitatively, the graph of the spectrum is similar to the graphs of $|h(e^{-i\omega})|^2$ for $h(L) = (1 - 0.5L^{12})^{-1}$ and $h(L) = (1 - 0.9L^{12})^{-1}$ which appear in Figure 4, the important difference being in the number of peaks and troughs.)

By the formula 2π = frequency $\times$ period, the frequency $\pi/2$ corresponds to cycles of length 4 -- one year in quarterly data. Since much of the variance in $\{w_t\}$ can be attributed to spectral power near the frequency $\pi/2$, the $\{w_t\}$ process will exhibit much seasonal variation.

B. It will be seen in Chapter XIV of the text (especially Exercise XIV.4) that one may find the optimal decision rule in such a problem by finding the decision rule for the associated certainty problem, and replacing those quantities which are in fact unknown by their mathematical expectations. Using the derivative formulas from Exercise IX.3, the Euler equation for the certainty problem is

$$f_0 - \left(f_1 + d(1 - \beta L^{-1})(1 - L)\right)n_t - w_t = 0.$$

Use the factorization

$$f_1 + d(1 - \beta L^{-1})(1 - L) = -\beta d L^{-1}(1 - \lambda_1 L)(1 - \beta^{-1}\lambda_1^{-1}L) \quad 0 < \lambda_1 < 1$$

and write the solution (see Section IX.8 of the text) as

$$n_t = \lambda_1 n_{t-1} + (1 - \beta\lambda_1)^{-1}d^{-1}\lambda_1 f_0 - d^{-1}\lambda_1 \Sigma_{j=0}^{\infty}(\beta\lambda_1)^j w_{t+j}, \ t \geq 1.$$

Now replace objects which are unknown at t -- w_{t+j} -- by their expected values -- $E_t w_{t+j}$:

$$n_t = \lambda_1 n_{t-1} + c - d^{-1}\lambda_1 \ \Sigma_{j=0}^{\infty}(\beta\lambda_1)^j E_t w_{t+j},$$

where $c = (1 - \beta\lambda_1)^{-1}d^{-1}\lambda_1 f_0$. Using formula (90) from Chapter XI of the text, and $(1 - \delta L^4) = a(L)$, we obtain

$$n_t = \lambda_1 n_{t-1} + c + \Sigma_{j=0}^{3} h_j w_{t-j}$$

where $h(L) = \Sigma_{j=0}^{\infty} h_j L^j$ is given by

$$h(L) = -d^{-1}\lambda_1 a(\beta\lambda_1)^{-1}[1 + \Sigma_{j=1}^{3}(\Sigma_{k=j+1}^{4}(\beta\lambda_1)^{k-j}a_k)L^j]$$

so that

$$h_0 = -d^{-1}\lambda_1 a(\beta\lambda_1)^{-1} = -d^{-1}\lambda_1/(1 - \delta(\beta\lambda_1)^4)$$

$$h_1 = -d^{-1}\lambda_1 a(\beta\lambda_1)^{-1}(\beta\lambda_1)^3\delta$$

$$h_2 = -d^{-1}\lambda_1 a(\beta\lambda_1)^{-1}(\beta\lambda_1)^2\delta$$

$$h_3 = -d^{-1}\lambda_1 a(\beta\lambda_1)^{-1}\beta\lambda_1\delta.$$

Notice that for each j, h_j is a function of λ_1, β, δ; $h_j = h_j(\beta\lambda_1,\delta)$. Writing the two equation system as

$$w_t = \delta w_{t-4} + \varepsilon_t$$

$$n_t = \lambda_1 n_{t-1} + c + \Sigma_{j=0}^{3} \ h_j(\beta\lambda_1,\delta)w_{t-j}$$

indicates clearly how the parameter δ from the wage equation impinges on the coefficients h_j in the decision rule. That is, the functions $h_j(\beta\lambda_1,\delta)$ embody the cross equation restrictions of rational expectations.

C. For convenience, suppose $f_0 = 0$ so that $c = 0$. Then notice that n_t is an exact function of w_t, w_{t-1}, ...:

$$n_t = (1 - \lambda_1 L)^{-1} h(L) w_t \equiv \sum_{j=0}^{\infty} H_j w_{t-j}.$$

Thus

$$P[n_t | w_t, w_{t-1}, \ldots] = (1 - \lambda_1 L)^{-1} h(L) w_t = n_t.$$

There is no error, so

$$P[n_t | w_t, w_{t\pm1}, w_{t\pm2}, \ldots] = P[n_t | w_t, w_{t-1}, \ldots]$$
$$= (1 - \lambda_1 L)^{-1} h(L) w_t,$$

and n_t fails to Granger cause w_t by Sims's theorem 2. (This is a case in which the moving average representation for the process $\{n_t, w_t\}$ is trivially triangular; there is only one noise -- ε_t -- in the system, so there is only one nonzero column in the moving average polynomial matrix for $\{n_t, w_t\}$.)

D. Using the decision rule (3),

$$n_t^a = (1 - \delta L^4) n_t = (1 - \delta L^4)(1 - \lambda_1 L)^{-1} h(L) w_t$$
$$= (1 - \lambda_1 L)^{-1} h(L)(1 - \delta L^4) w_t$$
$$= (1 - \lambda_1 L)^{-1} h(L) w_t^a$$
$$= (1 - \lambda_1 L)^{-1} h(L) \varepsilon_t.$$

Thus

$$P[n_t^a | w_t^a, w_{t-1}^a, \ldots] = (1 - \lambda_1 L)^{-1} h(L) w_t^a;$$

the coefficients in this projection are the same as those in $P[n_t | w_t, w_{t-1}, \ldots]$.

E. (i) The Euler equation for the certainty version of this problem is

$$f_0 - (f_1 + d(1 - \beta L^{-1})(1 - L))n_t^a - w_t^a = 0.$$

Thus the certainty decision rule is

$$n_t^a = \lambda_1 n_{t-1}^a + c - d^{-1}\lambda_1 \Sigma_{j=0}^{\infty}(\beta\lambda_1)^j w_{t+j}^a$$

where λ_1 and c are as above. Now replace w_{t+j}^a by $E_t w_{t+j}^a$ and note that $E_t w_{t+j}^a = E_t \varepsilon_{t+j} = 0$ for $j > 0$. Thus

$$n_t^a = \lambda_1 n_{t-1}^a + c - d^{-1}\lambda_1 w_t^a, \tag{4}$$

$$w_t^a = \varepsilon_t.$$

The cross-equation restriction here is that the lack of serial correlation in w_t^a dictates that there be no lags of w_t^a in (4).

(ii) Let $\tilde{h}(L) = -d^{-1}\lambda_1$. The econometrician expects the coefficients in $P[n_t^a | w_t^a, w_{t-1}^a, \ldots]$ to be given by the lag generating function $\tilde{h}(L)/(1 - \lambda_1 L)$, but they are in fact generated by $h(L)/(1 - \lambda_1 L)$. Lags (1, 2, and 3) of w_t^a belong in the decision rule, and the econometrician, thinking (4) to be the correct implication of the model of firms' behavior, will reject the model when he finds that an alternative hypothesis (which allows lags of w_t^a) fits the data better. (Alternatively, if the econometrician projected n_t^a on a constant, n_{t-1}^a, and w_t^a, he would find -- unexpectedly, since he believes (4) to be correct -- that his regression does not fit exactly. Further, the residual in this equation -- being a linear combination of ε_{t-1}, ε_{t-2}, and ε_{t-3} -- would be serially correlated. Unexpected serial correlation is often taken to be evidence against a model.)

* * *

23. A. To find the Wold representation for X, it is necessary to factor the covariance function. That is, one must find a function d(z), with $d_0 = 1$, and d(z) having no zeros on $|z| < 1$ and no poles on $|z| \leq 1$, where

$$g_X(z) = \sigma_a^2 d(z)d(z^{-1}).$$

Loosely speaking, finding the factorization amounts to finding the poles and zeros of $g_X(z)$. Specifically, let z_1, z_1^{-1}, ..., z_m, z_m^{-1} be the zeros of $g_X(z)$ (with $|z_j| \leq 1$, j = 1, ..., m) and let p_1, p_1^{-1}, ..., p_n, p_n^{-1} be the poles of $g_X(z)$ (with $|p_j| < 1$, j = 1, ..., n). Then

$$d(z) = \Pi_{j=1}^{m}(1 - z_j z)/\Pi_{j=1}^{n}(1 - p_j z).$$

Sections XI.15, 16, 17 of the text provide some additional discussion of the factorization problem.*

B. From the optimal filtering formulas, the optimal one-sided seasonal adjustment filter is given by

$$\theta(z) = [\sigma_a^2 d(z)]^{-1}[d(z^{-1})^{-1}g_{xX}(z)]_+,$$

while the two-sided filter (Problem 2) is given by

$$h(z) = [\sigma_a^2 d(z)d(z^{-1})]^{-1}g_{xX}(z) = g_X(z)^{-1}g_{xX}(z).$$

Since $X_t = x_t + u_t$ and x and u are orthogonal, $g_{xX}(z) = g_x(z) = g_X(z) - g_u(z)$. Thus

---

*The multivariate factorization problem is somewhat more complicated. For general discussions, see Rosanov, op. cit., Ch. I.10, and P. Whittle, Prediction and Regulation, 1983 (Second Edition), Minneapolis: The University of Minnesota Press, Ch. 9.3. Computer algorithms can be found in W.G. Tuel, "Computer Algorithm for Spectral Factorization of Rational Matrices," IBM Journal, 1968 (March): 163-170; and D.C. Youla, "On the Factorization of Rational Matrices, IRE Transactions on Information Theory, 1961 (July): 172-189.

$$\theta(z) = 1 - [\sigma_a^2 d(z)]^{-1}[d(z^{-1})^{-1} g_u(z)]_+$$

$$h(z) = 1 - [\sigma_a^2 d(z)]^{-1}[d(z^{-1})^{-1} g_u(z)] = 1 - g_u(z)/g_x(z).$$

C. Write

$$y_t = \alpha\Sigma_{j=0}^{\infty}\lambda^j P[x_{t+j}|x_t, x_{t-1}, \ldots]$$

and define s_t by

$$y_t = P[y_t|X_t, X_{t-1}, \ldots] + s_t;$$

note that by construction $Es_t X_{t-j} = 0$ for $j \geq 0$. The $\{y_t\}$ process can be represented as

$$\begin{aligned} y_t &= \alpha\Sigma_{j=0}^{\infty} \lambda^j P[x_{t+j}|X_t, X_{t-1}, \ldots] + s_t \\ &= \alpha\Sigma_{j=0}^{\infty} \lambda^j P[\theta(L)X_{t+j} + \varepsilon_{t+j}|X_t, X_{t-1}, \ldots] + s_t \\ &= \alpha\Sigma_{j=0}^{\infty} \lambda^j P[\theta(L)X_t|X_t, X_{t-1}, \ldots] + s_t \\ &\equiv q_t + s_t, \end{aligned}$$

where q_t is the solution to

$$q_t = \lambda P_t q_{t+1} + \alpha\theta(L)X_t.$$

The information set implicit in the operator P_t is $\{X_t, X_{t-1}, \ldots\} = \{a_t, a_{t-1}, \ldots\}$. We seek a process

$$q_t = h(L)X_t = e(L)a_t.$$

Using $q_t = e(L)a_t$, $P_t q_{t+1} = [L^{-1}e(L)]_+ a_t = L^{-1}(e(L) - e_0)a_t$, and $X_t = d(L)a_t$ in the formula for q_t, one obtains

$$e(L)a_t = \lambda L^{-1}(e(L) - e_0)a_t + \alpha\theta(L)d(L)a_t$$

which is required to hold for all realizations of $\{a_t\}$. Thus

$$e(L) = \lambda L^{-1}(e(L) - e_0) + \alpha\theta(L)d(L).$$

Evaluate this expression at $L = \lambda$ (see Exercise 12 and Section XI.19 of the text), to find

$$e_0 = \alpha\theta(\lambda)d(\lambda),$$

and

$$e(L) = \frac{\alpha[\theta(L)d(L) - \lambda L^{-1}\theta(\lambda)d(\lambda)]}{1 - \lambda L^{-1}}$$

or

$$h(L) = e(L)d(L)^{-1} = \alpha(1 - \lambda L^{-1})^{-1}\{\theta(L) - \lambda L^{-1}\theta(\lambda)d(\lambda)d(L)^{-1}\}.$$

D. Assume that $\theta(L)$ and $d(L)$ can be written

$$\theta(L) = \theta^a(L)/\theta^b(L)$$

$$d(L) = d^a(L)/d^b(L)$$

where θ^a, θ^b, d^a, d^b are each finite-order polynomials in the lag operator.* Write

$$h(L) = \frac{\alpha\theta^a(\lambda)d^a(\lambda)}{\theta^b(L)d^b(L)} \frac{1}{1 - \lambda^{-1}L}\left\{\frac{d^a(L)\theta^a(L)}{d^a(\lambda)\theta^a(\lambda)} - \lambda L^{-1} \frac{d^b(L)\theta^b(L)}{d^b(\lambda)\theta^b(\lambda)}\right\}$$

$$= \alpha\gamma(\lambda)d(L)^{-1}\delta(L)^{-1}(1 - \lambda^{-1}L)^{-1}\{\gamma(L)/\gamma(\lambda) - \lambda L^{-1}\delta(L)/\delta(\lambda)\}$$

---

*This assumption essentially restricts attention to x and X processes with rational spectra. Such a restriction is common, indeed practically necessary, in applied work.

where $\gamma(L) \equiv d^a(L)\theta^a(L)$, $\delta(L) \equiv d^b(L)\theta^b(L)$. Suppose that $\gamma(\cdot)$ is a polynomial of order s and $\delta(\cdot)$ is a polynomial of order r. Long division yields

$$\gamma(L)/(1 - \lambda L^{-1}) = \gamma_s L^s + (\gamma_{s-1} + \gamma_s\lambda)L^{s-1} + \dots$$

$$+ (\gamma_1 + \gamma_2\lambda + \dots + \gamma_s\lambda^{s-1})L + \gamma(\lambda)/(1 - \lambda L^{-1})$$

$$= \Sigma_{j=1}^{s}(\Sigma_{k=j}^{s}\gamma_k\lambda^{k-j})L^j + \gamma(\lambda)/(1 - \lambda L^{-1})$$

$$-\lambda L^{-1}\delta(L)/(1 - \lambda L^{-1}) = -\lambda L^{-1}\Sigma_{j=1}^{r}(\Sigma_{k=j}^{r}\delta_k\lambda^{k-j})L^j$$

$$- \lambda L^{-1}\delta(\lambda)/(1 - \lambda L^{-1}).$$

Then simple algebra yields

$$h(L) = \alpha\gamma(\lambda)d(L)^{-1}\delta(L)^{-1}\{\gamma(\lambda)^{-1}\ \Sigma_{j=1}^{s}\ \Sigma_{k=j}^{s}\gamma_k\lambda^{k-j}L^j$$

$$+ \delta(\lambda)^{-1}[\delta_o - \Sigma_{j=1}^{r-1}\ \Sigma_{k=j}^{r}\delta_k\lambda^{k-j}L^j]\}.$$

When $\theta(L) \equiv 1$ and $d^b(L) \equiv 1$, we have $\gamma(L) = 1$, $\gamma_j = 0$ for $j \geq 1$, $\delta(L) = d(L)^{-1}$, and $\delta_0 = 1$, so the formula reduces to the Hansen-Sargent formula ((90) in the text). If $\theta^b(L) = 1 = d^a(L)$ but $\theta^a(L) = \theta(L)$ is of order s,

$$h^*(L) = \alpha\ \Sigma_{j=1}^{s}\ \Sigma_{k=j}^{s}\theta_k\lambda^{k-j}L^j + \alpha\theta(\lambda)d(\lambda)\{1 - \Sigma_{j=1}^{r-1}\ \Sigma_{k=j}^{r}\delta_k\lambda^{k-j}L^j\}$$

is a finite-order polynomial (with order max(s,r-1)) from which the coefficients can be read directly. In the most general case, $\theta^b(L)d^a(L)h(L)$ is the above max(s,r-1)-order polynomial h^*, and, defining $f(L) \equiv \theta^b(L)d^a(L)$, the coefficients h_j can be generated via the recursion

$$h_0 = f_0^{-1} h_0^*,$$

$$h_j = f_0^{-1}(h_j^* - f_1 h_{j-1} - \dots - f_j h_0) \qquad j \geq 1.$$

E. The covariance generating function for $\tilde{x}_t$ is

$$\theta(z)\theta(z^{-1})\sigma_a^2 d(z)d(z^{-1}),$$

and we seek a factorization

$$\psi(z)\psi(z^{-1})\sigma_b^2 = \theta(z)\theta(z^{-1})\sigma_a^2 d(z)d(z^{-1})$$

with $\psi(0) = 1$, where $\psi(z)$ has no zeros on the open unit disk and no poles on the closed unit disk. Then the Wold representation for $\tilde{x}_t$ is

$$\tilde{x}_t = \psi(L)b_t$$

where $b_t = \tilde{x}_t - P[\tilde{x}_t | \tilde{x}_{t-1}, \dots]$, $Eb_t^2 = \sigma_b^2$, and $\Sigma_{j=0}^{\infty} \psi_j^2 < \infty$. If $\theta(z)$ has no zeros on $|z| < 1$, $\psi(L) = \theta_0^{-1}\theta(L)$ and $b_t = \theta_0 a_t$.† Thus, except for normalization,

$$\tilde{x}_t = \theta(L)d(L)a_t$$

is a Wold representation for $\tilde{x}_t$ whenever $\theta(z)$ has no zeros on $|z| < 1$.

F. Define $\tilde{q}_t$ by

$$\tilde{q}_t = \lambda P_t \tilde{q}_{t+1} + \alpha \tilde{x}_t$$

where the information set at t is $\{\tilde{x}_t, \tilde{x}_{t-1}, \dots\}$. Then using the Wold representation for $\tilde{x}_t$ and formula (90) from the text,

---

†The application of the "plussing" operator in the construction of the distributed lag operator in (5) ensures that it does not have poles on $|z| \leq 1$.

$$f(L)\tilde{x}_t = \tilde{q}_t = \alpha(1 - \lambda L^{-1})\{1 - \lambda^{-1}L\psi(\lambda)\psi(L)^{-1}\}\tilde{x}_t.$$

G. Using the relation $\tilde{x}_t = \theta(L)X_t$,

$$f(L)\tilde{x}_t = \alpha(1 - \lambda L^{-1})\{\theta(L) - \lambda L^{-1}\psi(\lambda)\psi(L)^{-1}\theta(L)\}X_t$$

which equals $h(L)X_t$ when

$$\psi(\lambda)\psi(L)^{-1}\theta(L) = \theta(\lambda)d(\lambda)d(L)^{-1},$$

i.e., when $\psi(L) = \theta(L)d(L)$ -- when $\theta(z)$ has no zeros on $|z| < 1$. The lack of zeros in $\theta(z)$ means that no information is lost in passing from X to $\tilde{x}$, because X_t can be recovered from $\theta(L)^{-1}\tilde{x}_t$, which involves only current and past $\tilde{x}$'s. Thus the information sets $\{\tilde{x}_t, \tilde{x}_{t-1}, \ldots\}$ and $\{X_t, X_{t-1}, \ldots\}$ are equivalent. Therefore, if agents actually respond to an unobserved signal, one will correctly characterize the restrictions agents' behavior imposes on observables by proceeding as though they are responding to an estimate of that signal when (i) the estimate has been extracted optimally, and (ii) the information in the estimate is equivalent to the information in the observables.

Notice that as the noise becomes small ($\sigma_u^2 \to 0$), the "adjustment" filter approaches the identity operator ($\theta(L) \to 1$). This explains why analysis of the seasonally adjusted data in Exercise 22 failed to reveal the restrictions across the raw series: there was no "noise", yet the adjustment filter $(1 - \delta L^4)$ was not unity. It was, in fact, invertible, (condition (ii) was satisfied), but it was not the result of projecting the variable (n_t) about which agents cared on the process (also n_t) seen by the econometrician (condition (i) was not satisfied).

H. (i) It is useful to begin by proving that y fails to Granger cause x. From (1), y_t is an <u>exact</u> function of $x_t, x_{t-1}, \ldots$. Write this function as

$$y_t = H(L)x_t$$

where $H(L) = \Sigma_{j=0}^{\infty} H_j L^j$. Thus

$$P[y_t | x_t, \ldots] = y_t$$
$$= P[y_t | x_t, x_{t\pm 1}, \ldots]$$

and y fails to Granger cause x.

By construction, the s_t in (7) is orthogonal to X_t, X_{t-1}, ... But there is no requirement that $Es_t X_{t+j} = 0$ for $j > 0$, and in general, there will be some $j > 0$ for which $Es_t X_{t+j} \neq 0$. But then $P[y_t | X_t, X_{t\pm 1}, \ldots] = h(L)X_t + P[s_t | X_t, X_{t\pm 1}, \ldots] \neq h(L)X_t = P[y_t | X_t, X_{t-1}, \ldots]$ and y Granger causes X. To argue more precisely, let the Wold representation of x_t be

$$x_t = c_x(L)\varepsilon_t^x$$

and that for u_t be

$$u_t = c_u(L)\varepsilon_t^u$$

where ε_t^x and ε_t^u are serially uncorrelated and $E\varepsilon_t^u \varepsilon_s^x = 0$ for all t, s (since x_s and u_t are orthogonal). Then

$$x_t = c_x(L)\varepsilon_t^x$$

$$X_t = c_x(L)\varepsilon_t^x + c_u(L)\varepsilon_t^u$$

is the Wold representation for (x_t, X_t). The distributed lag coefficient generating function for the projection of y_t on the entire X process is, using $y_t = H(L)x_t$,

$$H(z)c_x(z)c_x(z^{-1})/g_X(z) = H(z)g_x(z)/(g_x(z) + g_u(z))$$

which is in general two-sided. By Sims's theorem 2, y Granger causes X.

(ii) The process s_t is given by

$$s_t = \alpha P[\Sigma_{j=0}^{\infty}\lambda^j x_{t+j}|x_t, \ldots] - \alpha P[\Sigma_{j=0}^{\infty}\lambda^j x_{t+j}|X_t, \ldots],$$

the forecast error in projecting $\alpha P[\Sigma_{j=0}^{\infty} \lambda^j x_{t+j}|x_t, \ldots]$ on $\{X_t, X_{t-1}, \ldots\}$. Notice that s_t is a linear function of x_t, X_t, X_{t-1}, X_{t-1}, ... The information set $\{X_t, X_{t-1}, \ldots\}$ used in the construction of s_t does not include s_{t-1}, s_{t-2}, ..., so s_t will not generally be orthogonal to $\{s_{t-1}, s_{t-2}, \ldots\}$: s_t will generally be serially correlated.

(iii) Let $\gamma(L) = c(L)^{-1}$. Then $\eta_t = \gamma(L)s_t$, and

$$\begin{aligned} E\eta_t X_{t-j} &= E\gamma(L)s_t X_{t-j} = E(\gamma_0 s_t + \gamma_1 s_{t-1} + \ldots)X_{t-j} \\ &= \Sigma_{k=0}^{j}\gamma_k Es_{t-k}X_{t-j} + \Sigma_{k=j+1}^{\infty}\gamma_k Es_{t-k}X_{t-j} \\ &= \gamma_{j+1}Es_{t-j-1}X_{t-j} + \gamma_{j+2}Es_{t-j-2}X_{t-j} + \ldots \end{aligned}$$

since $Es_{t-k}X_{t-j} = 0$ for $k \le j$. Since s_{t-k} _may_ be correlated with _future_ X's, $E\eta_t X_{t-j}$ is not in general zero for $j \ge 0$.

(iv) It was shown in Exercise 3 that the process s_t has the forward Wold or "Dlow" representation $s_t = c(L^{-1})\tilde{\eta}_t$. Note that $\gamma(L^{-1}) = c(L^{-1})^{-1}$. Now $\tilde{\eta}_t = \gamma(L^{-1})s_t$ is a linear combination of current and _future_ s. Further, $Es_t X_{t-j} = 0$ for $j \ge 0$. Thus

$$\begin{aligned} E\tilde{\eta}_t X_{t-j} &= \gamma_0 Es_t X_{t-j} + \gamma_1 Es_{t+1}X_{t-j} + \ldots \\ &= 0 \qquad \text{for } j \ge 0. \end{aligned}$$

(v) Given (4) and (5), theory delivers the h(L) in (7) and the restrictions $Es_t X_{t-j} = 0$ for $j \ge 0$. But it also tells us something about the serial correlation properties of s_t. The Hayashi-Sims procedure allows the orthogonality conditions and the known serial correlation properties of s_t to be used simultaneously in estimation.

I. From (7),

$$E[y_t - h(L)X_t]X_{t-j} = 0 \qquad j \geq 0.$$

Given the known d(L) and $\theta(L)$, the polynomial h(L) depends only on the (unknown) parameters α and λ. To indicate the dependence, write

$$h(L) = h(L;\ \alpha,\lambda).$$

For some given α_g and λ_g, and a sample of length T from $(y_t,\ X_t)$, it is possible to compute

$$y_t - h(L;\ \alpha_g,\lambda_g)X_t$$

and sample versions of the orthogonality conditions

$$T^{-1}\Sigma_{t=1}^{T}[y_t - h(L;\ \alpha_g,\lambda_g)X_t]X_{t-j} = G_T(\alpha_g,\ \lambda_g)$$

for various $j \geq 0$. Then, since $E[y_t - h(L;\ \alpha_g,\lambda_g)X_t]X_{t-j} = 0$, one can think of estimating α and λ by choosing values for these parameters which make G_T "small." This procedure for estimating parameters of interest is known as the "Generalized Method of Moments" (it chooses parameters to set sample moments "close" to population moments) and is developed in L. Hansen, "Large Sample Properties of Generalized Method of Moments Estimators," Econometrica 50 (July, 1982): 1029-54. Hansen and Sargent, op. cit., discuss the application of the procedure to linear rational expectations models.

* * *

24. Note that

$$P[\Sigma_{j=0}^{\infty}\lambda^{j}x_{t+j+1}|x_t, \ldots] = \lambda^{-1}P[\Sigma_{j=0}^{\infty}\lambda^{i}x_{t+j} - x_t|x_t, \ldots]$$

$$= \lambda^{-1}P[\Sigma_{j=0}^{\infty} \lambda^{j}x_{t+j}|x_t, \ldots] - \lambda^{-1}x_t.$$

The first term is given by formula (90) from the text. Let a(L) be of order r. Then

$$P[\Sigma_{j=0}^{\infty}\lambda^{j}x_{t+j+1}|x_t, \ldots]$$

$$= (L - \lambda)^{-1}[c(L) - c(\lambda)]\varepsilon_t$$

$$= \lambda^{-1}a(\lambda)^{-1}[1 - a(\lambda) + \Sigma_{j=1}^{r-1} \Sigma_{k=j+1}^{r}\lambda^{k-j}a_k L^j]x_t.$$

* * *

25. A. Write

$$\bar{z}_t = z_t + \lim_{\beta\to 1} E_t \sum_{j=0}^{\infty} \beta^{j+1}\Delta z_{t+1+j}$$

$$= z_t + \lim_{\beta\to 1} E_t(-\Delta z_t + \Delta z_t + \beta\Delta z_{t+1} + \ldots)$$

$$= z_t - \Delta z_t + \lim_{\beta\to 1} E_t \sum_{j=0}^{\infty} \beta^{j}\Delta z_{t+j}$$

$$= z_t - \Delta z_t + \lim_{\beta\to 1} [\frac{Lc(L) - \beta c(\beta)}{L - \beta}]\varepsilon_t \qquad \text{(from formula (90))}$$

$$= z_t - c(L)\varepsilon_t + \frac{Lc(L) - c(1)}{L - 1}\varepsilon_t$$

$$= z_t + \{\frac{c(L) - c(1)}{L - 1}\}\varepsilon_t.$$

B. $(1 - L)\bar{z}_t = (1 - L)z_t - \{c(L) - c(1)\}\varepsilon_t$

$$= c(L)\varepsilon_t - c(L)\varepsilon_t + c(1)\varepsilon_t = c(1)\varepsilon_t.$$

C. $\bar{z}_t = \frac{c(L)}{1 - L}\varepsilon_t - \{\frac{c(L) - c(1)}{1 - L}\}\varepsilon_t$

$$= \frac{c(1)}{1 - L}\varepsilon_t = c(1)\frac{1}{1 - L}c(L)^{-1}(1 - L)z_t$$

$$= c(1)c(L)^{-1}z_t.$$

D. From (*),

$$z_t - \bar{z}_t = z_t - c(1)c(L)^{-1}z_t = (1 - c(1)/c(L))z_t.$$

E. Formula (**) might not be a Wold representation for s_t. If it is to be such a representation, the operator $(1 - L)^{-1}[c(L) - c(1)]$ must have no zeros inside the unit disk. But it is a simple matter to construct examples where this condition does not hold. For instance, let

$$c(L) = c_0 + c_1L + c_2L^2$$

and suppose $c_2 > 0 > c_1 > -2c_2$. Then

$$(1 - L)^{-1}[c(L) - c(1)] = -(c_1 + c_2)(1 + (c_1 + c_2)^{-1}c_2L)$$

which has a zero at $-(c_1 + c_2)/c_2$ inside the unit disk. This means that $(1 - L)^{-1}[c(L) - c(1)]$ does not have a square-summable inverse in nonnegative powers of L. In this case, $\{\varepsilon_t, \varepsilon_{t-1}, \ldots\}$ constitutes a larger information set than does $\{s_t, s_{t-1}, \ldots\}$, $\{\varepsilon_t\}$ is not fundamental for $\{s_t\}$, and (**) is not a Wold representation for $\{s_t\}$.

F. Suppose

$$s_{1t} = f(L)z_{1t}$$

$$s_{2t} = g(L)z_{2t}$$

and that z_2 fails to Granger cause z_1. The latter assumption is equivalent to the one-sidedness (in nonnegative powers of z) of the lag generating function

$$g_{21}(z)/g_{11}(z)$$

from the projection of z_{2t} on the entire $\{z_{1t}\}$ process. The cross-covariance generating function of s_2, s_1 is

$$g(z)f(z^{-1})g_{21}(z)$$

while the covariance generating function of s_1 is

$$f(z)f(z^{-1})g_{11}(z).$$

Thus the lag coefficient generating function for the projection of s_{2t} on $\{s_{1t}\}$ is

$$g(z)g_{21}(z)/f(z)g_{11}(z)$$

which will be one-sided in nonnegative powers of z whenever f(z) has a square summable inverse in nonnegative powers of z; that is, when f(z) has no zeros on $|z| < 1$. In light of the analysis in part E, f(z) may have zeros on $|z| < 1$; the failure of s_2 to Granger cause s_1 does not follow from the failure of z_2 to Granger cause z_1.

CHAPTER XIV

INVESTMENT UNDER UNCERTAINTY

EXERCISES

1. Assume that

$$J_{t+1} = \alpha J_t + \eta_{t+1}, \quad |\alpha| < 1/b,$$
$$u_{t+1} = \beta u_t + \varepsilon_{t+1}, \quad |\beta| < 1/b,$$

where $E_t\eta_{t+1} = \bar{\eta}$ and $E_t\varepsilon_{t+1} = \bar{\varepsilon}$. Use this information and (29) to calculate a "reduced form" for investment of the form

$$k_{t+j+1} - \lambda_1 k_{t+j} = \gamma_0 + \gamma_1 J_{t+1+j} + \gamma_2 u_{t+1+j}$$

giving explicit formulas for γ_0, γ_1, and γ_2 in terms of λ_1, d, λ_2, α, β, $\bar{\eta}$, and $\bar{\varepsilon}$.

2. (Certainty equivalence principle) Let x be a random variable with probability density g(x), and let α, a parameter, be set by a decision-maker. Let $f(x,\alpha)$ be concave and twice continuously differentiable. Consider <u>Problem 1</u>: choose α to maximize $Ef(x,\alpha) = \int f(x,\alpha)g(x)dx$.

A. Find the first-order necessary condition for choosing α.

B. Suppose that $f(x,\alpha) = (x,\alpha)A(x,\alpha)' + (x,\alpha)B$ where B is a 2 x 1 matrix, (x,α) is a 1 x 2 vector, and A is a 2 x 2 negative definite matrix. Prove that in this special case, choosing α to solve Problem 1 gives the same α as choosing α to solve the following <u>Problem 2</u>:

choose α to maximize $f(Ex,\alpha)$. The equivalence of these answers in the special case of a quadratic objective function is known as the "certainty equivalence" or separation principle.

3. (Eckstein (1983)) There is a large number n of identical farms producing corn. Each farm maximizes

$$E_0 \sum_{t=0}^{\infty} b^t \{p_{t+1}y_{t+1} - c_0 a_t - \frac{c_1}{2} a_t^2 - c_2 a_t a_{t-1} - w_t a_t\} \tag{1}$$

subject to a_{-1} given. Here c_0, c_1, $c_2 > 0$, $0 < b < 1$, a_t is acres planted at t, y_{t+1} is output at time (t+1), p_{t+1} is the price of corn at (t+1), and w_t is the cost of fertilizer applied per acre. Output is produced subject to the constant returns to scale production function

$$y_{t+1} = fa_t, \qquad f > 0. \tag{2}$$

The demand curve for corn is

$$p_{t+1} = \beta_0 - \beta_1 Y_{t+1} + u_{t+1} \tag{3}$$

where β_0, $\beta_1 > 0$, Y_{t+1} is total output at (t+1), $(Y_{t+1} \equiv ny_{t+1})$ and u_{t+1} is a random shock to demand. Assume that u_t follows the Markov process

$$u_t = \rho u_{t-1} + \varepsilon_t$$

$|\rho| < 1$, where ε_t is a "white noise", with $E\varepsilon_t = 0$, $E\varepsilon_t^2 = \sigma_\varepsilon^2$, $E\varepsilon_t\varepsilon_{t-j} = 0$ for $j \neq 0$. Assume that the fertilizer cost w_t follows the moving average process

$$w_t = d_0\eta_t + d_1\eta_{t-1}$$

where η_t is a serially uncorrelated random variable with mean zero. The farm is assumed to maximize (1) by choosing a linear contingency plan for setting a_t. At time t, the farm is assumed to see w_t, $w_{t-1}, \ldots$, u_t, $u_{t-1}, \ldots$, a_{t-1}, and industry-wide initial acreage A_{t-1} ($\equiv na_{t-1}$).

A. Carefully define a rational expectations equilibrium for this industry.

B. Describe how to compute a rational expectations equilibrium. Get as far as you can in computing the equilibrium for the following parameter values:

$$\beta_1 = 10^{-6} \qquad c_1 = 20$$

$$n = 10^6 \qquad c_2 = 5$$

$$f = 1 \qquad b = 0.8$$

(Find the equilibrium in terms of the unspecified parameters, i.e., d_0, d_1, etc.)

C. Describe the effect on the equilibrium law of motion of A_t of a change in the fertilizer-cost process to the form

$$w_t = g_0\varepsilon_t + g_1\varepsilon_{t-1} + g_2\varepsilon_{t-2}$$

where ε_t is a white noise.

4. A small country produces one good, bananas, under competitive conditions. There is free entry into the industry within the country. The price of bananas, p_t, is determined exogenously to the country and is a stochastic process with Wold moving average representation

$$p_t = c(L)\varepsilon_t, \tag{1}$$

where $c(L) = \Sigma_{j=0}^{\infty} c_j L^j$, ε_t is fundamental for p_t and $c(L)^{-1}$ exists as square summable in nonnegative powers of L. Output of bananas at t, y_t, is determined via the single-factor production function

$$y_t = f(L)n_t \tag{2}$$

where $f(L) = \Sigma_{j=0}^{\infty} f_j L^j$, where $\Sigma_{j=0}^{\infty} f_j^2 < +\infty$, and n_t is employment. Each competitive firm faces a wage rate w_t, which it takes parametrically. For the country (industry) as a whole, however, the wage rate obeys the upward sloping supply schedule

$$w_t = \beta_0 + \beta_1 N_t, \qquad \beta_0, \beta_1 > 0, \tag{3}$$

where N_t is total employment of labor in the country's banana industry. (Either of the following specifications for N_t will do. First, $N_t = mn_t$, where m is the number of firms, and n_t is the employment of a representative firm, "fractional" values of n_t and m being acceptable. Second, there is a continuum of firms with $N_t = \int n_t(w)du(w)$, where $u(\cdot)$ is a measure over firms' employment). The representative firm faces p_t and w_t parametrically, and solves the following optimum problem

$$\max E_0 \sum_{t=0}^{\infty} \{p_t f(L)n_t - w_t n_t\} \tag{4}$$

subject to (1) with $\{p_t, p_{t-1}, \ldots\}$ being known at time t. Here E_t is conditional expectation given information at time t. Notice that there are constant returns to scale.

A. Find the "marginal expected present value" of employing an additional worker at time t.

B. Close the model by appealing to free entry, and impose the equilibrium condition that wages adjust, via (3), to insure zero expected present value. Derive the equilibrium condition restricting the wage process w_t in a form

$$w_t = E_t \sum_{j=0}^{\infty} h_j p_{t+j}$$

giving an explicit expression for the h_j's.

C. Assume that

$$f(L) = \frac{1}{1 - \lambda L}, \qquad |\lambda| < 1 \tag{*}$$

$$c(L) = \frac{1}{1 - \rho_1 L - \rho_2 L^2} \tag{**}$$

where the zeros of $(1 - \rho_1 z - \rho_2 z^2)$ lie outside the unit circle. Under these special specifications, derive a representation for the equilibrium wage process of the form

$$w_t = \sum_{j=0}^{\infty} g_j p_{t-j}, \tag{5}$$

giving explicit formulas for the g_j's as functions of $(\lambda, \rho_1, \rho_2)$.

D. Describe how representation (5) would change if a banana cartel were formed (one that excluded our country as a competitive fringe producer) that changed $c(L)$ from the form (**) to the form

$$c(L) = 1 + 0.99L.$$

How does this experiment illustrate Lucas's critique of pre-1973 econometric policy evaluation procedures?

5. Stabilizing Prices vs. Quantities. Consider an industry consisting of n identical firms that produce a single good. Output y_t of the representative firm is related to its capital k_t by $y_t = fk_t$, $f > 0$. The representative firm maximizes

$$E_0 \sum_{t=0}^{\infty} \beta^t \{p_t y_t - (w_t + \tau_t)k_t - (d/2)(k_t - k_{t-1})^2\}, \qquad 0 < \beta < 1$$

where E_t is the expectations operator conditional on observations known at t, p_t is the price of the good, w_t is the rental rate on capital, τ_t is a specific tax-subsidy on capital, and $d > 0$ reflects costs of rapid adjustment. The demand curve is given by

$$p_t = A_0 - A_1 Y_t + u_t; \qquad A_0, A_1 > 0$$

where $Y_t = ny_t = nfk_t = fK_t$, and where u_t is a random shock to demand. Assume that w_t is a random process

$$w_t = \bar{\omega} + \varepsilon_{wt}$$

where ε_{wt} is a serially independent random variable with mean zero and constant variance. Assume that u_t is a serially indpendent random variable with mean zero and constant variance. At time t, the representative firm knows

$$\{k_{t-1}, K_{t-1}, w_t, w_{t-1}, \ldots, u_t, u_{t-1}, \ldots, \tau_t, \tau_{t-1}, \ldots\}.$$

A. Initially assume that $\tau_t = 0$ for all t, so that capital is neither taxed nor subsidized. Define a <u>rational expectations competitive equilibrium</u>, and display the equilibrium law of motion for K_t.

B. Now suppose that the govenment sets τ_t as a linear function of

$$\{u_{t-1}, u_{t-2}, \ldots, \varepsilon_{wt-1}, \varepsilon_{wt-2}, \ldots\}.$$

with a constant term of zero (this makes the subsidy-tax average out to zero over long periods of time). First, find a linear feedback law for τ_t that minimizes the variance of the <u>stationary</u> distribution of industry output Y_t (i.e., assume that the linear feedback rule has been operating forever to calculate the variance of Y). Second, find a linear feedback law for τ_t that minimizes the stationary variance of p_t. (Hint: Write the equilibrium law of motion for K_t in the form $K_t = g_0 + g_1(L)u_t + g_2(L)\varepsilon_{wt}$ and proceed.)

C. Under what more general assumption about the serial correlation pattern of the demand shock $\{u_t\}$ would the "objective" of minimizing the stationary variance of price lead to a different decision rule for τ_t than the objective of minimizing the stationary variance of quantity?

D. Is it a good goal for policy to minimize the stationary variance of price? Of quantity?

6. An industry consists of a large number of n firms, produces a single good, and faces a demand schedule

$$p_t = A_0 - A_1 Y_t + u_t, \qquad A_0, A_1 > 0 \tag{1}$$

where p_t is the price at t, Y_t is total industry output at t, and u_t is a serially uncorrelated random process with mean zero. There are n identical firms, each with cost function

$$c_t = c_0 + c_1 y_t + \frac{c_2}{2} y_t^2 + \frac{c_3}{2}(y_t - y_{t-1})^2 + \frac{c_4}{2}(Y_t - Y_{t-1})^2 + J_t y_t + \tau_t y_t \qquad c_0, c_1, c_2, c_3, c_4 > 0. \tag{2}$$

Here y_t is a representative firm's output, and $Y_t = ny_t$; J_t is a stochastic process representing the effects of factor prices on costs, and τ_t is a tax-subsidy rate set by the goverment. Assume that

$$J_t = \lambda J_{t-1} + \varepsilon_t, \qquad |\lambda| < 1 \tag{3}$$

where ε_t is a serially uncorrelated random process with mean zero. The tax parameter τ_t is set by the government according to the feedback rule

$$\tau_t = \delta_0 + \delta_1 y_t + \delta_2 y_{t-1} \tag{4}$$

where δ_0, δ_1, δ_2 are constants. Each firm's tax rate thus depends on the firm's own output, a dependence recognized by the firm. In (2), the term $(c_4/2)(Y_t - Y_{t-1})^2$ reflects costs of adjusting industry-wide output over and above those taken into account by individual firms. There is thus an externality.

A representative firm maximizes

$$E \sum_{t=0}^{\infty} \beta^t \{p_t y_t - c_t\}, \qquad 0 < \beta < 1 \tag{5}$$

with y_{-1} and Y_{-1} given.

A. Define a rational expectations competitive equilibrium.

B. Compute the rational expectations competitive equilibrium.

C. Consider the "social planning" problem of maximizing the expected value of discounted consumer surplus plus producer surplus. (In formulating the social costs of production, omit the term $\tau_t y_t$ from the cost function (2)). For arbitrary settings of $(\delta_0, \delta_1, \delta_2)$ does the rational expectations competitive equilibrium solve this social planning problem?

D. Find values of $(\delta_0, \delta_1, \delta_2)$ (if they exist) that make the rational expectations competitive equilibrium solve the social planning problem.

7. The duck decoy industry is under investigation by the Anti-Trust Division of the Justice Department. One group of economists in the Division thinks that there is a collusive conspiracy among the n firms in the industry to set price and quantity as though the industry were a monopoly. A second group argues that the industry is competitive. For

$s = 1,\ldots,T$, time series data are available on industry output, Y_s, the price of duck decoys, p_s, aggregate capital at time s, K_s, and the rental rate on capital, w_s.

The industry consists of a fixed number of n identical firms. Duck decoys are produced according to the production function

$$y_t = fk_t, \qquad f > 0 \tag{1}$$

where y_t is output of the representative firm, and k_t is the capital stock of the representative firm at t. Aggregate output is

$$Y_t = fK_t \tag{2}$$

where

$$Y_t = ny_t, \; K_t = nk_t. \tag{3}$$

The demand for duck decoys obeys

$$p_t = A_0 - A_1Y_t + u_t, \qquad A_0 > 0, \; A_1 > 0 \tag{4}$$

where u_t is a random shock to demand with Wold moving average representation

$$u_t = \frac{1}{1 - \rho L}\varepsilon_{ut}, \qquad |\rho| < 1 \tag{5}$$

where ε_{ut} is a white noise with mean zero and variance σ_u^2. The rental rate on capital w_t is governed by the upward sloping supply curve to the industry

$$w_t = B_0 + B_1K_t, \qquad B_0 > 0, \; B_1 > 0. \tag{6}$$

The net cash flow at time t of the representative firm is

$$\pi(t) = p_ty_t - w_tk_t - (d/2)(k_t - k_{t-1})^2. \tag{7}$$

The present value of the representative firm's cash flow is

$$E_0 \sum_{t=0}^{\infty} b^t \pi(t), \qquad 0 < b < 1. \tag{8}$$

At time t, the firm takes k_{t-1}, u_t, $u_{t-1}, \ldots$, as given.

A. Define a rational expectations competitive equilibrium.

B. Compute the rational expectations competitive equilibrium.

C. What "social planning problem" does the rational expectations equilibrium implicitly solve?

D. Define a collusive or monopolistic rational expectations equilibrium.

E. Compute the monopolistic rational expectations equilibrium.

F. Show that the "feedback coefficient" of K_t on K_{t-1} is smaller in the monopolistic than in the competitive equilibrium. (Hint, a graphical argument will suffice.)

G. Suppose that the Justice Department economists know the values of f, n, b, d. However, they do not know the values of (B_0, B_1, A_0, A_1) and would have to estimate them econometrically from observations on $(Y_s, K_s, s = 1, \ldots, T)$. (The Justice Department has no reliable data on P_s or w_s). Given the information available to the economists, is it possible for them to determine whether the industry is behaving competitively or monopolistically?

H. Suppose that the Justice Department economists know the values f, n, b, d. However, they do not know the values of (B_0, B_1, A_0, A_1) and would have to estimate them econometrically from observations on $(Y_s, K_s, p_s, w_s, s = 1, \ldots, T)$. Given the information now assumed to be available to the economists, is it possible for them to determine whether the industry is behaving competitively or monopolistically?

SOLUTIONS

1. It will prove useful to begin by deriving a formula for $E_t J_{t+j}$. Now

$$E_t J_{t+1} = \alpha E_t J_t + E_t \eta_{t+1} = \alpha J_t + \bar{\eta}$$

$$E_t J_{t+2} = \alpha E_t J_{t+1} + E_t \eta_{t+2}$$

$$= \alpha^2 J_t + \alpha\bar{\eta} + \bar{\eta}$$

since, by the law of iterated expectations,

$$E_t \eta_{t+2} = E_t(E_{t+1}\eta_{t+2}) = E_t\bar{\eta} = \bar{\eta}.$$

Continuing in the above manner, one finds

$$E_t J_{t+j} = \alpha^j J_t + (\alpha^{j-1} + \alpha^{j-2} + \ldots + 1)\bar{\eta}$$

$$= \alpha^j J_t + \frac{1 - \alpha^j}{1 - \alpha}\bar{\eta}.$$

Similarly,

$$E_t u_{t+j} = \beta^j u_t + \frac{1 - \beta^j}{1 - \beta}\bar{\varepsilon}.$$

Equation (29) can be written

$$k_{t+j+1} = \lambda_1 k_{t+j} - \frac{\lambda_1}{d}\sum_{i=0}^{\infty} \lambda_2^{-i} E_{t+j+1} J_{t+j+1+i}$$

$$+ \frac{b\lambda_1}{d}\sum_{i=0}^{\infty} \lambda_2^{-i} E_{t+j+1} J_{t+j+2+i} + \frac{f_0\lambda_1}{d}\sum_{i=0}^{\infty} \lambda_2^{-i} E_{t+j+1} u_{t+j+1+i}$$

$$+ \frac{A_0 f_0 \lambda_1}{d}\sum_{i=0}^{\infty} \lambda_2^{-i}$$

$$= \lambda_1 k_{t+j} - \frac{\lambda_1}{d}\sum_{i=0}^{\infty} \lambda_2^{-i}(\alpha^i J_{t+j+1} + \frac{1 - \alpha^i}{1 - \alpha}\bar{\eta})$$

$$+ \frac{b\lambda_1\lambda_2}{d}[-J_{t+j+1} + \sum_{i=0}^{\infty} \lambda_2^{-i} E_{t+j+1} J_{t+j+1+i}]$$

$$+ \frac{f_0\lambda_1}{d} \sum_{i=0}^{\infty} \lambda_2^{-i}[\beta^i u_{t+j+1} + \frac{1 - \beta^i}{1 - \beta}\bar{\varepsilon}] + \frac{A_0 f_0 \lambda_1}{d(1 - \lambda_2^{-1})}$$

$$= \lambda_1 k_{t+j} + \frac{-\lambda_1}{d} \sum_{i=0}^{\infty} \lambda_2^{-i}(\alpha^i J_{t+j+1} + \frac{1 - \alpha^i}{1 - \alpha}\bar{\eta})$$

$$- \frac{1}{d}J_{t+j+1} - \frac{f_0\lambda_1}{d}[\frac{1}{1 - \beta\lambda_2^{-1}}u_{t+j+1} + \frac{\bar{\varepsilon}}{(1 - \beta)(1 - \lambda_2^{-1})}$$

$$- \frac{\bar{\varepsilon}}{(1 - \beta)(1 - \beta\lambda_2^{-1})}] + \frac{A_0 f_0 \lambda_1}{d(1 - \lambda_2^{-1})} ,$$

since $\lambda_1\lambda_2 = b^{-1}$, $|\alpha\lambda_2^{-1}| < 1$, and $|\beta\lambda_2^{-1}| < 1$. Simplifying the infinite series and collecting terms, one obtains an expression of the form

$$k_{t+j+1} - \lambda_1 k_{t+j} = \gamma_0 + \gamma_1 J_{t+j+1} + \gamma_2 u_{t+j+1}$$

where

$$\gamma_0 = \frac{-\lambda_1}{d}[\frac{\bar{\eta}}{(1 - \alpha)}(\frac{1}{1 - \lambda_2^{-1}} - \frac{1}{1 - \alpha\lambda_2^{-1}})]$$

$$- \frac{f_0\lambda_1}{d}[\frac{\bar{\varepsilon}}{(1 - \beta)}(\frac{1}{1 - \lambda_2^{-1}} - \frac{1}{1 - \beta\lambda_2^{-1}})] + \frac{A_0 f_0 \lambda_1}{d(1 - \lambda_2^{-1})}$$

$$\gamma_1 = \frac{-\lambda_1}{d(1 - \alpha\lambda_2^{-1})} - \frac{1}{d}$$

$$\gamma_2 = - \frac{f_0\lambda_1}{d(1 - \beta\lambda_2^{-1})} .$$

* * *

2. A. By Leibniz's rule,

$$\frac{\partial}{\partial\alpha}Ef(x,\alpha) = \frac{\partial}{\partial\alpha}\int f(x,\alpha)g(x)dx = \int\frac{\partial f}{\partial\alpha}(x,\alpha)g(x)dx,$$

since the limits of integration do not depend on α. Thus, the first order necessary condition for α to maximize $Ef(x,\alpha)$ is

$$\int\frac{\partial f}{\partial\alpha}(x,\alpha)g(x)dx = 0.$$

This condition is also sufficient, since by the concavity of $f(x,\alpha)$ and the positivity of the density function $g(x)$,

$$\int\frac{\partial^2}{\partial\alpha^2}f(x,\alpha)g(x)dx < 0.$$

B. $f(x,\alpha) = (x \quad \alpha)A(x \quad \alpha)' + (x \quad \alpha)B$. Let

$$A = \begin{bmatrix} a_{11} & a_{12} \\ a_{21} & a_{22} \end{bmatrix}, \quad B = \begin{bmatrix} B_1 \\ B_2 \end{bmatrix}.$$

Now

$$f(x,\alpha) = (x \quad \alpha)\begin{bmatrix} a_{11} & a_{12} \\ a_{21} & a_{22} \end{bmatrix}\begin{bmatrix} x \\ \alpha \end{bmatrix} + (x \quad \alpha)\begin{bmatrix} B_1 \\ B_2 \end{bmatrix}$$

$$= (x \quad \alpha)\begin{bmatrix} a_{11}x + a_{12}\alpha \\ a_{21}x + a_{22}\alpha \end{bmatrix} + B_1x + B_2\alpha$$

$$= a_{11}x^2 + a_{12}\alpha x + a_{21}\alpha x + a_{22}\alpha^2 + B_1x + B_2\alpha.$$

Consider Problem 1:

$$\max_\alpha Ef(x,\alpha) = \max_\alpha \int f(x,\alpha)g(x)dx.$$

Using the results of part A, the maximizing α solves

$$\int (a_{12}x + a_{21}x + 2a_{22}\alpha + B_2)g(x)dx = 0$$

or, equivalently,

$$\alpha = -\frac{B_2 + (a_{12} + a_{21})Ex}{2a_{22}} .$$

Now consider Problem 2:

$$\max_\alpha f(Ex,\alpha).$$

From above,

$$f(Ex,\alpha) = a_{11}(Ex)^2 + \alpha(a_{12} + a_{21})Ex + a_{22}\alpha^2 + B_1Ex + B_2\alpha.$$

The maximizing α solves

$$(a_{12} + a_{21})Ex + 2a_{22}\alpha + B_2 = 0$$

or, equivalently,

$$\alpha = -\frac{B_2 + (a_{12} + a_{21})Ex}{2a_{22}}$$

which is the same as the α which maximizes $Ef(x,\alpha)$. Notice that in general $\max_\alpha Ef(x,\alpha) \neq \max_\alpha f(Ex,\alpha)$. However, when the function $f(\cdot)$ is quadratic, $\text{argmax}_\alpha Ef(x,\alpha)$ <u>will</u> equal $\text{argmax}_\alpha f(Ex,\alpha)$.*

*"$\text{argmax}_a g(x,a)$" means "the 'argument' a which maximizes $g(x,a)$."

* * *

3. Each farmer maximizes

$$E_0 \sum_{t=0}^{\infty} b^t \{p_{t+1} y_{t+1} - c_0 a_t - \frac{c_1}{2} a_t^2 - c_2 a_t a_{t-1} - w_t a_t\} \tag{1}$$

subject to a_{-1} given,

$$y_{t+1} = f a_t \text{ (so that } Y_{t+1} = f A_t). \tag{2}$$

The demand curve is

$$p_{t+1} = \beta_0 - \beta_1 Y_{t+1} + u_{t+1} \tag{3}$$

with

$$u_t = \rho u_{t-1} + \varepsilon_t, \tag{3'}$$

$\{\varepsilon_t\}$ white noise and

$$w_t = g_0 \xi_t + g_1 \xi_{t-1} + g_2 \xi_{t-2}. \tag{3''}$$

(For part B, set $g_2 = 0$, $g_0 = d_0$, $g_1 = d_1$).

A. A rational expectations competitive equilibrium is a pair of stochastic processes $\{\bar{p}_t\}_{t=0}^{\infty}$ and $\{\bar{a}_t\}_{t=0}^{\infty}$ such that the following two conditions hold:

(i) Given the representative farm's strategy for planting $\{\bar{a}_t\}$, the stochastic process for prices $\{\bar{p}_t\}$ clears the corn market, i.e.,

$$\bar{p}_t = \beta_0 - \beta_1 n f \bar{a}_t + u_t.$$

(ii) When farmers face $\{\bar{p}_t\}$ parametrically, the stochastic process $\{\bar{a}_t\}$ maximizes expected present value (1).

An alternative definition of a rational expectations equilibrium (alluded to in footnote 10 in the text) involves the fulfillment of individuals' expectations. In particular, the representative farmer is assumed to believe that industry-wide acreage follows

$$A_t = H_0 + H_1A_{t-1} + \sum_{i=0}^{\infty} J_iw_{t-i} + \sum_{i=0}^{\infty} K_iu_{t-i}. \tag{P}$$

This is the farmer's "perception." (At t, the farmer sees A_{t-1}; w_t, w_{t-1}, ...; u_t, u_{t-1}, ...; a_{t-1}.) Using (2) in (3), $p_{t+1} = \beta_0 - \beta_1fA_t + u_{t+1}$. Using this and (2) in (1) write

$$E_0\sum_{t=0}^{\infty} b^t\{[\beta_0 - \beta_1fA_t + u_{t+1}]fa_t - c_0a_t - \frac{c_1}{2}a_t^2 - c_2a_ta_{t-1} - w_ta_t\}. \tag{4}$$

The farmer's problem is to choose $\{a_t\}$ to maximize (4) subject to the laws of motion (3'), (3"), and the perception (P), with knowledge (at t) of a_{t-1}, A_{t-1} and $\{w_t, w_{t-1}, \ldots; u_t, u_{t-1}, \ldots\}$. The solution to this problem is a linear contingency plan of the form

$$a_t = h_0 + h_1a_{t-1} + h_2A_{t-1} + \sum_{i=0}^{\infty} j_iw_{t-i} + \sum_{i=0}^{\infty} k_iu_{t-i}, \tag{R}$$

i.e., "reality." Then a <u>rational expectations competitive equilibrium</u> is a pair of functions (P) and (R) such that

$$A_t = na_t$$

identically, where A_t is given by (P) and a_t is given by (R). The equality between perception and reality can be seen to hold if

$$H_0 = nh_0,\ H_1 = (h_1 + nh_2),\ J_i = nj_i,\ k_i = nk_i.$$

Notice that expectations are fulfilled in such an equilibrium: given beliefs (P), agents undertake actions (R) which cause the beliefs to be justified.

B. Equilibrium laws of motion for (p_{t+1}, a_t) are calculated as follows: First, substitute (2) into (1) and calculate the Euler equations for the representative farm. Then substitute for p_{t+1} using (3) and solve this new Euler equation for a_t. Second, multiply the $\{a_t\}$ from the first step by nf and use the result in (3) to get the equilibrium price.

Notice that since $c_1 \neq 0$ (and $\beta_1 \neq 0$), the present value of the farm will diminish without bound if $\{a_t\}$ grows too rapidly; the optimal number of units of land planted will be of mean exponential order less than $1/\sqrt{b}$:

$$E_0 \Sigma_{t=0}^{\infty} b^t a_t^2 < \infty.$$

Using the derivative formulas from Exercise IX.3, the first order condition for choosing a_0 is

$$E_0\{fp_1 - c_0 - c_1a_0 - (L + bL^{-1})c_2a_0 - w_0\} = 0,$$

which depends on E_0a_1. How is a_1 to be chosen? The first order condition for the choice of a_1, given information available at $t = 1$ is

$$E_1\{fp_2 - c_0 - c_1a_1 - (L + bL^{-1})c_2a_1 - w_1\} = 0,$$

which depends on E_1a_2. But the choice of a_2 depends on E_2a_3, and so on. Evidently, the optimal $\{a_t\}$ process is given by the appropriate (in terms of exponential order) solution to

$$- c_0 - (1 + c_1B^{-1} + bc_2B^{-2})E_ta_{t-1} + fE_tp_{t+1} - E_tw_t = 0, \quad t \geq 0.$$

Thus

$$E_t a_{t+1} + \frac{c_1}{bc_2} a_t + \frac{1}{b} a_{t-1} = E_t \frac{p_{t+1} f - c_0 - w_t}{bc_2}.$$

Using (3) in the demand equation,

$$p_{t+1} = \beta_0 - \beta_1 nfa_t + u_{t+1}.$$

Use this in the previous equation to obtain

$$E_t a_{t+1} + \frac{c_1}{bc_2} a_t + \frac{1}{b} a_{t-1} = E_t \frac{f(\beta_0 - \beta_1 nfa_t + u_{t+1}) - c_0 - w_t}{bc_2}$$

or

$$E_t a_{t+1} + \left(\frac{c_1}{bc_2} + \frac{\beta_1 nf^2}{bc_2}\right) a_t + \frac{1}{b} a_{t-1} = \frac{f\beta_0 - c_0}{bc_2} + E_t \frac{fu_{t+1}}{bc_2} - E_t \frac{w_t}{bc_2} .$$

Using the specified parameter values,

$$E_t a_{t+1} + \left(\frac{21}{4}\right) a_t + \frac{5}{4}\, a_{t-1} = \frac{\beta_0 - c_0}{4} + \frac{1}{4} E_t u_{t+1} - \frac{1}{4} E_t w_t$$

or

$$(B^{-1} + 5)(B^{-1} + \tfrac{1}{4}) E_t a_{t-1} = \text{const} + \frac{1}{4} E_t u_{t+1} - \frac{1}{4} E_t w_t .$$

Then use the forward inverse of $(B^{-1} + 5)$ to get

$$(1 + \tfrac{1}{4}L) a_t = \text{const} + \frac{1}{20(1 - \frac{1}{-5B})} E_t u_{t+1} - \frac{1}{20(1 - \frac{1}{-5B})} E_t w_t + \gamma_0 5^t,$$

where γ_0 is an undetermined constant. But the exponential order condition on $\{a_t\}$ will be violated unless $\gamma_0 = 0$. Then

$$(1 + \tfrac{1}{4}L) a_t = \text{const} + \frac{1}{20} \sum_{j=0}^{\infty} (-\tfrac{1}{5})^j E_t u_{t+1+j} - \frac{1}{20} \sum_{j=0}^{\infty} (-\tfrac{1}{5})^j E_t w_{t+j} .$$

To evaluate the two terms on the right hand side, note

$$(1)\ \Sigma\lambda^j E_t u_{t+1+j} = \lambda^0 E_t u_{t+1} + \lambda^1 E_t u_{t+2} + \ldots$$

$$= \frac{1}{\lambda}(-u_t + u_t + \lambda E_t u_{t+1} + \lambda^2 E_t u_{t+2} + \ldots)$$

$$= \frac{1}{\lambda}(-u_t + \Sigma\lambda^j E_t u_{t+j})$$

$$= \frac{1}{\lambda}(-u_t + \frac{1}{1 - \lambda\rho} u_t) \qquad \text{(by (3').)}$$

Since $\lambda = -\frac{1}{5}$, we have

$$\frac{1}{20}\sum_{j=0}^{\infty}(-\frac{1}{5})^j E_t u_{t+1} = \frac{1}{20}(-5)(-u_t + \frac{1}{1 + \frac{\rho}{5}} u_t)$$

$$= -\frac{1}{4}(\frac{1 - (1 + \frac{\rho}{5})}{1 + \frac{\rho}{5}})u_t = \frac{\rho/20}{1 + \frac{\rho}{5}} u_t.$$

$$(2)\ \Sigma\lambda^j E_t w_{t+j}:$$

$$w_t = g_0\varepsilon_t + g_1\varepsilon_{t-1} + g_2\varepsilon_{t-2}$$

$$E_t w_t = w_t$$

$$\lambda E_t w_{t+1} = \lambda(g_1\varepsilon_t + g_2\varepsilon_{t-1}) = \frac{\lambda(g_1 + g_2 L)}{g_0 + g_1 L + g_2 L^2}\, w_t$$

$$\lambda^2 E_t w_{t+2} = \lambda^2 g_2 \varepsilon_t = \frac{\lambda^2 g_2}{g_0 + g_1 L + g_2 L^2}\, w_t$$

$$\lambda^j E_t w_{t+j} = 0 \qquad \text{for all } j > 2.$$

Then

$$\Sigma\lambda^j E_t w_{t+j} = \left(1 + \frac{\lambda(g_1 + g_2L)}{g_0 + g_1L + g_2L^2} + \frac{\lambda^2 g_2}{g_0 + g_1L + g_2L^2}\right)w_t$$

$$= \frac{[(g_0 + \lambda g_1 + \lambda^2 g_2) + (g_1 + \lambda g_2)L + g_2L^2}{g_0 + g_1L + g_2L^2}\, w_t .$$

With $\lambda = -\frac{1}{5}$,

$$\Sigma\lambda^j E_t w_{t+j} = \frac{[(g_0 - \frac{1}{5}g_1 + \frac{1}{25}g_2) + (g_1 - \frac{g_2}{5})L + g_2L^2]w_t}{g_0 + g_1L + g_2L^2}.$$

Then

$$A_t = na_t = -\frac{n}{4}a_{t-1} + \text{const} + \frac{\frac{\rho}{20}}{1 + \frac{\rho}{5}}\, nu_t$$

$$- \frac{n}{20}\,\frac{[(g_0 - \frac{g_1}{5} + \frac{g_2}{25}) + (g_1 - \frac{g_2}{5})L + g_2L^2]w_t}{g_0 + g_1L + g_2L^2} . \qquad (5)$$

For part B,

$$A_t = na_t = -\frac{n}{4}a_{t-1} + \text{const} + \frac{\frac{\rho}{20}}{1 + \frac{\rho}{5}} nu_t - \frac{n}{20}\,\frac{[(d_0 - \frac{d_1}{5}) + d_1L]w_t}{d_0 + d_1L} . \qquad (6)$$

C. In an economy in which $\{w_t\}$ evolves according to $w_t = (d_0 + d_1L)\varepsilon_t$, the mapping from fertilizer cost to acreage is given by (6). In an economy in which $w_t = (g_0 + g_1L + g_2L^2)\varepsilon_t$, the response of current acreage to fertilizer costs is given by (5). Thus the equilibria are different; the specific values of a_0, a_1,... will almost surely be different, but more importantly, the mapping from $\{w_t\}$ to $\{a_t\}$ will be different. A change in the fertilizer cost process changes acres planted because the w's change and because the coefficients in the equilibrium law of motion for A_t change.

* * *

4. A. The marginal cost of an additional worker at t is w_t. To determine the marginal revenue generated by the worker, note that the additional worker at t generates f_0 extra units of ouptut at t (for which the firm expects to receive $f_0 p_t$), f_1 extra units of output at t+1 (for which the firm expects--on the basis of information available at time t--to receive $f_1 E_t p_{t+1}$), f_2 extra units of output at t+2, etc. Thus the firm expects an additional worker employed during period t to generate $E_t f(L^{-1}) p_t$ in extra revenue. The "marginal expected present value" of employing an additional worker at time t is therefore

$$MEPV_t = E_t f(L^{-1}) p_t - w_t = \Sigma_{j=0}^{\infty} f_j E_t p_{t+j} - w_t.$$

Of course, the $MEPV_t$ can be found directly by differentiating the present value expression (4) with respect to n_t, using the derivative formulas of Exercise 3 in Chapter IX.

B. Entry will occur so long as the reward for increasing the number of individuals in banana production is positive; i.e., until $MEPV_t = 0$. Thus

$$w_t = E_t \Sigma_{j=0}^{\infty} h_j p_{t+j} = E_t \Sigma_{j=0}^{\infty} f_j p_{t+j}$$

so that $h_j = f_j$, $j \geq 0$. Using (3),

$$N_t = \beta_1^{-1}(-\beta_0 + E_t \Sigma_{j=0}^{\infty} f_j p_{t+j})$$

which determines aggregate employment. Industry output is then given by $Y_t = f(L) N_t$. (The size of any individual firm is indeterminate, owing to the free entry and constant returns to scale assumptions.)

C. If $f(L) = (1 - \lambda L)^{-1}$, then $f_j = \lambda^j$. Then

$$w_t = E_t \Sigma_{j=0}^{\infty} \lambda^j p_{t+j}$$

$$= (1 - \lambda L^{-1})^{-1}(1 - \lambda^{-1}L^{-1}c(L)^{-1})p_t,$$

$$= (1 - \rho_1\lambda - \rho_2\lambda^2)^{-1}[1 + \rho_2\lambda L]p_t,$$

from formula (XI.90).

D. If, in place of (**), $c(L) = 1 + 0.99L$,

$$w_t = E_t p_t + \lambda E_t p_{t+1}$$

$$= p_t + \lambda(0.99)\varepsilon_t$$

$$= (1 + 0.99\lambda + 0.99L)\Sigma_{j=0}^{\infty}(-0.99)^j p_{t-j}. \tag{6}$$

Thus not only will prices and wages be different in the two regimes, the _mapping_ from prices to wages will be different. Lucas's point, in this context, is that the practice, common in 1973, of using estimates of the g's in (5) obtained under the (**) regime to predict the consequences of a change to the $c(L) = 1 + 0.99L$ regime, is incorrect. Equation (6) describes the wage process under the "99" regime; correctly predicting the consequences of the regime change requires knowledge of the mapping from the price process to the wage process.

* * *

5. A. A rational expectations competitive equilibrium is a _pair_ of stochastic processes $\{\bar{p}_t\}_{t=0}^{\infty}$ and $\{\bar{k}_t\}_{t=0}^{\infty}$ such that the following two conditions hold:

(i) when the representative firm faces the price process $\{\bar{p}_t\}$ as a price-taker, the process $\{\bar{k}_t\}$ maximizes the expected present value of its net cash flow,

(ii) Given the capital process $\{\bar{k}_t\}$, the price process $\{\bar{p}_t\}$ clears the output market, i.e.,

$$\bar{p}_t = A_0 - A_1 Y_t + u_t = A_0 - A_1 nf\bar{k}_t + u_t.$$

To find the equilibrium, note first that since $A_1 > 0$, the optimal capital process will have the exponential order property $E_0 \Sigma_{t=0}^{\infty} \beta^t k_t^2 < \infty$. Next, differentiate the present value relation with respect to k_t to obtain the Euler equation

$$E_t\{fp_t - (w_t + \tau_t) - d(1 - \beta L^{-1})(1 - L)k_t\} = 0.$$

Substituting from the demand curve and rearranging, one obtains

$$E_t\{-f^2 nA_1 - d(1 - \beta L^{-1})(1 - L)\}k_t = w_t + \tau_t - (fA_0 + fu_t).$$

or

$$E_t\{-f^2 nA_1 L^{-1} - d(1 - \beta L^{-1})(L^{-1} - 1)\}k_{t-1} = E_t\{\tau_t + w_t - fu_t - fA_0\}$$

which can be written

$$\{-f^2 nA_1 B^{-1} - d(1 - \beta B^{-1})(B^{-1} - 1)\}E_t k_{t-1} = E_t\{\tau_t + w_t - fu_t - fA_0\}.$$

Now factor the polynomial,

$$-f^2 nA_1 B^{-1} - d(1 - \beta B^{-1})(B^{-1} - 1) = d\beta(B^{-1} - \lambda_1)(B^{-1} - \lambda_2)$$

where, as usual, $0 < \lambda_1 < 1 < \beta^{-1} < \lambda_2$ and $\lambda_2^{-1} = \beta\lambda_1$. Thus,

$$-(1 - \lambda_1 L)k_t = (d\beta)^{-1}(\lambda_2 - B^{-1})^{-1}$$
$$\times E_t\{\tau_t + \varepsilon_{wt} - fu_t + \bar{\omega} - fA_0\} + \Gamma\lambda_2^t,$$

where Γ is a constant. But unless $\Gamma = 0$, the exponential order condition will be violated. Thus

$$-(1 - \lambda_1 L)k_t = d^{-1}\lambda_1(1 - \beta\lambda_1 B^{-1})^{-1}E_t\{\tau_t + \varepsilon_{wt} - fu_t\}$$

$$- d^{-1}\lambda_1(1 - \beta\lambda_1)^{-1}(fA_0 - \bar{\omega}).$$

When $\tau_t = 0$, the equilibrium law of motion for $\{k_t\}$ is

$$k_t = \lambda_1 k_{t-1} - d^{-1}\lambda_1\{\varepsilon_{wt} - fu_t\} - d^{-1}\lambda_1(1 - \beta\lambda_1)^{-1}(fA_0 - \bar{\omega})$$

(recall that $\{\varepsilon_{wt}\}$ and $\{u_t\}$ are serially uncorrelated.) The equilibrium law of motion for $\{K_t\}$ is obtained by multiplying the one for $\{k_t\}$ by n.

B. Suppose τ_t is set according to

$$\tau_t = \Sigma_{j=1}^{\infty} F_{uj}u_{t-j} + \Sigma_{j=1}^{\infty} F_{wj}\varepsilon_{wt-j} = F_u(L)u_t + F_w(L)\varepsilon_{wt}.$$

Now write

$$\tau_t + \varepsilon_{wt} - fu_t = G_u(L)u_t + G_w(L)\varepsilon_{wt}$$

where $G_{u0} = -f$, $G_w(0) = 1$, $G_{uj+1} = F_{uj}$, and $G_{wj+1} = F_{wj}$ for $j \geq 0$. Then using formula (XI.90),

$$-(1 - \lambda_1 L)k_t = d^{-1}\lambda_1(1 - \beta\lambda_1 L^{-1})^{-1}\{[G_u(L) - \beta\lambda_1 L^{-1}G_u(\beta\lambda_1)]u_t$$

$$+ [G_w(L) - \beta\lambda_1 L^{-1}G_w(\beta\lambda_1)]\varepsilon_{wt}\}$$

$$- d^{-1}\lambda_1(1 - \beta\lambda_1)^{-1}(fA_0 - \bar{\omega}),$$

so that

$$Y_t = -nfd^{-1}\lambda_1\{\frac{G_u(L) - \beta\lambda_1 L^{-1}G_u(\beta\lambda_1)}{(1 - \lambda_1 L)(1 - \beta\lambda_1 L^{-1})}u_t + \frac{G_w(L) - \beta\lambda_1 L^{-1}G_w(\beta\lambda_1)}{(1 - \lambda_1 L)(1 - \beta\lambda_1 L^{-1})}\varepsilon_{wt}\}$$

$$+ nfd^{-1}\lambda_1(1 - \beta\lambda_1)^{-1}(fA_0 - \bar{\omega}).$$

The problem of the policymaker is to choose $G_{u1}, G_{u2}, \ldots, G_{w1}, G_{w2}, \ldots$ to minimize the variance of $\{Y_t\}$. Put another way, the policymaker must choose functions $G_u(L)$ and $G_w(L)$ to minimize the variance of $\{Y_t\}$, subject to the constraints $G_u(0) = -f$, $G_w(0) = 1$. Let $H_k(L) = nfd^{-1}\lambda_1 G_k(L)$ for $k = u, w$, and let $\lambda = \lambda_1$, $\theta = \beta\lambda_1$. Then, assuming that $\{u_t\}$ and $\{\varepsilon_{wt}\}$ are mutually independent,

$$\mathrm{var}(Y_t) = \mathrm{var}\{\frac{H_u(L) - \theta L^{-1}H_u(\theta)}{(1 - \lambda L)(1 - \theta L^{-1})}u_t\} + \mathrm{var}\{\frac{H_w(L) - \theta L^{-1}H_w(\theta)}{(1 - \lambda L)(1 - \theta L^{-1})}\varepsilon_{wt}\},$$

$$\mathrm{var}(p_t) = A_1^2\mathrm{var}\{(-A_1^{-1} + [\frac{H_u(L) - \theta L^{-1}H_u(\theta)}{(1 - \lambda L)(1 - \theta L^{-1})}])u_t\}$$

$$+ \mathrm{var}\{\frac{H_w(L) - \theta L^{-1}H_w(\theta)}{(1 - \lambda L)(1 - \theta L^{-1})}\varepsilon_{wt}\}.$$

Consider the generic problem of choosing $H(L) = \Sigma_{j=0}^{\infty}H_j L^j$, given H_0, to minimize

$$\mathrm{var}\{c + [(1 - \lambda L)(L - \theta)]^{-1}[LH(L) - \theta H(\theta)]\}e_t$$

where $\{e_t\}$ is white noise. It is useful to define $g(L)$ by $LH(L) - \theta H(\theta) = (1 - \lambda L)(L - \theta)g(L)$ and consider the problem of choosing $g(L) = \Sigma_{j=0}^{\infty}g_j L^j$ to minimize

$$\mathrm{var}\{c + g(L)\}u_t = ((c + g_0)^2 + g_1{}^2 + g_2{}^2 + \ldots)\sigma_u^2.$$

The constraint on $H(L)$ (i.e., the given H_0) restricts $g(L)$: notice that

$$\frac{d}{dz}[zH(z) - \theta H(\theta)]|_{z=0} = H_0$$

so that

$$H_0 = [(1 - \lambda z)(z - \theta)g'(z) + (1 + \theta\lambda - 2\lambda z)g(z)]|_{z=0} \tag{1}$$

$$= -\theta g_1 + (1 + \theta\lambda)g_0,$$

which gives the restriction on $g(z)$. Since for $j \geq 2$ the g_j may be set freely, it is clear that the variance is minimized when $g_j = 0$ for $j \geq 2$. What remains is to choose g_1 to minimize

$$[c + (H_0 + \theta g_1)/(1 + \theta\lambda)]^2 + g_1^2;$$

the optimal g_1 is

$$g_1 = -[c + H_0\theta/(1 + \theta\lambda)^2]\{(1 + \theta\lambda)^2/[\theta^2 + (1 + \theta\lambda)^2]\}. \tag{2}$$

The optimal g_0 is of course obtained from the constraint involving H_0, g_1, and g_0. To determine the associated H_j's, note that

$$zH(z) - \theta H(\theta) = (z - \theta)[H(\theta) + (H_1 + \theta H_2)z + H_2z^2]$$

$$= (z - \theta)(1 - \lambda z)(g_0 + g_1z)$$

which gives, upon equating like powers of z,

$$H(\theta) = g_0$$

$$H_1 + H_2\theta = g_1 - \lambda g_0$$

$$H_2 = -\lambda g_1.$$

The first of these equations is redundant, as it can be obtained from the other two using the restriction $H_0 = -\theta g_1 + (1 + \theta\lambda)g_0$. Thus

$$H_2 = -\lambda g_1 \tag{3}$$

$$H_1 = (1 + \theta\lambda)g_1 - \lambda g_0. \tag{4}$$

The F_{uj} and F_{wj} can be found as follows:

(a) to find F_{wj}, set $H_0 = nfd^{-1}\lambda_1$, $c = 0$ and solve (2) for g_1^w. Then use (1) to find g_0^w. Use these values for g_0 and g_1 in (3) and (4) to get $F_{w1} = H_1^w$, $F_{w2} = H_2^w$. Set $F_{wj} = 0$ for $j \geq 3$. These settings for F_{wj} should be used whether prices or quantities are being stabilized. (Recall that u_t and ε_{wt} were assumed independent, and note that $\{\varepsilon_{wt}\}$ affects prices only via its effect on quantities--minimizing its effect on one minimizes its effect on the other.)

(b) to find F_{uj},

(i) to stabilize quantities, set $H_0 = -f^2nd^{-1}\lambda_1$, $c = 0$ and solve (2) for g_1^q. Then use (1) to find g_0^q. Use these values for g_0 and g_1 in (3) and (4) to get $F_{u1} = H_1^q$, $F_{u2} = H_2^q$. Set $F_{uj} = 0$ for $j \geq 3$.

(ii) to stabilize prices, follow step (i) with $c = -A_1^{-1}$ instead of $c = 0$.

Notice that the two regimes (price stabilization and quantity stabilization) involve identical responses to non-demand shocks, and responses to demand shocks which differ quantitatively, but not (much) qualitatively.

C. If the demand shock is serially correlated, the two rules will differ qualitatively. To see this, note that in the notation used above, the quantity stabilization rule would require minimization of Σg_j^2, while the price stabilization rule would require minimization of $\Sigma_{j=0}^{\infty}(-A_1^{-1}c_j + g_j)^2$ (where the demand shock has Wold representation

$u_t = \Sigma_{k=0}^{\infty} c_k \varepsilon_{ut-j}$.) In general, the price stabilization rule would involve responses to many more lags of the demand shock.*

D. There is nothing in particular to recommend price or quantity stabilization in this model. A better objective would involve maximizing consumer plus producer surplus; but since the competitive equilibrium is Pareto optimal, this would mean setting $\tau_t = 0$ for all t.

* * *

6. A. A rational expectations competitive equilibrium is a <u>pair</u> of stochastic processes $\{\bar{p}_t\}_{t=0}^{\infty}$ and $\{\bar{y}_t\}_{t=0}^{\infty}$ such that the following two conditions hold:

(i) When the representative firm faces the price process $\{\bar{p}_t\}$ as a price taker, the process $\{\bar{y}_t\}$ maximizes the expected present value of its net cash flow (5),

(ii) Given the output process $\{\bar{y}_t\}$, the price process $\{\bar{p}_t\}$ clears the market, i.e.,

$$\bar{p}_t = A_0 - A_1 Y_t + u_t = A_0 - A_1 n\bar{y}_t + u_t.$$

B. To compute the equilibrium, note first that since A_1, $c_2 > 0$, the optimal output process will have the exponential order property $E_0 \Sigma_{t=0}^{\infty} \beta^t y_t^2 < \infty$. Next, using the derivative formulas from Exercise IX.3,

---

*It turns out that the methods used in parts A and B can be applied, with some modification, to solve problems in which there are positive costs associated with fluctuations in policy variables, and even to solve the sorts of dynamic games considered in Chapter XV. See C. Whiteman, "Spectral Utility, Wiener-Hopf Techniques, and Rational Expectations," <u>Journal of Economic Dynamics and Control</u> 9 (1985): 225-240, and "Analytical Policy Design Under Rational Expectations," <u>Econometrica</u> 54 (1986): 1387-1405.

differentiate the present value relation (5) with respect to y_t to obtain the Euler equation

$$E_t\{p_t - c_1 - c_2 y_t - c_3(1 - \beta L^{-1})(1 - L)y_t - J_t - \delta_0$$
$$- [\delta(\beta L^{-1}) + \delta(L)]y_t\} = 0$$

where $\delta(L) = \delta_1 + \delta_2 L$. Notice that the representative firm ignores the effect its own actions have on $(Y_t - Y_{t-1})^2$, but exploits the effect its own output has on the tax rate τ_t. Substituting from the demand curve and rearranging, one obtains

$$\{(-nA_1 - c_2)B^{-1} - c_3(1 - \beta B^{-1})(B^{-1} - 1) - (2\delta_1 B^{-1} + \beta\delta_2 B^{-2} + \delta_2)\}E_t y_{t-1}$$
$$= E_t\{J_t - u_t + c_1 + \delta_0 - A_0\}.$$

Notice that if λ^{-1} is a zero of the polynomial in braces on the left, $\beta\lambda$ is also; write

$$\lambda_0(\lambda - B^{-1})(\beta^{-1}\lambda^{-1} - B^{-1})E_t y_{t-1} = E_t\{J_t - u_t + c_1 - A_0\}$$

where $\lambda_0 = \beta(c_3 - \delta_2)$. If δ_1 is too small (i.e., too negative), then λ may be complex, with $|\lambda| = 1/\sqrt{\beta}$. In the real case, take λ to be the smaller root, and write

$$(\lambda - B^{-1})E_t y_{t-1} = \lambda_0^{-1}\beta\lambda(1 - \beta\lambda B^{-1})^{-1}E_t\{J_t - u_t + c_1 + \delta_0 - A_1\}$$
$$+ \Gamma(\beta\lambda)^{-t}$$

where Γ is a constant. But unless $\Gamma = 0$, the exponential order condition will be violated. Thus set $\Gamma = 0$ to get

$$y_t = \lambda y_{t-1} - \lambda_0^{-1}\beta\lambda\Sigma_{j=0}^{\infty}(\beta\lambda)^j\, E_t\{J_{t+j} - u_{t+j}\}$$
$$- \lambda_0^{-1}\beta\lambda(1 - \beta\lambda)^{-1}(c_1 + \delta_0 - A_0).$$

Equilibrium output for the industry is obtained by multiplying this $\{y_t\}$ by n; the equilibrium price is then obtained from the demand schedule (1).

C. The social planning problem is to maximize the expected discounted area under the demand curve less the expected discounted social costs of production, i.e.,

$$E_0\Sigma_{t=0}^{\infty}\beta^t\{\int_0^{ny_t}(A_0 - A_1x + u_t)dx - n(c_t - \tau_t y_t)\}.$$

Notice that the social costs are "paid" plant-by-plant, so that the social cost at t of operating n plants is nc_t.* The social planning problem is thus to maximize

$$E_0\Sigma_{t=0}^{\infty}\beta^t\{A_0 ny_t - \frac{A_1}{2}n^2y_t^2 + ny_tu_t - nc_0 - nc_1y_t - \frac{c_2}{2}ny_t^2$$
$$- \frac{c_3}{2}n(y_t - y_{t-1})^2 - \frac{c_4}{2}n^3(y_t - y_{t-1})^2 - nJ_ty_t\}.$$

The "per-firm" Euler equation for the social planning problem is

$$E_t\{A_0 - nA_1y_t + u_t - c_1 - c_2y_t - c_3(1 - \beta L^{-1})(1 - L)y_t$$
$$- c_4n^2(1 - \beta L^{-1})(1 - L)y_t - J_t\} = 0,$$

which is in general different from the Euler equation for the competitive firm; in general, the competitive equilibrium will not solve the social planning problem.

---

*Requiring that the social planner not change the number of plants sidesteps the following unappealing aspect of the problem: the optimal size of a plant is zero. For a given output Y, it would be less costly to produce it in n+1 plants than n because (contemporaneous and adjustment) costs depend on the square of the output of the representative firm. In this example, the smaller the better.

D. When $\delta_0 = 0$ and

$$\delta(\beta L^{-1}) + \delta(L) = c_4 n^2(1 - \beta L^{-1})(1 - L),$$

the Euler equation for the competitive equilibrium coincides with the one for the social planning problem. Thus, given the tax policy $\tau_t = \delta_0 + \delta_1 y_t + \delta_2 y_{t-1}$, with

$$\delta_0 = 0$$

$$\delta_1 = n^2 c_4 (1 + \beta)/2$$

$$\delta_2 = -c_4 n^2,$$

the regulated competitive equilibrium is optimal.

* * *

7. A. A rational expectations competitive equilibrium is a <u>triple</u> of stochastic processes $\{\bar{p}_s\}_{s=0}^{\infty}$, $\{\bar{w}_s\}_{s=0}^{\infty}$ and $\{\bar{k}_s\}_{s=0}^{\infty}$ such that the following two conditions hold:

(i) when the representative firm faces the price processes $\{\bar{p}_s\}$ and $\{\bar{w}_s\}$ as a price taker, the process $\{\bar{k}_s\}$ maximizes the expected present value of net cash flow (8),

(ii) given the representative firm's capital sequence $\{\bar{k}_s\}$, the prices $\{\bar{p}_s\}$ and $\{\bar{w}_s\}$ clear the output and factor markets; i.e.,

$$\bar{p}_t = A_0 - A_1 Y_t + u_t = A_0 - A_1 n f \bar{k}_t + u_t$$

and

$$\bar{w}_t = B_0 + B_1 K_t = B_0 + B_1 n \bar{k}_t .$$

B. Using (1) and (7) in (8), the present value of the representative firm's net cash flow becomes

$$E_0 \sum_{t=0}^{\infty} b^t \{p_t f k_t - w_t k_t - (d/2)(k_t - k_{t-1})^2\}.$$

The Euler equations for maximizing this expression are

$$E_t[p_t f - w_t - d(1 - L)(1 - bL^{-1})]k_t = 0 \qquad t = 0, 1, \ldots \tag{9}$$

or

$$p_t f - w_t + d(1 - B^{-1})(1 - bB^{-1})E_t k_{t-1} = 0 \qquad t = 0, 1, 2, \ldots .$$

Substituting for p_t and w_t from (4) and (6) and rearranging,

$$[-(nf^2A_1 + nB_1)B^{-1} + d(1 - B^{-1})(1 - bB^{-1})]E_t k_{t-1} = -A_0 f + B_0 - fu_t$$

for $t = 0, 1, 2, \ldots$. Factor the polynomial in B^{-1} as

$$db(\gamma_1 - B^{-1})(\gamma_2 - B^{-1}) = -(nf^2A_1 + nB_1)B^{-1} + d(1 - B^{-1})(1 - bB^{-1})$$

and take $|\gamma_1| < 1$ and $\gamma_2 = 1/b\gamma_1$ without loss of generality. Now operate on both sides of the equation involving $E_t k_{t-1}$ with $(\gamma_2 - B^{-1})^{-1}$ to get

$$(\gamma_1 - B^{-1})E_t k_{t-1} = (db)^{-1}(\gamma_2 - B^{-1})^{-1}E_t(-A_0 f + B_0 - fu_t) + c\gamma_2^t$$

where c is an undetermined constant. But since A_1, $B_1 > 0$, the optimal $\{k_t\}$ must be of mean exponential order less than $1/\sqrt{b}$. This forces the choice $c = 0$. Then

$$k_t - \gamma_1 k_{t-1} = -(\gamma_1/d)[(-A_0 f + B_0)/(1 - b\gamma_1) - f \sum_{j=0}^{\infty} (\gamma_1 b)^i E_t u_{t+i}]$$

or, using (5),

$$k_t - \gamma_1 k_{t-1} = -(\gamma_1/d)\{(-A_0 f + B_0)/(1 - b\gamma_1) - [f/(1 - \rho\gamma_1 b)]u_t\}$$

which is the law of motion for the capital stock of the representative firm. The equilibrium laws of motion for $\{k_t\}$, $\{p_t\}$, and $\{w_t\}$ can be calculated using this expression, (1) - (3), and (4) and (6).

C. As in Section 5 of Chapter XIV of the text, the competitive equilibrium maximizes the sum of consumer and producer surplus--in this case the discounted area under the demand curve for the industry's output, less the discounted area under the supply curve the industry faces, less discounted industry adjustment costs. Thus, it may be verified that the Euler equations for maximizing

$$E_0 \sum_{t=0}^{\infty} b^t \{\int_0^{nfk_t} (A_0 - A_1 x + u_t)dx - \int_0^{nk_t} (B_0 + B_1 v)dv - (nd/2)(k_t - k_{t-1})^2\}$$

are given by (9). Notice that the social planner "pays" adjustment costs at the firm level.

D. A collusive arrangement among the n firms of the industry naturally extends to the factor market; an n-plant monopolist would exploit (6) as well as (4). Using these two equations in (7) and using the result in (8), the objective function for the n-plant monopolist becomes

$$E_0 \sum_{t=0}^{\infty} b^t \{[A_0 - A_1 nfk_t + u_t]nfk_t - [B_0 + B_1 nk_t]nk_t - (nd/2)(k_t - k_{t-1})^2\} \qquad (10)$$

where k_t is per-plant output at t. Notice that the monopolist pays adjustment costs at the plant level.

A monopolistic rational expectations equilibrium is a <u>triple</u> of sequences $\{\bar{p}_s\}_{s=0}^{\infty}$, $\{\bar{w}_s\}_{s=0}^{\infty}$, $\{\bar{k}_s\}_{s=0}^{\infty}$ such that the following two conditions hold:

(i) when the monopolist faces the stochastic process $\{u_t\}$, the sequence $\{\bar{k}_s\}$ maximizes the expected present value of net cash flow (10),

(ii) given the monopolist's per-plant capital stock $\{\bar{k}_t\}$, the prices $\{\bar{p}_s\}_{s=0}^{\infty}$ and $\{\bar{w}_s\}_{s=0}^{\infty}$ clear the output and factor markets; i.e.,

$$\bar{p}_t = A_0 - A_1 Y_t + u_t = A_0 - A_1 f\bar{K}_t + u_t$$

and

$$\bar{w}_t = B_0 + B_1\bar{K}_t.$$

E. The Euler equations for maximizing (10) are

$$E_t[A_0 nf - nB_0 + nfu_t - 2A_1 n^2 f^2 k_t - 2B_1 n^2 k_t$$
$$- nd(1 - L)(1 - bL^{-1})k_t] = 0$$

for $t \geq 0$, or

$$[-(2nf^2A_1 + 2nB_1)B^{-1} + d(1 - B^{-1})(1 - bB^{-1})]E_t k_{t-1}$$
$$= -A_{0f} + B_0 - fu_t \qquad (11)$$

for $t = 0, 1, \ldots$. As in part A, factor the polynomial in B^{-1} as

$$db(\mu_1 - B^{-1})(\mu_2 - B^{-1}) = -(2nf^2A_1 + 2nB_1)B^{-1} + d(1 - B^{-1})(1 - bB^{-1})$$

and take $|\mu_1| < 1$ and $\mu_2 = 1/b\mu_1$. Then, as above,

$$k_t = \mu_1 k_{t-1} - (\mu_1/d)\{(-A_0 f + B_0)/(1 - b\mu_1) - [f/(1 - \rho\mu_1 b)]u_t\}$$

is the law of motion for per-plant capital. Laws of motion for the price of output and the rental rate on capital may now be calculated from (4) and (6).

F. Notice that $\mu_1\mu_2 = \gamma_1\gamma_2 = b^{-1}$, but

$$\mu_1 + \mu_2 = (db)^{-1}[2nf^2A_1 + 2n\beta_1 + d(1 + b)]$$

$$> (db)^{-1}[nf^2A_1 + nB_1 + d(1 + b)] = \gamma_1 + \gamma_2.$$

Further, μ_1, μ_2, γ_1, and γ_2 are all positive. Referring to Figure 4 in Chapter IX, it is clear that the larger the sum of the factors ($-\phi/b$ in Figure 4) the smaller is the small factor. Thus $\mu_1 < \gamma_1$.

G. Even with data on $\{u_t\}$, it is not possible to determine whether the industry is competitive or collusive. To see this, notice that

$$E_t(K_{t+1} - (\lambda_1 + \lambda_2)K_t + b^{-1}K_{t-1} - \lambda_0 - fu_t) = 0 \tag{12}$$

where in the competitive case $\lambda_i = \gamma_i$ while in the collusive case $\lambda_i = \mu_i$. Equation (12) defines a set of orthogonality conditions

$$EK_{t-j}(K_{t+1} - (\lambda_1 + \lambda_2)K_t + b^{-1}K_{t-1} - \lambda_0 - fu_t) = 0 \qquad j \geq 0$$

which can be used (as in Exercise 23 of Chapter XI) to estimate the unknown parameters λ_0 and $(\lambda_1 + \lambda_2)$. Thus it will be possible to obtain an estimate of the sum of the inverses of the roots of the relevant polynomial, but without more information, it will not be possible to determine whether $nf^2A_1 + nB_1$ or twice this quantity enters the sum--it will not be possible to determine whether the industry is behaving competitively or monopolistically.

Without data on $\{u_t\}$, matters are even more difficult. One may note that for either industry structure,

$$(1 - \lambda_1 L)(1 - \rho L)K_t = \text{constant} + \text{error}_t$$

is a projection equation, where "error" is proportional to ε_u. After computing the inverses of the roots of the polynomial in the lag operator polynomial induced by the projection of K_t on K_{t-1} and K_{t-2}, the Justice Department will have two numbers to assign to the "deep" parameters λ_1 and ρ. Which is which? Even if this quandary can be resolved, one would still only know the sum $(\lambda_1 + b^{-1}\lambda_1^{-1})$, not whether $nf^2A_1 + nB$, or twice this amount enters the sum, and the competition-collusion question would remain open.

H. Given data on prices and rental rates, (4) and (6) can be estimated along with the law of motion for k_t, and estimates of A_1 and B_1 can be obtained. These, and knowledge of d, b, n, and f, will enable the Justice Department to determine whether the sum of roots is $\mu_1 + \mu_2$ (monopoly) or $\gamma_1 + \gamma_2$ (competition).

CHAPTER XV

DYNAMIC OPTIMAL TAXATION

EXERCISES

1. (Interpretation of the model of Section 2 as permitting only a tax on new investment.)

Modify the example of Section 2 so that the government now imposes a tax only on new investment. The tax collected at t is $\gamma_t(k_t - k_{t-1})$.

A. Show that the market equilibrium now satisfies the following counterpart of (2):

$$k_t = \lambda k_{t-1} - \frac{\lambda}{d}\frac{1}{1 - \lambda bL^{-1}}\{J_t - bJ_{t+1} - f_0u_t - A_0f_0 + \gamma_t - b\gamma_{t+1}\}. \quad (2')$$

B. The government's problem is to choose a $\{\gamma_t\}_{t=0}^{\infty}$ sequence maximizing

$$\sum_{t=0}^{\infty} b^t\{[A_0f_0nk_t - (\tfrac{1}{2})A_1(f_0^2n^2k_t^2) + f_0nu_tk_t - nJ_t(k_t - k_{t-1})$$
$$- (\tfrac{1}{2})nd(k_t - k_{t-1})^2]$$

subject to (2'), (4), and the sequence of budget constraints

$$B_{t+1} = b^{-1}(g_t + B_t - \gamma_t(k_t - k_{t-1})) \qquad t \geq 0, \qquad (3')$$

with $B_0 = 0$. Formulate the Lagrangian associated with this problem, and show that the first order necessary conditions are given by the system

$$\begin{bmatrix} 0 & \mu(1 - L) & \frac{-\lambda}{d}\frac{(1 - L)}{1 - \lambda L} \\ \mu(1 - bL^{-1}) & \frac{-nd}{\lambda}(1 - \lambda bL^{-1})(1 - \lambda L) & -(1 - \lambda bL^{-1}) \\ \frac{-\lambda}{d}\frac{(1 - bL^{-1})}{1 - \lambda bL^{-1}} & -(1 - \lambda L) & 0 \end{bmatrix} \begin{bmatrix} y_t \\ k_t \\ \theta_t \end{bmatrix} = \begin{bmatrix} 0 \\ s_t \\ \frac{\lambda}{dn}\frac{1}{1 - \lambda bL^{-1}} s_t \end{bmatrix} \qquad (*)$$

where μ and $\{\theta_t\}_{t=0}^{\infty}$ are nonnegative multipliers.

C. Show that the solution of this problem for $t \geq 1$ is given by (22), (27), (29), (23) and $\gamma_t = (1 - bL^{-1})\tau_t$, where τ_t is given by (23), (29). Show that the present scheme raises an identical stream of revenue as the scheme in Section 2.

2. (Tax-smoothing)

Consider a model in which private agents maximize

$$\sum_{t=0}^{\infty} b^t\{u_t c_t - (u_2/2)c_t^2 - u_3 n_t - (u_4/2)n_t^2 - \tau_t n_t\} \qquad (1)$$

$$u_1,\ u_2,\ u_3,\ u_4 > 0 \qquad 0 < b < 1$$

subject to

$$c_t = fn_t,\ f > 0 \qquad u_1 f - u_3 > 0. \qquad (2)$$

Here c_t is consumption, n_t is employment, and τ_t is a tax rate on employment.

A government chooses τ_t to maximize the welfare of the representative private agent

$$\sum_{t=0}^{\infty} b^t\{u_1c_t - (u_2/2)c_t^2 - u_3n_t - (u_4/2)n_t^2\}$$

subject to (2), and

$$B_{t+1} = b^{-1}(B_t + g_t - \tau_t n_t), \quad t \geq 0, \quad B_0 = 0.$$

Here $\{g_t\}_{t=0}^{\infty}$ is a known sequence of exponential order less than $1/\sqrt{b}$. The government also takes as given private agents' rules for selecting (n_t,c_t) as a function of $\{\tau_s\}_{s=0}^{\infty}$.

A. Formulate and solve the government's optimal taxation problem.

B. Show that if an optimal plan exists, it involves setting $\tau_t = \tau$ for all $t \geq 0$.

3. Show that if $d = 0$, the solution of the problem of Section 2 is time consistent.

SOLUTIONS

1. A. With the tax on new investment,

$$v_0' = \Sigma_{t=0}^{\infty} b^t\{p_t f_0 k_t - (J_t + \gamma_t)(k_t - k_{t-1}) - (d/2)(k_t - k_{t-1})^2\}$$

which differs from v_0 in that the term involving τ_t does not appear, and in that the J_t in v_0 has been replaced by $J_t + \gamma_t$ in v_0'. Expression (2') then follows immediately from (2).

B. The Lagrangean is now

$$\begin{aligned} L = \Sigma_{t=0}^{\infty} b^t\{&[A_0 f_0 n k_t - (\tfrac{1}{2})A_1 f_0^2 n^2 k_t^2 + f_0 n u_t k_t \\ &- nJ_t(k_t - k_{t-1}) - (\tfrac{1}{2})nd(k_t - k_{t-1})^2] \\ &+ \theta_t[\lambda k_{t-1} - d^{-1}\lambda(1 - \lambda bL^{-1})^{-1}((1 - \lambda bL^{-1})(J_t + \gamma_t) \\ &- f_0 u_t - A_0 f_0) - k_t] \\ &+ \mu_t[bB_{t+1} - B_t - g_t + \gamma_t(k_t - k_{t-1})]\} \end{aligned}$$

where $\{\theta_t\}_{t=0}^{\infty}$ and $\{\mu_t\}_{t=0}^{\infty}$ are sequences of nonnegative multipliers. Differentiating with respect to k_t, γ_t, and B_{t+1} we obtain the Euler equations

$$\begin{aligned} -A_1 f_0^2 n^2 k_t - nd(1 - bL^{-1})(1 - L)k_t + \lambda bL^{-1}\theta_t - \theta_t& \\ + (1 - bL^{-1})\mu_t\gamma_t = s_t& \end{aligned} \tag{7'}$$

$$d^{-1}\lambda(1 - \lambda L)^{-1}(1 - L)\theta_t - \mu_t(1 - L)k_t = 0 \tag{8'}$$

$$(b - bL^{-1})\mu_t = 0 \tag{9'}$$

for $t \geq 0$, where

$$s_t \equiv -A_0 f_0 n - f_0 n u_t + n(1 - bL^{-1})J_t. \tag{11'}$$

The polynomial in L operating on k_t in (7') is identical to the one in the text, and the factorization is thus immediate. Further, (9') yields $\mu_t = \mu_{t+1} = \mu$ for all t, also as in the text.

Using the definition of s_t in (2') yields

$$d^{-1}\lambda(1 - \lambda bL^{-1})^{-1}(1 - bL^{-1})\gamma_t + (1 - \lambda L)k_t = -(\lambda/dn)(1 - \lambda bL^{-1})^{-1}s_t. \qquad (12')$$

Multiplying (8') by -1 and using $\mu_t = \mu$ yields

$$\mu(1 - L)k_t - d^{-1}\lambda(1 - \lambda L)^{-1}(1 - L)\theta_t = 0. \qquad (13')$$

Finally, using the polynomial factorization and constant μ in (7') yields

$$\mu(1 - bL^{-1})\gamma_t - nd\lambda^{-1}(1 - \lambda bL^{-1})(1 - \lambda L)k_t - (1 - \lambda bL^{-1})\theta_t = s_t. \qquad (14')$$

Writing equations (12'), (13'), and (14') in polynomial matrix notation yields (*).

C. The solution asserted in the problem statement is incorrect. To see this, suppose it happens that $s_t = 0$ for all t. In this case, firms wish to drive k_t to zero over time, and they succeed in doing so. In the capital tax economy, from equations (27) and (22) in the text,

$$k_0 = (n + 2\mu)^{-1}(n + \mu)\lambda k_{-1}$$

$$k_t = \lambda^t k_0.$$

Since $\mu \geq 0$, $k_0 \leq k_{-1}$. Notice also from equation (23) that $\tau_t = 0$ for $t \geq 1$. At $t = 0$,

$$\tau_0 = (n + 2\mu)^{-1} d\mu k_{-1};$$

the government attempts to finance its entire stream of expenditures by initial period taxation. If this is feasible, the formula

$$G = \tau_0 k_0$$

determines $\mu > 0$.

The assertion in the text is that $\gamma_t = (1 - bL^{-1})\tau_t$ (which yields $\gamma_0 = \tau_0$, $\gamma_t = 0$ for $t \geq 1$), that $\{k_t\}$ continues to be given by (22) and (27), and that the stream of revenue $\{\gamma_t(k_t - k_{t-1})\}$ matches the previous $\{\tau_t k_t\}$. But as was indicated above, $\mu \geq 0$ implies $k_0 \leq k_{-1}$, and the "stream" of revenue in the investment tax economy is $\gamma_0(k_0 - k_{-1})$, which is nonpositive for any $\mu \geq 0$. This contradicts the assertion; the two economies evidently behave differently in general.

To determine how the investment tax economy behaves, notice that the equations (12'), (13'), (14') derived in part B above can be written in the compact form

$$A(L)C(bL^{-1})^T C(L)[(1 - bL^{-1})\gamma_t \quad k_t \quad \theta_t]^T = \bar{s}_t$$

where C(L) is the polynomial matrix (defined in the text) associated with the capital tax problem, and $A(L) = \mathrm{diag}[(1 - L), 1, 1]$. Operating on both sides of the above equation yields

$$C(bL^{-1})^T C(L)[(1 - bL^{-1})\gamma_t \quad k_t \quad \theta_t]^T = A(L)^{-1}\bar{s}_t + [q \quad 0 \quad 0]^T$$

where q is an as-yet undetermined constant.* Finally, since $A(L)^{-1}\bar{s}_t = 0$,

$$C(L)[(1 - bL^{-1})\gamma_t \quad k_t \quad \theta_t]^T = [C(bL^{-1})^{-1}]^T\bar{s}_t + [C(b)^{-1}]^T[q \quad 0 \quad 0]^T$$

which, if $(1 - bL^{-1})\gamma_t$ is interpreted as τ_t, is the expression in the text for the capital tax economy, amended by the vector of constants $[C(b)^{-1}]^T[q \quad 0 \quad 0]^T$. Apparently, the transition equations for the investment tax economy will differ from those of the capital tax economy by a set of constants.

Instead of seeking the factorization $C(bL^{-1})^TC(L)$, it is possible to obtain the transition equations for the investment tax economy by pursuing the "alternative" direct method outlined in the text. First, solve (12') for γ_t to get

$$\gamma_t = -(1 - bL^{-1})^{-1}n^{-1}s_t \qquad (17')$$

$$- d\lambda^{-1}(1 - bL^{-1})^{-1}(1 - \lambda bL^{-1})(1 - \lambda L)k_t \qquad t \geq 0.$$

Next, consider (13'): this is the fundamental source of the difference between the two economies. The equation is

$$\mu(1 - L)k_t - d^{-1}\lambda(1 - \lambda L)^{-1}(1 - L)\theta_t = 0, \qquad t \geq 0. \qquad (13')$$

Then

$$\mu k_t - d^{-1}\lambda(1 - \lambda L)^{-1}\theta_t = q, \qquad t \geq 0$$

where q is a constant. From (13') evaluated at $t = 0$, $q = -\mu k_{-1}$. Thus

---

*Suppose $(1 - L)x_t - (1 - L)y_t = 0$ for $t \geq 0$. Then $x_t - y_t$ for $t \geq 0$, and $q = x_{-1} - y_{-1}$.

$$\theta_t = d\lambda^{-1}\mu(1 - \lambda L)k_t - \mu k_{-1}, \qquad t \geq 1. \tag{18'}$$

Notice that (18') differs from (18) by a constant. Evidently, and in accord with intuition, if $k_{-1} = 0$, the two economies will behave identically. Proceeding as in the text, substitute (17') and (18') into (14') and solve for k_t to get

$$(1 - \lambda L)k_t = \frac{-(1 + \mu/n)}{(2\mu + n)} \frac{\lambda}{d} \frac{1}{1 - \lambda bL^{-1}} s_t + \frac{\mu(1 - \lambda)}{2\mu + n} k_{-1} \qquad t \geq 1. \tag{19'}$$

Note that (19') differs from (19) by a constant. Now substitute (19') into (17') and (18'), and solve for γ_t and θ_t to get

$$\gamma_t = \frac{-\mu/n}{(2\mu + n)} \frac{1}{1 - \lambda bL^{-1}} s_t - \frac{(1 - \lambda b)d\mu(1 - \lambda)}{(1 - b)\lambda(2\mu + n)} k_{-1} \qquad t \geq 1 \tag{20'}$$

$$\theta_t = \frac{-\mu(1 + \mu/n)}{(2\mu + n)} \frac{1}{1 - \lambda bL^{-1}} \frac{1}{-\lambda bL^{-1}} s_t \tag{21'}$$

$$- \frac{(\mu + n)d}{(2\mu + n)\lambda}(1 - \lambda)\mu k_{-1} \qquad t \geq 1$$

which differ from (20) and (21) by constants.

The next task is to solve for k_0, τ_0, and θ_0. For $t = 0$, (13') is

$$\mu k_0 = \lambda d^{-1}\theta_0 + \mu k_{-1}. \tag{25'}$$

Now operate on both sides of (12') by $-\lambda^{-1}dn(1 - \lambda bL^{-1})$ and add the result to (14') to get

$$\gamma_t = (\mu + n)^{-1}(1 - bL^{-1})^{-1}(1 - \lambda bL^{-1})\theta_t \qquad t \geq 0. \tag{26'}$$

Substitute (26') for γ_t in (12') and evaluate at $t = 0$:

$$(\mu + n)^{-1}\lambda d^{-1}\theta_0 + (k_0 - \lambda k_{-1}) = -\lambda(dn)^{-1}(1 - \lambda bL^{-1})^{-1}s_0.$$

Use (25') to eliminate θ_0 from this equation, and solve for k_0:

$$k_0 = \frac{(n+\mu)}{(n+2\mu)}\lambda k_{-1} - \frac{\lambda}{dn}\frac{(n+\mu)}{(n+2\mu)}\frac{1}{1-\lambda bL^{-1}}s_0 + \frac{\mu}{2\mu+n}k_{-1}. \qquad (27')$$

Now substitute (25') into (27') and solve for θ_0:

$$\theta_0 = d\mu\frac{(n+\mu)}{(n+2\mu)}k_{-1} - \frac{\mu}{n}\frac{(n+\mu)}{(n+2\mu)}\frac{1}{1-\lambda bL^{-1}}s_0 \qquad (28')$$

$$- d\lambda^{-1}\mu\frac{(n+\mu)}{(n+2\mu)}k_{-1}.$$

Finally, use (21') for θ_t, $t \geq 1$, and (28') for θ_0 in (26') to get

$$\gamma_0 = d\mu\frac{(n+\mu)}{(n+2\mu)}k_{-1} - \frac{\mu}{n}\frac{(n+\mu)}{(n+2\mu)}\frac{1}{1-\lambda bL^{-1}}s_0 \qquad (29')$$

$$- \mu d\frac{(n+\mu)}{(n+2\mu)}(\lambda^{-1} - b(1-\lambda))k_{-1}.$$

The last step is to set μ so that the $\{\gamma_t, k_t\}_{t=0}^{\infty}$ sequences given by (19'), (20'), (27'), (29') satisfy the government budget constraint.

* * *

2. It is necessary to begin by finding private agents' contingency plan for setting employment. Since $c_t = fn_t$, individuals seek to maximize

$$\Sigma_{t=0}^{\infty} b^t\{(u_1 f - u_3)n_t - (\tfrac{1}{2})(u_2 f^2 + u_4)n_t^2 - \tau_t n_t\}$$

by choice of $\{n_t\}_{t=0}^{\infty}$. The first order condition for choosing n_t is

$$u_1 f - u_3 - (u_2 f^2 + u_4)n_t - \tau_t = 0 \qquad t = 0, 1, \ldots .$$

Thus agents' contingency plan for setting n_t is

$$n_t = v_2^{-1}v_1 - v_2^{-1}\tau_t \qquad (3)$$

where $v_1 = u_1 f - u_3$, $v_2 = u_2 f^2 + u_4$. Notice that since $v_1 > 0$, employment will be positive in the absence of taxation.

A. To find the optimal tax scheme, form the Lagrangean

$$L = \Sigma_{t=0}^{\infty} b^t \{v_1 n_t - (\tfrac{1}{2}) v_2 n_t^2 + \theta_t [v_2^{-1} v_1 - v_2^{-1} \tau_t - n_t]$$

$$+ \mu_t [bB_{t+1} - B_t - g_t + \tau_t n_t]\}$$

where $\{\theta_t\}_{t=0}^{\infty}$ and $\{\mu_t\}_{t=0}^{\infty}$ are sequences of nonnegative multipliers. Notice that the government takes as given agents' contingency plan for setting employment.* The first order conditions for setting $\{n_t\}_{t=0}^{\infty}$, $\{\tau_t\}_{t=0}^{\infty}$, $\{B_t\}_{t=1}^{\infty}$ are:

$$v_1 - v_2 n_t - \theta_t + \mu_t \tau_t = 0 \tag{4}$$

$$-v_2^{-1} \theta_t + \mu_t n_t = 0 \tag{5}$$

$$(b - bL^{-1}) \mu_t = 0 \tag{6}$$

for $t \geq 0$. Equation (6) gives $\mu_t = \mu$ for all t. Then (5) gives $\theta_t = v_2 \mu n_t$. Using this in (4) and recalling (3) yields

$$- (1 + \mu) v_2 n_t + \mu \tau_t = -v_1 \tag{7}$$

$$n_t + v_2^{-1} \tau_t = v_2^{-1} v_1. \tag{3}$$

The solution to these two equations is

---

*Since there are no costly adjustment or "time-to-get-utility" elements in this problem, one period is like any other from the representative agent's viewpoint. While the important analogy is between (3) and equation (2) of Section 2 of the text, it happens here that (3) is also the representative agent's decision rule for setting {n} -- a decision rule which (uncharacteristically) involves only "deep" parameters of preferences.

$$n_t = v_2^{-1} v_1[(1 + \mu)/(1 + 2\mu)] \tag{8}$$

$$\tau_t = v_1\mu/(1 + 2\mu). \tag{9}$$

Finally, we seek a μ for which the budget constraint holds, i.e.,

$$G = \Sigma_{t=0}^{\infty} b^t n_t \tau_t = (1 - b)^{-1} v_1^2 v_2^{-1} \mu(1 + \mu)(1 + 2\mu)^{-2}. \tag{10}$$

B. Provided (10) has a solution* for $\mu \geq 0$, (9) is the optimal tax, and clearly $\tau_t = \tau \equiv v_1\mu/(1 + 2\mu)$ for all t.

* * *

3. When d = 0, the link between decisions made at different dates is broken, controls at t will not affect returns in earlier periods, and the optimal plan will be time consistent. The policymaker is not tempted to exploit his influence on agents' intertemporal margins in different ways at different dates because there are no intertemporal margins about which agents care. (This was the case in Exercise 2; the plan (9) in that exercise would be followed no matter when the game started.)

To see the result in more detail, one begins with a derivation of the analogue of (2) in the text for for the d = 0 case. The first order condition for maximizing (1) with respect to $\{k_t\}$ when d = 0 is given by

$$f_0 p_t - (1 - bL^{-1})J_t - \tau_t = 0.$$

---

*The maximum present value of revenue (achieved by driving the multiplier to infinity) is $v_1^2/[4(1 - b)v_2]$. If G exceeds this amount, it is not feasible to finance the given stream of government expenditures.

Using the demand function in this equation yields the following description of the equilibrium volume of capital:

$$k_t = (-A_1 n f_0)^{-1}\{(1 - bL^{-1})J_t - f_0 u_t - f_0 A_0 + \tau_t\}. \tag{2'}$$

Notice that <u>future</u> tax rates do not affect k_t.

The Lagrangean associated with the optimal tax is

$$\begin{aligned} L' = \Sigma_{t=0}^{\infty} b^t\{&A_0 f_0 n k_t - (\tfrac{1}{2})A_1 f_0^2 n^2 k_t^2 + f_0 n u_t k_t - nJ_t(k_t - k_{t-1}) \\ &+ \theta_t[-(-A_1 n f_0)^{-1}\{(1 - bL^{-1})J_t - f_0 u_t - f_0 A_0 + \tau_t\} - k_t] \\ &+ \mu_t[bB_{t+1} - g_t - B_t + \tau_t k_t]\}, \end{aligned}$$

where $\{\theta_t\}_{t=0}^{\infty}$, $\{\mu_t\}_{t=0}^{\infty}$ are sequences of nonnegative multipliers. The Euler equations associated with choices of $\{k_t\}_{t=0}^{\infty}$, $\{\tau_t\}_{t=0}^{\infty}$, $\{B_t\}_{t=1}^{\infty}$ are

$$A_0 f_0 n - A_1 f_0^2 n^2 k_t + f_0 n u_t - n(1 - bL^{-1})J_t - \theta_t + \mu_t \tau_t = 0 \tag{7'}$$

$$(-A_1 n f_0)^{-1}\theta_t + \mu_t k_t = 0 \tag{8'}$$

$$\mu_{t+1} - \mu_t = 0. \tag{9'}$$

Equation (9') implies $\mu_t = \mu$ for all t. Then (2'), (7'), and (8') yield the analogues of (12), (13), and (14):

$$\mu k_t - (A_1 n f_0)^{-1}\theta_t = 0 \tag{13'}$$

$$\mu\tau_t - A_1 f_0^2 n^2 k_t - \theta_t = s_t \tag{14'}$$

$$-(A_1 n f_0)^{-1}\tau_t - k_t = (-A_1 n f_0)^{-1} s_t. \tag{12'}$$

Writing these equations in matrix notation yields the analogue of (15') or (16'):

$$W(\tau_t \quad k_t \quad \theta_t)' = (0 \quad s_t \quad (-A_1 n f_0)^{-1} s_t)' = \bar{s}_t \tag{16'}$$

where the W in (16') is a matrix of constants. Thus

$$(\tau_t \quad k_t \quad \theta_t)' = W^{-1}\bar{s}_t, \qquad t \geq 0;$$

equilibrium capital and the optimal tax depend only upon current $\bar{s}_t$.

The solution of the first "remainder" problem gives rise to equations (7'), (8') and (9') for $t \geq 1$. Thus (16') holds for $t \geq 1$. Therefore, it is optimal, at $t = 1$, to follow through with the initial, time 0 "plan" for (k_1, τ_1) [given by the solution to (16') for $t = 1$], and the optimal tax strategy is time consistent.

CHAPTER XVI

THE PHILLIPS CURVE

EXERCISE

Supply in an individual market that gets relative demand shock z_t is governed by

$$y_t(z) = \gamma\{p_t(z) - E[p_t | I_t(z)]\}, \qquad \gamma > 0$$

where $p_t(z) = p_t + z_t$, and

$$p_t = \sum_{j=0}^{\infty} v_j \varepsilon_{t-j} = \int p_t(z) g(z_t) dz_t, \qquad v_0 = 1, \qquad \sum_{j=0}^{\infty} v_j^2 < \infty$$

where $Ez_t\varepsilon_s = 0$ for all t and s, and ε and z are serially independent processes with means of zero. Here $y_t(z)$ is the log of supply in market z, $p_t(z)$ is the log of price in market z, p_t is the average log price level and $g(z_t)$ is the probability density of z_t. We assume that z and ε are each normal random variates with means of zero. Information in market z, $I_t(z)$, consists of the following three elements: Ω_{t-1}, observations on all lagged prices and quantities in <u>all</u> markets; $p_t(z)$, the current own-market price; and the current market price $p_t(z')$ in one other market. Assume that different markets have statistically independent and identically distributed z's.

A. Derive a Phillips curve of the form

$$y_t = \phi(p_t - E[p_t | \Omega_{t-1}])$$

where $y_t = \int y_t(z_t)g(z_t)dz_t$. Give a formula for ϕ in terms of γ and the variances of ε_t and z_t.

B. Is your value for ϕ larger or smaller than the value that Lucas derived by assuming that $I_t(z)$ consisted only of the two bits of information Ω_{t-1} and $p_t(z_t)$? Can you guess what would happen to the slope ϕ if agents in market z were permitted to see current prices in n markets, as n becomes larger and larger? Heuristically explain what is going on here to affect the slope ϕ.

SOLUTION

A. The model is:

$y_t(z) = \gamma\{p_t(z) - E[p_t|I_t(z)]\}$, $\gamma > 0$ supply in market z

$p_t(z) = p_t + z_t$ demand in market z

$p_t(z') = p_t + z_t'$ demand in market z'

$I_t(z) = [\Omega_{t-1}, p_t(z), p_t(z')]$ information at t in market z.

Since all random variables are distributed normally, conditional expectations and linear least squares projections coincide. First decompose p_t: since $p_t = \sum_{j=0}^{\infty} v_j \varepsilon_{t-j}$,

$$p_t = E[p_t|\Omega_{t-1}] + \varepsilon_t,$$

where ε_t is orthogonal to Ω_{t-1}. By assumption, $Ez_t\varepsilon_t = 0$. Then write

$$p_t(z) = E[p_t|\Omega_{t-1}] + \varepsilon_t + z_t.$$

Thus $E[p_t(z)|\Omega_{t-1}] = E[p_t|\Omega_{t-1}]$ because ε_t is orthogonal to Ω_{t-1} by the orthogonality condition, and $E[z_t|\Omega_{t-1}] = 0$ because $\{z_t\}$ is serially independent. Write

$$E[p_t|I_t(z)] = E[p_t|\Omega_{t-1}, p_t(z), p_t(z')].$$

Now group $p_t(z)$ and $p_t(z')$ together and use the Kalman filter (recursive projection) formula to get

$$E[p_t|I_t(z)] = E[p_t|\Omega_{t-1}] + E[p_t - E(p_t|\Omega_{t-1})|p_t(z) - E(p_t(z)|\Omega_{t-1}), p_t(z') - E(p_t(z')|\Omega_{t-1})]$$

$$= E[p_t|\Omega_{t-1}] + E[\varepsilon_t|\varepsilon_t + z_t, \varepsilon_t + z_t']$$

$$= E[p_t|\Omega_{t-1}] + a_1(\varepsilon_t + z_t) + a_2(\varepsilon_t + z_t')$$

where a_1 and a_2 are given by the normal equations:

$$E\begin{bmatrix} \varepsilon_t + z_t \\ \varepsilon_t + z_t' \end{bmatrix}(\varepsilon_t) = E\begin{bmatrix} \varepsilon_t + z_t \\ \varepsilon_t + z_t' \end{bmatrix}[(\varepsilon_t + z_t) \quad (\varepsilon_t + z_t')]\begin{bmatrix} a_1 \\ a_2 \end{bmatrix}$$

or

$$\begin{bmatrix} \sigma_\varepsilon^2 \\ \sigma_\varepsilon^2 \end{bmatrix} = E\begin{bmatrix} (\varepsilon_t + z_t)^2 & (\varepsilon_t + z_t)(\varepsilon_t + z_t') \\ (\varepsilon_t + z_t')(\varepsilon_t + z_t) & (\varepsilon_t + z_t')^2 \end{bmatrix}\begin{bmatrix} a_1 \\ a_2 \end{bmatrix}$$

which becomes

$$\begin{bmatrix} \sigma_\varepsilon^2 \\ \sigma_\varepsilon^2 \end{bmatrix} = \begin{bmatrix} \sigma_\varepsilon^2 + \sigma_z^2 & \sigma_\varepsilon^2 \\ \sigma_\varepsilon^2 & \sigma_\varepsilon^2 + \sigma_z^2 \end{bmatrix}\begin{bmatrix} a_1 \\ a_2 \end{bmatrix}$$

since z_t and z_t' are identically distributed. Thus

$$\begin{bmatrix} a_1 \\ a_2 \end{bmatrix} = \frac{1}{(\sigma_\varepsilon^2 + \sigma_z^2)^2 - \sigma_\varepsilon^4}\begin{bmatrix} \sigma_\varepsilon^2 + \sigma_z^2 & -\sigma_\varepsilon^2 \\ -\sigma_\varepsilon^2 & \sigma_\varepsilon^2 + \sigma_z^2 \end{bmatrix}\begin{bmatrix} \sigma_\varepsilon^2 \\ \sigma_\varepsilon^2 \end{bmatrix}$$

$$= \frac{1}{\sigma_z^4 + 2\sigma_\varepsilon^2\sigma_z^2}\begin{bmatrix} \sigma_\varepsilon^2\sigma_z^2 \\ \sigma_\varepsilon^2\sigma_z^2 \end{bmatrix}$$

$$= \frac{\sigma_\varepsilon^2}{\sigma_z^2 + 2\sigma_\varepsilon^2}\begin{bmatrix} 1 \\ 1 \end{bmatrix}.$$

Thus

$$E[p_t|I_t(z)] = E[p_t|\Omega_{t-1}] + \frac{\sigma_\varepsilon^2}{\sigma_z^2 + 2\sigma_\varepsilon^2}\{p_t(z) - E[p_t(z)|\Omega_{t-1}]\}$$

$$+ \frac{\sigma_\varepsilon^2}{\sigma_z^2 + 2\sigma_\varepsilon^2}\{p_t(z') - E[p_t(z')|\Omega_{t-1}]\}.$$

Substitute this expression into the supply function to get (with $\alpha = \sigma_\varepsilon^2/(\sigma_z^2 + 2\sigma_\varepsilon^2)$)

$$y_t(z) = \gamma\big[p_t(z) - E[p_t|\Omega_{t-1}] - \alpha\{p_t(z) - E[p_t|\Omega_{t-1}]\} - \alpha\{p_t(z') - E[p_t|\Omega_{t-1}]\}\big]$$

since $E[p_t(z)|\Omega_{t-1}] = E[p_t|\Omega_{t-1}]$. Then

$$y_t(z) = \gamma[p_t(z) - \alpha p_t(z) - \alpha p_t(z') - (1 - 2\alpha)E(p_t|\Omega_{t-1})].$$

Now take expected values (integrate with respect to the density of z -- this aggregates markets). Let $\int y_t(z)g(z)dz = y_t$. Notice that

$$Ep_t(z) = \int p_t(z)g(z)dz = Ep_t(z') = p_t.$$

Thus

$$y_t = \gamma(1 - 2\alpha)(p_t - E[p_t|\Omega_{t-1}])$$

$$= \phi(p_t - E[p_t|\Omega_{t-1}])$$

where $\phi = \gamma(1 - 2\alpha) = \gamma\big[1 - 2[\sigma_\varepsilon^2/(\sigma_z^2 + 2\sigma_\varepsilon^2)]\big] = \gamma\sigma_z^2/(\sigma_z^2 + 2\sigma_\varepsilon^2)$.

B. The slope in Lucas's case was $\gamma\sigma_z^2/(\sigma_z^2 + \sigma_\varepsilon^2)$. Clearly,

$$\frac{\gamma\sigma_z^2}{\sigma_z^2 + 2\sigma_\varepsilon^2} < \frac{\gamma\sigma_z^2}{\sigma_z^2 + \sigma_\varepsilon^2}.$$

As agents see prices in an increasingly large number (n) of markets, the slope becomes

$$\lim_{n\to\infty} \frac{\gamma\sigma_z^2}{\sigma_z^2 + n\sigma_\varepsilon^2} = 0$$

in which case $y_t = 0$. As agents get more and more information about prices in other markets, they get better and better estimates of the average price level until in the limit they know p_t exactly and cannot be "fooled" at all; that is, the Phillips curve becomes vertical.

CHAPTER XVII

OPTIMAL MONETARY POLICY

EXERCISES

1. Consider the system formed by (1), (2), and (3') where (1) is replaced by

$$y_t = \gamma(p_t - {}_tp^*_{t-1}) + \lambda y_{t-1} + \alpha({}_tp^*_{t-1} - p_{t-1}) + u_t$$

where $\alpha > 0$ and where u_t and ε_t have the same properties assumed in the text. Calculate the optimal feedback rule for m_t, using the objective function in the text. Show that the neutrality theorem fails.

2. Consider the system formed by (1), (2), and (3') with (3') replaced by

$${}_tp^*_{t-1} = E[p_t|\Omega_{t-1}] + \xi_t$$

where ξ_t is the term reflecting random deviations from rationality and satisfying $E[\xi_t|\Omega_{t-1}] = 0$. Assume that the public and the government share the same information set. Find the optimal control rule for m_t. Does the neutrality theorem hold?

3. Complete the model on page 460 by assuming the fixed-weight expectations schemes

$$ {}_tp^*_{t-1} = vp_{t-1}, \qquad {}_{t+1}p^*_{t-1} = wp_{t-1}, $$

where v and w are parameters that remain fixed in the face of variations in the rule. Assume that the authority is interested in minimizing $E_{t-1}(y_t - y^*)^2$ by choosing a feedback rule <u>either</u> of the form

$$ r_t = H\Omega_{t-1} \qquad \text{or} \qquad m_t = G\Omega_{t-1} $$

where H and G are vectors conformable to the authority's information set Ω_{t-1}, which consists of observations on all <u>lagged</u> endogenous and exogenous variables (and therefore on lagged values of the disturbances, too, since the authority knows the model). You may assume that u_t, ε_{1t} and ε_{2t} are pairwise uncorrelated. Then prove that:

A. Whether the authority should use the interest rate rule or the money supply rule depends on the variances of u, ε_1, and ε_2 and the slopes of the IS and LM curves.

B. The more stable is the IS curve relative to the LM curve and the steeper is the IS relative to the LM curve, the more likely is it that the authority will want to use the interest rate as its instrument. (Poole (1970) and Bailey (1971) are useful references on the problem addressed in this exercise.)

4. Let m_t be the log of the money supply and y_t be the level of real output. To test whether "money is a veil" in the long run, a researcher proposes to estimate the final form

$$ y_t = \sum_{j=0}^{\infty} h_t m_{t-j} + \text{residual}_t $$

and to test whether $\sum_{j=0}^{\infty} h_j = 0$. If this sum is zero, he plans to conclude that "money is a veil." Otherwise, he will conclude that in the long run "money matters." Critically discuss the virtues and defects of this research strategy from the standpoint of economic theory. (Feel free to introduce sample models to make your case.)

5. Consider an economy described by the following equations:

$$C_t = \left(\frac{1.80}{\sqrt{2}} - 0.81\right)Y_{t-1} + 100,$$

$$I_t = 0.81(Y_{t-1} - Y_{t-2}) + \varepsilon_t + 10,$$

and

$$Y_t = C_t + I_t + G_t,$$

where C, I, Y, and G are consumption, investment, GNP, and government purchases, respectively; and $\{\varepsilon_t\}$ is a "white-noise" process with mean $E[\varepsilon_t] = 0$ and variance $\sigma^2 = E[\varepsilon_t^2]$. The units of time are quarters. Suppose that the government sets G_t at the constant level $\bar{G}$ every period.

A. Is the economy one with a business cycle? If so, what is the average period of the cycle as measured by the period of the cycles in the covariogram of GNP?

B. Suppose now that G_t is set so that fiscal policy leans against the wind. In particular, the government employs the "feedback rule"

$$G_t = 10 - \lambda(Y_{t-1} - Y_{t-2}), \qquad \lambda > 0.$$

Show how variations in λ will affect the behavior of GNP. Can λ be set so that there are no "business cycles," defined as cycles in the covariogram of GNP?

C. Suppose that the government uses the feedback rule

$$G_t = 10 + \lambda_1 Y_{t-1} + \lambda_2 Y_{t-2}.$$

What values of λ_1 and λ_2 minimize the variance of GNP? (Hint: write Y_t in the form:

$$Y_t = \text{constant} + \sum_{i=0}^{\infty} w_i \varepsilon_{t-i}$$

and see how the w_i depend on λ_1 and λ_2.)

6. Consider the macroeconomic model

$$m_t - p_t = \tau y_t + u_t \qquad \text{(portfolio balance)}$$

$$y_t = \gamma(p_t - E_{t-1}p_t) + \lambda y_{t-1} + \varepsilon_t \qquad \text{(aggregate supply)}$$

$$\gamma > 0, \; 0 < \lambda < 1,$$

where m is the log of money, p is the log of the price level, y is real GNP, τ is one minus the marginal income tax rate, and $\{u_t\}$ and $\{\varepsilon_t\}$ are serially uncorrelated and mutually uncorrelated covariance stationary random processes. Here $E_{t-1}p_t$ is the linear least squares projection of p_t on lagged p's, y's, and m's.

A. Prove that in this model, Friedman's "no-feedback" rule for setting m is as good as any other rule from the point of view of the objective: minimize $E_{t-1}(y_t - y^*)^2$ where y* is given.

B. Determine whether the tax parameter τ influences $E_{t-1}(y_t - y^*)^2$. If it does, what value of τ minimizes this objective?

C. Determine whether the tax parameter τ influences $E_{t-1}y_t$. Would your answer change if τ were permitted to depend on time and say be determined via a feedback rule?

7. An economy is described by the following equations:

$$C_t = c_1 Y_{t-1} + u_{1t} \qquad 0 < c_1 < 1$$

$$I_t = a_0 + a_1(Y_{t-1} - Y_{t-2}) + a_2 r_t + u_{2t} \qquad a_2 < 0 < a_1$$

$$m_t = b_1 r_t + b_2 Y_{t-1} + v_t \qquad b_1 < 0,\ b_2 > 0$$

$$C_t + I_t = Y_t$$

where C_t is consumption at t, I_t is investment, Y_t is GNP, r_t is the interest rate, and m_t is the money supply; u_{1t}, u_{2t} and v_t are serially uncorrelated random variables (white noises) that are mutually independent (i.e., u_{1t}, u_{2t}, and v_t are pairwise uncorrelated), with variances σ^2_{u1}, σ^2_{u2}, and σ^2_v.

The monetary authority desires to minimize the mean squared error: $E(Y_t - Y^*)^2$ where Y^* is the target level of GNP. To achieve this end, the monetary authority considers two alternative strategies. The first is to peg the money supply via the feedback rule

$$m_t = \Lambda_0 + \lambda_1 Y_{t-1} + \lambda_2 Y_{t-2} + \lambda_3 Y_{t-3} \qquad (*)$$

where Λ_0, λ_1, λ_2, λ_3 are parameters to be chosen. The second is to peg the interest rate via the feedback rule:

$$r_t = \Delta_0 + \delta_1 Y_{t-1} + \delta_2 Y_{t-2} + \delta_3 Y_{t-3}. \qquad (\dagger)$$

A. Compute the optimal values of Λ_0, λ_1, λ_2 and λ_3. What is the mean squared error attained under this rule?

B. Compute the optimal values of Δ_0, δ_1, δ_2, and δ_3 assuming that the interest rate rule (†) is used. What is the mean squared error attained under this rule?

C. What should the monetary authority do, peg r or peg m? What feature of the above model is critical in accounting for this result?

SOLUTIONS

1. Define $E[p_t|\Omega_{t-1}] \equiv E_{t-1}p_t$. Then the system becomes

$$y_t = \gamma(p_t - E_{t-1}p_t) + \lambda y_{t-1} + \alpha(E_{t-1}p_t - p_{t-1}) + u_t$$

$$m_t - p_t = y_t + \varepsilon_t.$$

The supply equation can be rewritten as

$$y_t = (\gamma - \alpha L)p_t + (\alpha - \gamma)E_{t-1}p_t + \lambda y_{t-1} + u_t,$$

while the portfolio balance equation can be rearranged to get

$$p_t = m_t - y_t - \varepsilon_t$$

which can then be used to calculate $E_{t-1}p_t$:

$$E_{t-1}p_t = E_{t-1}m_t - E_{t-1}y_t.$$

By substituting these results into the supply equation, one obtains

$$\begin{aligned} y_t &= (\gamma - \alpha L)(m_t - y_t - \varepsilon_t) + (\alpha - \gamma)(E_{t-1}m_t - E_{t-1}y_t) + \lambda y_{t-1} + u_t \\ &= \gamma m_t - \gamma y_t - \gamma\varepsilon_t - \alpha m_{t-1} + \alpha y_{t-1} + \alpha\varepsilon_{t-1} \\ &\quad + (\alpha - \gamma)E_{t-1}m_t - (\alpha - \gamma)E_{t-1}y_t + \lambda y_{t-1} + u_t \end{aligned}$$

or

$$\begin{aligned} y_t = {} & \frac{\gamma}{1 + \gamma}m_t - \frac{\alpha}{1 + \gamma}m_{t-1} + \frac{\alpha - \gamma}{1 + \gamma}E_{t-1}m_t + \frac{\alpha + \lambda}{1 + \gamma}y_{t-1} \\ & - \frac{\alpha - \gamma}{1 + \gamma}E_{t-1}y_t - \frac{\gamma}{1 + \gamma}\varepsilon_t + \frac{\alpha}{1 + \gamma}\varepsilon_{t-1} + \frac{1}{1 + \gamma}u_t \end{aligned}$$

which is a reduced form for y_t. The authorities seek to minimize the function $E_{t-1}(y_t - y^*)^2 = (E_{t-1}y_t - y^*)^2 + E_t(y_t - E_{t-1}y_t)^2$. To do this, they first minimize the bias squared, $(E_{t-1}y_t - y^*)^2$. In fact, they will succeed in setting this quantity to zero: using the reduced form for y_t,

$$E_{t-1}y_t = \frac{\gamma}{1+\gamma}E_{t-1}m_t - \frac{\alpha}{1+\gamma}m_{t-1} + \frac{\alpha-\gamma}{1+\gamma}E_{t-1}m_t + \frac{\alpha+\lambda}{1+\gamma}y_{t-1}$$

$$- \frac{\alpha-\gamma}{1+\gamma}E_{t-1}y_t + \frac{\alpha}{1+\gamma}\varepsilon_{t-1}$$

or

$$E_{t-1}y_t = \frac{1+\gamma}{1+\alpha}\left(\frac{\alpha}{1+\gamma}E_{t-1}m_t - \frac{\alpha}{1+\gamma}m_{t-1} + \frac{\alpha+\lambda}{1+\gamma}y_{t-1} + \frac{\alpha}{1+\gamma}\varepsilon_{t-1}\right).$$

Since the authorities control $E_{t-1}m_t$, $E_{t-1}y_t$ can be made to equal y^*:

$$y^* = \frac{\alpha}{1+\alpha}E_{t-1}m_t - \frac{\alpha}{1+\alpha}m_{t-1} + \frac{\alpha+\lambda}{1+\alpha}y_{t-1} + \frac{\alpha}{1+\alpha}\varepsilon_{t-1}.$$

Thus the authorities set

$$E_{t-1}m_t = \frac{1+\alpha}{\alpha}\left(y^* + \frac{\alpha}{1+\alpha}m_{t-1} - \frac{\alpha+\lambda}{1+\alpha}y_{t-1} - \frac{\alpha}{1+\alpha}\varepsilon_{t-1}\right)$$

$$= \frac{1+\alpha}{\alpha}y^* + m_{t-1} - \frac{\alpha+\lambda}{\alpha}y_{t-1} - \varepsilon_{t-1}$$

which gives $(E_{t-1}y_t - y^*)^2 = 0$. But

$$y_t - E_{t-1}y_t = \frac{\gamma}{1+\gamma}[m_t - E_{t-1}m_t] - \frac{\gamma}{1+\gamma}\varepsilon_t + \frac{1}{1+\gamma}u_t.$$

Clearly, $E_{t-1}(y_t - E_{t-1}y_t)^2$ is minimized when $m_t - E_{t-1}m_t = 0$. Thus, the authorities will set m_t according to the feedback rule

$$m_t = \frac{1+\alpha}{\alpha}y^* + m_{t-1} - \frac{\alpha+\lambda}{\alpha}y_{t-1} - \varepsilon_{t-1}. \qquad (*)$$

With this rule in effect, the value of the objective function is

$$E_{t-1}(y_t - y^*)^2 = \left(\frac{\gamma}{1+\gamma}\right)^2\text{var}(\varepsilon_t) + \left(\frac{1}{1+\gamma}\right)^2\text{var}(u_t)$$

while y_t evolves according to

$$y_t = E_{t-1}y_t + (y_t - E_{t-1}y_t)$$

$$= y^* - \frac{\gamma}{1+\gamma}\varepsilon_t + \frac{1}{1+\gamma}u_t.$$

Thus the use of the uniquely optimal feedback rule (*) has eliminated the serial correlation in y_t. Clearly, the neutrality theorem fails.

* * *

2. The model is

$$y_t = \gamma(p_t - {}_tp^*_{t-1}) + \lambda y_{t-1} + u_t \qquad \gamma > 0 \tag{1}$$

$$m_t - p_t = y_t + \varepsilon_t \tag{2}$$

$${}_tp^*_{t-1} = E[p_t|\Omega_{t-1}] + \xi_t. \tag{3'}$$

To find the reduced form for y_t, first substitute (3') into (1) to get

$$y_t = \gamma(p_t - E[p_t|\Omega_{t-1}] - \xi_t) + \lambda y_{t-1} + u_t.$$

Notice that $E[y_t|\Omega_{t-1}] = \lambda y_{t-1}$ since $E[\xi_t|\Omega_{t-1}] = E[u_t|\Omega_{t-1}] = 0$. Now (2) gives

$$p_t = m_t - y_t - \varepsilon_t$$

whereby

$$E[p_t|\Omega_{t-1}] = E[m_t|\Omega_{t-1}] - E[y_t|\Omega_{t-1}]$$

$$= E[m_t|\Omega_{t-1}] - \lambda y_{t-1}.$$

Thus, using (2) again,

$$p_t - E[p_t|\Omega_{t-1}] = m_t - y_t - \varepsilon_t - E[m_t|\Omega_{t-1}] + \lambda y_{t-1}$$

and the reduced form for y_t is

$$y_t = \gamma(m_t - E[m_t|\Omega_{t-1}] - y_t - \varepsilon_t + \lambda y_{t-1} - \xi_t) + \lambda y_{t-1} + u_t$$

or

$$y_t = \frac{\gamma}{1+\gamma}(m_t - E[m_t|\Omega_{t-1}]) + \lambda y_{t-1} + \frac{1}{1+\gamma}u_t - \frac{\gamma}{1+\gamma}(\varepsilon_t + \xi_t),$$

an expression very much like equation (20) of the text. It should be clear from this expression that the neutrality theorem holds, as only unexpected (not systematic) movements in the money supply affect output.

The optimal monetary rule is found as follows. First, from the reduced form above,

$$E[y_t|\Omega_{t-1}] = \lambda y_{t-1}$$

since $E[\xi_t|\Omega_{t-1}] = 0$ by assumption. Thus, as in Section XVII.3 of the text, the bias squared is independent of the parameters of the money supply rule, the optimal policy is

$$m_t = E[m_t|\Omega_{t-1}],$$

and the neutrality theorem holds.

* * *

3. Upon substitution of the fixed-weight expectations schemes, the model becomes

$$y_t = \gamma(p_t - vp_{t-1}) + \lambda y_{t-1} + u_t \qquad \gamma > 0 \tag{21}$$

$$m_t - p_t = y_t + br_t + \varepsilon_{1t} \qquad b < 0 \tag{22}$$

$$y_t = c[r_t - (wp_{t-1} - p_t)] + \varepsilon_{2t} \qquad c < 0. \tag{23}$$

The LM curve is obtained by using (22) to eliminate p_t from (21):

$$y_t = \gamma(m_t - y_t - br_t - \varepsilon_{1t} - vp_{t-1}) + \lambda y_{t-1} + u_t$$

or

$$y_t = -\frac{\gamma b}{1+\gamma} r_t + \frac{\gamma}{1+\gamma} m_t - \frac{\gamma v}{1+\gamma} p_{t-1} + \frac{\lambda}{1+\gamma} y_{t-1} - \frac{\gamma}{1+\gamma} \varepsilon_{1t} + \frac{1}{1+\gamma} u_t. \tag{LM}$$

Graphed with r_t as a function of y_t, the curve has slope $-\frac{1+\gamma}{\gamma b} > 0$. For given values of r_t, increases in m_t increase y_t; that is, the LM curve shifts right when the money supply increases.

To obtain an IS curve in which r_t is a function of y_t but not p_t, use (23) to eliminate p_t from (21):

$$y_t = \gamma(\frac{1}{c} y_t - \frac{1}{c}\varepsilon_{2t} - r_t + wp_{t-1} - vp_{t-1}) + \lambda y_{t-1} + u_t$$

or

$$y_t = -\frac{\gamma c}{c-\gamma} r_t + \frac{\gamma c(w-v)}{c-\gamma} p_{t-1} + \frac{\lambda c}{c-\gamma} y_{t-1} - \frac{\gamma}{c-\gamma}\varepsilon_{2t} + \frac{c}{c-\gamma} u_t. \tag{IS}$$

Graphed with r_t as a function of y_t, the IS curve has slope

$$-\frac{c-\gamma}{\gamma c} < 0.$$

A. Under the interest rate rule, the IS curve is a reduced form for y_t. To find the optimal rule, one first minimizes the bias squared. Now

$$(E_{t-1}y_t - y^*)^2 = (-\frac{\gamma c}{c-\gamma} E_{t-1} r_t + \frac{\gamma c(w-v)}{c-\gamma} p_{t-1} + \frac{\lambda c}{c-\gamma} y_{t-1} - y^*)^2$$

since $E_{t-1}\varepsilon_{2t} = E_{t-1}u_t = 0$. Clearly, the bias can be set to zero by setting

$$r_t = -\frac{c - \gamma}{\gamma c}y^* + (w - v)p_{t-1} + \frac{\lambda}{\gamma}y_{t-1},$$

i.e., by a rule of the form $H\Omega_{t-1}$. Under such a rule, the mean squared error becomes

$$E_{t-1}(y_t - y^*)^2 = E_{t-1}(y_t - E_{t-1}y_t)^2 + (E_{t-1}y_t - y^*)^2$$

$$= E_{t-1}\left(-\frac{\gamma}{c - \gamma}\varepsilon_{2t} + \frac{c}{c - \gamma}u_t\right)^2$$

$$= \left(\frac{\gamma}{c - \gamma}\right)^2\sigma^2_{\varepsilon_2} + \left(\frac{c}{c - \gamma}\right)^2\sigma^2_u.$$

Under the money supply rule, the LM curve is <u>not</u> a reduced form for y_t since it contains the endogenous variable r_t. The reduced form for y_t is obtained by using the IS schedule to eliminate r_t from the LM schedule. First, rearrange the IS schedule

$$r_t = \frac{\gamma - c}{\gamma c}y_t + \frac{\lambda}{\gamma}y_{t-1} + (w - v)p_{t-1} - \frac{1}{c}\varepsilon_{2t} + \frac{1}{\gamma}u_t,$$

and substitute the result into the LM schedule to get

$$y_t = -\frac{\gamma b}{1 + \gamma}\left[\frac{\gamma - c}{\gamma c}y_t + \frac{\lambda}{\gamma}y_{t-1} + (w - v)p_{t-1} - \frac{1}{c}\varepsilon_{2t} + \frac{1}{\gamma}u_t\right]$$

$$+ \frac{\gamma}{1 + \gamma}m_t - \frac{\gamma v}{1 + \gamma}p_{t-1} + \frac{\lambda}{1 + \gamma}y_{t-1} - \frac{\gamma}{1 + \gamma}\varepsilon_{1t} + \frac{1}{1 + \gamma}u_t.$$

Since y_t is a function of m_t, it is clear from the above expression that the authority can, on average, "hit" its target y^*: it can set the bias to zero by setting m_t as a function of y^*, p_{t-1}, and y_{t-1}. Under such a rule, the mean squared error becomes

$$E_{t-1}(y_t - E_{t-1}y_t)^2 = E_{t-1}\left(\frac{\gamma b}{c(1 + \gamma)}\varepsilon_{2t} + \frac{1 - b}{1 + \gamma}u_t - \frac{\gamma}{1 + \gamma}\varepsilon_{1t}\right)^2$$

$$= \left(\frac{\gamma b}{c(1 + \gamma)}\right)^2\sigma^2_{\varepsilon_2} + \left(\frac{1 - b}{1 + \gamma}\right)^2\sigma^2_u + \left(\frac{\gamma}{1 + \gamma}\right)^2\sigma^2_{\varepsilon_1}.$$

The interest rate rule will dominate the money supply rule when

$$\frac{1}{c^2}\left[\left(\frac{\gamma b}{(1+\gamma)}\right)^2 - \left(\frac{c\gamma}{c-\gamma}\right)^2\right]\sigma^2_{\varepsilon_2} + \left[\left(\frac{1-b}{1+\gamma}\right)^2 - \left(\frac{c}{c-\gamma}\right)^2\right]\sigma^2_u$$

$$+ \left(\frac{\gamma}{1+\gamma}\right)^2\sigma^2_{\varepsilon_1} > 0.$$

Whether the authority should choose one rule over the other depends upon $\sigma^2_{\varepsilon_1}$, $\sigma^2_{\varepsilon_2}$, σ^2_u, and the slopes of the LM and IS curves,

$$\left(\frac{\gamma b}{1+\gamma}\right)^{-1} \text{ and } \left(\frac{-c\gamma}{c-\gamma}\right)^{-1}.$$

B. The above expression is likely to be positive (the authority is likely to choose the interest rate rule) when $\sigma^2_{\varepsilon_1}$ is large relative to $\sigma^2_{\varepsilon_2}$, i.e., when the IS curve is stable relative to the LM curve, and when

$$\left(\frac{\gamma b}{1+\gamma}\right)^2 > \left(\frac{c\gamma}{c-\gamma}\right)^2$$

or

$$\left(\frac{c-\gamma}{c\gamma}\right)^2 > \left(\frac{1+\gamma}{\gamma b}\right)^2;$$

i.e., when the IS curve is steep relative to the LM curve.

* * *

4. The strategy is defective because simple models can be constructed in which deterministic movements in the money supply have no effect on real output -- money is a veil -- yet the sum of the coefficients, $\Sigma_{j=0}^{\infty} h_j$, is positive. Consider the simple model

$$y_t = \gamma(p_t - E_{t-1}p_t) + u_t \quad (\gamma > 0) \qquad \text{(Phillips curve)} \qquad (1)$$

$$m_t - p_t = y_t + \varepsilon_t \qquad \text{(portfolio balance)} \qquad (2)$$

$$m_t = \lambda m_{t-1} + e_t \quad (0 < \lambda < 1) \qquad \text{(money supply process)} \qquad (3)$$

where all variables have the standard definitions and it is assumed that u_t and ε_t are mutually and serially independent and orthogonal to $\{m_t, m_{t\pm1}, m_{t\pm2}, \ldots\}$. Using (2), and taking expectations,

$$E_{t-1}p_t = E_{t-1}m_t - E_{t-1}y_t.$$

Using (3), and again taking expectations, the above equation becomes

$$\begin{aligned} E_{t-1}p_t &= \lambda m_{t-1} - E_{t-1}y_t \\ &= \lambda m_{t-1}, \end{aligned}$$

since $E_{t-1}y_t = 0$ from (1). Using the above result and (2),

$$p_t - E_{t-1}p_t = m_t - y_t - \varepsilon_t - \lambda m_{t-1}.$$

Substituting this into (1), one obtains

$$y_t = \gamma(m_t - \lambda m_{t-1}) - \gamma y_t - \gamma\varepsilon_t + u_t$$

or

$$y_t = \frac{\gamma}{1+\gamma}m_t - \frac{\gamma\lambda}{1+\gamma}m_{t-1} + v_t \tag{4}$$

where $v_t \equiv \frac{1}{1+\gamma}(u_t - \gamma\varepsilon_t)$. Clearly, $Ev_tm_{t-s} = 0$ for all s. Thus (4) is a regression equation of the form

$$y_t = \sum_{j=0}^{\infty} h_jm_{t-j} + \text{residual}_t.$$

The researcher will recover

$$\begin{aligned} h_0 &= \gamma/(1+\gamma) \\ h_1 &= -\gamma\lambda/(1+\gamma) \\ h_j &= 0 \text{ for } j \geq 2 \end{aligned}$$

and conclude that $\Sigma_{j=0}^{\infty} h_j > 0$ (since $h_0 + h_1 = \frac{\gamma(1 - \lambda)}{1 + \gamma} > 0$). But equations (1) and (2) imply

$$y_t = \gamma(p_t - E_{t-1}m_t) + u_t$$
$$= \gamma(m_t - E_{t-1}m_t) - \gamma y_t - \gamma\varepsilon_t + u_t$$

or

$$y_t = \frac{\gamma}{1 + \gamma}(m_t - E_{t-1}m_t) + v_t \tag{5}$$

which is a reduced form confirming that deterministic movements in the money supply do not affect output. In this case money <u>is</u> a veil even though $\Sigma_{j=0}^{\infty}h_j > 0$.

The defect in the research strategy is symptomatic of the "observational equivalence" problem explained by Thomas J. Sargent in "The Observational Equivalence of Natural and Unnatural Rate Theories of Macroeconomics," <u>Journal of Political Economy</u>, 1976, vol. 34, no. 3, 631-640. The point of his paper is that though the reduced forms (4) and (5) fit the data equally well, (they have the same error terms) if the parameters of (4) are invariant to policy interventions money is <u>not</u> a veil while if the parameters of (5) are so invariant, money <u>is</u> a veil. A proper analysis requires a study of the stability of the two reduced forms across changes in policy regimes. Some evidence, favoring the invariance of reduced forms like (5), is presented by Salih Neftci and Thomas Sargent in "A Little Bit of Evidence on the Natural Rate Hypothesis from the U.S." <u>Journal of Monetary Economics</u>, 1978, Vol. 4, 315-319.

* * *

5. The reduced form for Y_t can be found by substituting the consumption and investment functions into the goods market equilibrium condition:

$$Y_t = (\frac{1.8}{\sqrt{2}} - 0.81)Y_{t-1} + 100 + 0.81(Y_{t-1} - Y_{t-2}) + \varepsilon_t + 10 + G_t$$

$$= 0.9\sqrt{2}Y_{t-1} - 0.81Y_{t-2} + 110 + G_t + \varepsilon_t$$

or

$$(1 - 0.9\sqrt{2}L + 0.81L^2)Y_t = 110 + G_t + \varepsilon_t.$$

The characteristic equation can be factored as

$$(1 - 0.9\sqrt{2}L + 0.81L^2) = \left[1 - \frac{0.9\sqrt{2}}{2}(1 + i)L\right]\left[1 - \frac{0.9\sqrt{2}}{2}(1 - i)L\right].$$

A. When $G_t = \bar{G}$, the covariogram of Y_t is given by the Yule-Walker equation (see Chapter XI, Section 2)

$$(1 - 0.9\sqrt{2}L + 0.81L^2)C_Y(\tau) = 0.$$

Since the roots of the characteristic equation are complex, the covariogram will display oscillations--the economy possesses a business cycle. Since

$$\frac{0.9\sqrt{2}}{2}(1 + i) = 0.9\, e^{i\frac{\pi}{4}},$$

the covariogram of Y_t obeys

$$C_Y(\tau) = K_1(0.9)^\tau\cos\frac{\pi}{4}\tau + K_2(0.9)^\tau\sin\frac{\pi}{4}\tau.$$

The period (p) of oscillation of the cycles in this covariogram is governed by $\frac{\pi}{4}p = 2\pi$, which gives $p = 8$. Since time is measured in quarters, the economy possesses business cycles two years long.

B. When G_t is set according to the feedback rule, output is described by

$$[1 - (0.9\sqrt{2} - \lambda)L + (0.81 - \lambda)L^2]Y_t = 120 + \varepsilon_t.$$

Business cycles of length two years occur when, as above, $\lambda = 0$. When $\lambda = 0.81$, the covariogram of Y_t is described by

$$C_Y(\tau) = (0.9\sqrt{2} - 0.81)C_Y(\tau - 1).$$

In this case, there are no oscillations in the covariogram and thus, according to the definition in Section XI.2 of the text, no business cycle.* The cycle can be eliminated by other choices of λ as well. All that is required is that the characteristic equation

$$1 - (0.9\sqrt{2} - \lambda)L + (0.81 - \lambda)L^2 = 0$$

have <u>real</u> roots. This will occur so long as (recalling the general solution for the roots of a quadratic equation)

$$(0.9\sqrt{2} - \lambda)^2 - 4(0.81 - \lambda) > 0$$
$$2(0.81) - 1.8\sqrt{2}\lambda + \lambda^2 - 4(0.81) + 4\lambda > 0$$
$$\lambda^2 + (4\lambda - 1.8\sqrt{2}\lambda) - 2(0.81) > 0;$$

i.e., for values of λ greater than (λ is restricted to be positive)

$$\tfrac{1}{2}[-(4 - 1.8\sqrt{2}) + \{(4 - 1.8\sqrt{2})^2 + 8(0.81)\}^{\frac{1}{2}}] = 0.68.$$

C. In this case, output is governed by the equation

$$[1 - (0.9\sqrt{2} + \lambda_1)L + (0.81 - \lambda_2)L^2]Y_t = 120 + \varepsilon_t.$$

---

*However, the economy <u>will</u> have a business cycle in the sense of Section XI.11: GNP will have the typical spectral shape (it is a first order autoregression with an AR parameter of nearly 0.5) and the variables Y, C, I, G will be highly coherent at the low business cycle frequencies (in fact, since there is only one noise, the variables will be perfectly coherent at all frequencies).

Let $t_1 = (0.9\sqrt{2} + \lambda_1)$ and $t_2 = -(0.81 - \lambda_2)$. Then, ignoring transient terms, output can be written

$$Y_t = \text{constant} + \sum_{i=0}^{\infty} w_i \varepsilon_{t-i},$$

where (see Section IX.2)

$$w_0 = 1$$

$$w_i = \frac{S_1}{S_1 - S_2} S_1^i - \frac{S_2}{S_1 - S_2} S_2^i \qquad \text{for } i \geq 1$$

$$= S_1^i + S_1^{i-1} S_2 + \ldots + S_2^i$$

and

$$(1 - S_1 L)(1 - S_2 L) = 1 - t_1 L - t_2 L^2.$$

The variance of Y_t is

$$\sigma_Y^2 = \sigma_\varepsilon^2 \sum_{i=0}^{\infty} w_i^2$$

which is minimized when $w_i = 0$ for $i \geq 1$. But this will occur when $S_1 = S_2 = 0$, which occurs when $t_1 = t_2 = 0$. Thus the variance-minimizing choices of λ_1 and λ_2 are those which cause output to be white noise: $\lambda_1 = -0.9\sqrt{2}$ and $\lambda_2 = 0.81$.*

* * *

*Notice that according to any of the three definitions advanced in Chapter XI, the feedback rule has eliminated the business cycle.

6. A. Rearrange the portfolio balance schedule to get

$$p_t = m_t - \tau y_t - u_t.$$

Applying the expectations operator,

$$E_{t-1}p_t = E_{t-1}m_t - \tau E_{t-1}y_t.$$

Then, using the aggregate supply function,

$$E_{t-1}p_t = E_{t-1}m_t - \tau\lambda y_{t-1}.$$

The above expressions can be used in place of p_t and $E_{t-1}p_t$ in the aggregate supply function to obtain the reduced form for y_t:

$$\begin{aligned} y_t &= \gamma(m_t - \tau y_t - u_t - E_{t-1}m_t + \tau\lambda y_{t-1}) + \lambda y_{t-1} + \varepsilon_t \\ &= \gamma(m_t - E_{t-1}m_t) - \gamma\tau y_t + \lambda(\gamma\tau + 1)y_{t-1} - \gamma u_t + \varepsilon_t \\ &= \frac{\gamma}{1 + \gamma\tau}(m_t - E_{t-1}m_t) + \lambda y_{t-1} - \frac{\gamma}{1 + \gamma\tau}u_t + \frac{1}{1 + \gamma\tau}\varepsilon_t. \end{aligned}$$

Anticipated movements in the money supply clearly do not affect output. Indeed, the bias squared is

$$(E_{t-1}y_t - y^*)^2 = (\lambda y_{t-1} - y^*)^2$$

as in Section XVII.3 of the text. Thus the optimal money supply rule is the one which minimizes $E_{t-1}(y_t - E_{t-1}y_t)^2$, i.e., $m_t = E_{t-1}m_t$. Any deterministic rule for setting m is as good as any other from the point of view of minimizing the mean squared error of output about y^*.

B. The mean squared error can be decomposed in the standard way:

$$E_{t-1}(y_t - y^*)^2 = (E_{t-1}y_t - y^*)^2 + E_{t-1}(y_t - E_{t-1}y_t)^2$$

$$= (\lambda y_{t-1} - y^*)^2 + E_{t-1}(\frac{-\gamma}{1 + \gamma\tau}u_t + \frac{1}{1 + \gamma\tau}\varepsilon_t)^2$$

using the results above and assuming $m_t = E_{t-1}m_t$. Thus the value of the objective function is

$$(\lambda y_{t-1} - y^*)^2 + (\frac{\gamma}{1 + \gamma\tau})^2\sigma_u^2 + (\frac{1}{1 + \gamma\tau})^2\sigma_\varepsilon^2$$

which clearly depends on τ. The mean squared error is minimized with respect to τ when $\tau = 1$, or when the marginal tax rate is zero.

C. From the aggregate supply curve,

$$E_{t-1}y_t = \lambda y_{t-1}$$

regardless of how the tax parameter τ is set. A change from a constant-τ regime to one in which the tax parameter is determined via a feedback rule would influence p_t and y_t through the portfolio balance schedule, but would not affect $E_{t-1}y_t$.

* * *

7. The consumption and investment functions can be substituted into the goods market equilibrium condition to get

$$Y_t = c_1Y_{t-1} + u_{1t} + a_0 + a_1(Y_{t-1} - Y_{t-2}) + a_2r_t + u_{2t}$$

or

$$Y_t = (c_1 + a_1)Y_{t-1} - a_1Y_{t-2} + a_0 + a_2r_t + u_{1t} + u_{2t}$$

which is much like an IS curve, as $a_2 < 0$. The other equation of the model,

$$m_t = b_1 r_t + b_2 Y_{t-1} + v_t$$

serves as an "LM curve," as $b_2 > 0 > b_1$.

A. Under the money supply rule, the IS schedule is not a reduced form for output. Therefore, rearrange the LM curve

$$r_t = \frac{1}{b_1}(m_t - b_2 Y_{t-1} - v_t)$$

and substitute the result into the IS curve to get

$$Y_t = (c_1 + a_1)Y_{t-1} - a_1 Y_{t-2} + a_0 + \frac{a_2}{b_1}(m_t - b_2 Y_{t-1} - v_t) + u_{1t} + u_{2t}$$

$$= \left(c_1 + a_1 - \frac{a_2 b_2}{b_1}\right)Y_{t-1} - a_1 Y_{t-2} + a_0 + \frac{a_2}{b_1}m_t + u_{1t} + u_{2t} - \frac{a_2}{b_1}v_t.$$

The money supply is to be set via the deterministic rule (*). We also know that the optimal deterministic rule minimizes the bias squared $(E_{t-1}Y_t - Y^*)^2$. From above

$$E_{t-1}Y_t = \left(c_1 + a_1 - \frac{a_2 b_2}{b_1}\right)Y_{t-1} - a_1 Y_{t-2} + a_0 + \frac{a_2}{b_1}E_{t-1}m_t.$$

The bias is zero when

$$E_{t-1}m_t = \frac{b_1}{a_2}\left[Y^* - a_0 - \left(c_1 + a_1 - \frac{a_2 b_2}{b_1}\right)Y_{t-1} + a_1 Y_{t-2}\right].$$

Thus the optimal feedback rule for m_t is of the form

$$m_t = \Lambda_0 + \lambda_1 Y_{t-1} + \lambda_2 Y_{t-2} + \lambda_3 Y_{t-3}$$

with

$$\Lambda_0 = \frac{b_1}{a_2}(Y^* - a_0)$$

$$\lambda_1 = -\frac{b_1}{a_2}(c_1 + a_1 - \frac{a_2 b_2}{b_1})$$

$$\lambda_2 = \frac{a_1 b_1}{a_2}$$

$$\lambda_3 = 0.$$

Under this rule, the value of the objective function is

$$E_{t-1}(Y_t - Y^*)^2 = (E_{t-1}Y_t - Y^*)^2 + E_{t-1}(Y_t - E_{t-1}Y_t)^2$$

$$= 0 + E_{t-1}(u_{1t} + u_{2t} - \frac{a_2}{b_1}v_t)^2$$

$$= \sigma_{u1}^2 + \sigma_{u2}^2 + (\frac{a_2}{b_1})^2\sigma_v^2.$$

B. Under the interest rate rule, the IS curve is a reduced form for output. The optimal rule minimizes the bias squared:

$$(E_{t-1}Y_t - Y^*)^2 = [(c_1 + a_1)Y_{t-1} - a_1Y_{t-2} + a_0 + a_2E_{t-1}r_t - Y^*]^2.$$

Clearly, this quantity is zero when

$$E_{t-1}r_t = \frac{1}{a_2}[Y^* - a_0 - (c_1 + a_1)Y_{t-1} + a_1Y_{t-2}].$$

Thus the optimal feedback rule for r_t is of the form

$$r_t = \Delta_0 + \delta_1Y_{t-1} + \delta_2Y_{t-2} + \delta_2Y_{t-3}.$$

with

$$\Delta_0 = \frac{1}{a_2}(Y^* - a_0)$$

$$\delta_1 = -\frac{c_1 + a_1}{a_2}$$

$$\delta_2 = \frac{a_1}{a_2}$$

$$\delta_3 = 0.$$

Under this rule, the value of the objective is

$$\begin{aligned} E_{t-1}(Y_t - Y^*)^2 &= (E_{t-1}Y_t - Y^*)^2 + E_{t-1}(Y_t - E_{t-1}Y_t)^2 \\ &= 0 + E_{t-1}(u_{1t} + u_{2t})^2 \\ &= \sigma^2_{u1} + \sigma^2_{u2}. \end{aligned}$$

C. The authority should peg r, as the mean squared error under the r rule is smaller than that under the m rule. The reason is that though r_t influences Y_t directly via the IS curve, m_t can only influence current output by first influencing r_t along the LM curve--an influence confounded by the error term v_t. In the language of Problem XVII.3, the r rule is superior because the IS curve is much steeper than the LM curve, which is horizontal in (r_t, Y_t) space.

CHAPTER XVIII

ASPECTS OF THE NEW CLASSICAL MACROECONOMICS

EXERCISE

Consider the following modified version of the model of Section 3. The representative firm continues to maximize $v_t = E_t \sum_{j=0}^{\infty} b^j \Pi_{t+j}$ where Π_{t+j} remains defined as

$$\Pi_{t+j} = (f_0 + a_{t+j})\tilde{n}_{t+j} - \frac{f_1}{2}\tilde{n}^2_{t+j} - \frac{d}{2}(\tilde{n}_{t+j} - \tilde{n}_{t+j-1})^2 - w_{t+j}\tilde{n}_{t+j}.$$

The firm maximizes v_t by choosing a contingency plan for $\tilde{n}_t$ as a function of $\tilde{n}_{t-1}$ and current and lagged values of w and a.

The representative household's problem is modified by the presence of a government that taxes or subsidizes it. The household's problem is to maximize

$$E_t \sum_{j=0}^{\infty} b^j[u_0 c_{t+j} - (\delta_0 + \varepsilon_{t+j})n_{t+j} - \frac{\delta_1}{2}n^2_{t+j} - \frac{\delta_2}{2}(n_{t+j} + \gamma n_{t+j-1})^2]$$

subject to

$$c_{t+j} = w_{t+j}n_{t+j} + \Pi_{t+j} - \tau_{t+j}n_{t+j} - \theta n^2_{t+j}.$$

Here the government is imagined to collect an employment tax-subsidy in the amount

$$T_{t+j} = \tau_{t+j}n_{t+j} + \theta n^2_{t+j}$$

and to remit the proceeds back to workers in a lump sum fashion. Thus, the tax is devised solely to induce or correct distortions in marginal conditions. The government is imagined to choose a contingency plan for τ_{t+j}, given its information, and to set θ in order to obtain its objectives.

Assume that $\{\varepsilon\}$ and $\{a\}$ are mutually uncorrelated white noises.

A. Suppose that the government desires to minimize the stationary variance of employment, and that it constrains itself to choosing among stationary contingency plans for τ_{t+j}. Then determine the optimal rule for taxes, and characterize the variance and serial correlation properties of equilibrium employment under the following alternative assumptions.

(i) Assume that θ is constrained to be zero (a constitutional amendment prohibits "quadratic taxation"). Further assume that the government has an information lag relative to private agents, and must select its contingency plan for τ_{t+j} as a linear function of <u>lagged</u> a's and ε's:

$$\tau_{t+j} = v_1(L)a_{t+j-1} + v_2(L)\varepsilon_{t+j-1},$$

where $v_1(L)$ and $v_2(L)$ are each one-sided in nonnegative powers of L. The government aims to minimize the stationary variance of $\{n\}$ over choices of $v_1(L)$ and $v_2(L)$.

(ii) Assume that θ is constrained to be zero, but that there is no information lag, so that now

$$\tau_{t+j} = w_1(L)a_{t+j} + w_2(L)\varepsilon_{t+j}$$

where $w_1(L)$ and $w_2(L)$ are chosen by the government to minimize the variance of n and are both one-sided in nonnegative powers of L.

(iii) Assume now that the government is constrained to set $\tau_{t+j} = 0$ for all t+j, but that it is free to set θ at any value it wants in order to minize the stationary variance of {n}.

B. Prove that all three optimal tax schemes that you derived in (i), (ii), and (iii) eradicate the "business cycle."

C. Now suppose that the government's objective is to maximize welfare of the representative agent in the economy. Derive the optimal setting for θ and the optimal contingency plan for τ_{t+j}. Under this plan, might there still be a business cycle?

SOLUTION

Using the constraint to eliminate c_t from (1), the household's problem becomes one of choosing a contingency plan for $\{n_t\}$ to maximize

$$E_t \Sigma_{j=0}^{\infty} b^j \{u_0(w_{t+j} n_{t+j} + \Pi_{t+j}) - (\delta_0 + \varepsilon'_{t+j}) n_{t+j} - (\tfrac{1}{2})\delta'_1 n^2_{t+j} \quad (9')$$
$$- (\tfrac{1}{2})(n_{t+j} + \gamma n_{t+j-1})^2\}$$

where

$$\varepsilon'_{t+j} = \varepsilon_{t+j} + \tau_{t+j}$$

$$\delta'_1 = \delta_1 + \theta,$$

and n_{t-1} is given. By observing the formal similarity between this problem and the one in the text, it is possible to deduce that equilibrium employment is described by the following analogue of (17):

$$bE_{t+j} n_{t+j+1} + W' n_{t+j} + n_{t+j-1} = \quad (17')$$
$$(u_0 d - \delta_2 \gamma)^{-1} [\varepsilon_{t+j} + \tau_{t+j} + \delta_0 - u_0 f_0 - u_0 a_{t+j}]$$

where

$$W' = (-u_0(f_1 + d(1 + b)) - \delta_1 - \theta - \delta_2 - \gamma^2 \delta_2 b)/(u_0 d - \delta_2 \gamma).$$

A. (i). When $\theta = 0$, $W' = W$. Then from (19),

$$n_{t+j+1} = \mu_1 n_{t+j} - (u_0 d - \delta_2 \gamma)^{-1} \mu_1 \Sigma_{i=0}^{\infty} \mu_2^{-i} E_{t+j+1} \{\varepsilon_{t+j+i+1} \quad (19')$$
$$+ \tau_{t+j+i+1} + \delta_0 - u_0 f_0 - u_0 a_{t+j+i+1}\}.$$

The problem now becomes one of choosing

$$\tau_{t+j} = v_1(L) a_{t+j-1} + v_2(L) \varepsilon_{t+j-1}$$

to minimize $\mathrm{var}(n_{t+j})$, where $\{n_{t+j}\}$ is given by (19'). This is formally equivalent to Exercise 5B of Chapter XIV, i.e., find $H(L) = \Sigma_{j=0}^{\infty} H_j L^j$, subject to given H_0, to minimize

$$\mathrm{var}\ \{\frac{H(L) - \theta L^{-1} H(\theta)}{(1 - \lambda L)(1 - \theta L^{-1})} u_t\}$$

where $\{u_t\}$ is white noise, and $\lambda = \mu_1$, $\theta = \mu_2^{-1}$. The solution to this problem was found to be to set H_1 and H_2 so that

$$(1 - \lambda L)^{-1}(1 - \theta L^{-1})^{-1}[H(L) - \theta L^{-1} H(\theta)] = g_0 + g_1 L$$

with g_0 and g_1 given by

$$g_1 = -H_0 \theta / \{\theta^2 + (1 + \theta\lambda)^2\}$$

$$g_0 = (H_0 + \theta g_1)/(1 + \theta\lambda).$$

In the present case, with $\lambda = \mu_1$, $\theta = \mu_2^{-1}$, set $H_0 = -u_0$ to find g_0^a, g_1^a, and the coefficients in the polynomial $v_1(L)$; and set $H_0 = 1$ to find g_0^ε, g_1^ε, and the coefficients in the polynomial $v_2(L)$. Then the minimum variance employment process is

$$n_{t+j+1} = -(u_0 d - \delta_2 \gamma)^{-1} \mu_1 \{g_0^\varepsilon \varepsilon_{t+j+1} + g_1^\varepsilon \varepsilon_{t+j} + g_0^a a_{t+j+1} + g_1^a a_{t+j} + \delta_0 - u_0 f_0\}.$$

Notice that $\{n_{t+j}\}$ is a first-order moving average and is thus serially correlated.

(ii) When there is no information lag, it is clear from (19') that variance in $\{n_{t+j}\}$ can be eliminated completely by setting $\tau_{t+j} = -\varepsilon_{t+j} + u_0 a_{t+j}$ for all $j \geq 0$. Then the employment process is deterministic, and given by

$$n_{t+j+1} = \mu_1 n_{t+j} - (u_0 d - \delta_2\gamma)^{-1}\mu_1(\delta_0 - u_0 f_0).$$

(iii) In this case, (17') becomes

$$bE_{t+j}n_{t+j+1} + W'n_{t+j} + n_{t+j-1} =$$
$$(u_0 d - \delta_2\gamma)^{-1}[\varepsilon_{t+j} + \delta_0 - u_0 f_0 - u_0 a_{t+j}] \equiv s_t.$$

The policymaker, by appropriate choice of θ, can set W' to any desired value. Writing the factorization

$$1 + b^{-1}W'B + b^{-1}B^2 = (1 - \mu_1^\theta B)[1 - (1/b\mu_1^\theta)B]$$

(μ_1^θ denotes the dependence of the factor on the value of θ) and referring to Figure 4 of Chapter IX, it is clear that the policymaker can choose θ so that μ_1^θ takes on any desired value in the interval $[-1/\sqrt{b}, 1/\sqrt{b}]$. Now by analogy to (19'),

$$n_{t+j+1} = \mu_1^\theta n_{t+j} - (u_0 d - \delta_2\gamma)^{-1}\mu_1^\theta \Sigma_{i=0}^{\infty}(b\mu_1^\theta)^i E_{t+j+1}s_{t+j+i+1}.$$

By driving $|\theta| \to \infty$, the policymaker drives $|\mu_1^\theta| \to 0$ and obtains "bliss"--zero employment variance; employment is given by the deterministic sequence $n_{t+j} = 0$ for $j \geq 0$.

B. Under schemes (ii) and (iii), the "cycle" -- serial correlation in employment or higher spectral power at business cycle frequencies than at (some) others -- is completely eliminated; employment is deterministic in each case. The cycle is not quite eliminated in case (i). It is feasible to eliminate serial correlation (produce a flat spectrum) in employment, but not optimal from the point of view of minimizing the variance in employment.* Of course, the tax policy will in general achieve a large reduction in fluctuations in employment.

C. The competitive equilibrium is optimal in the example; the optimal tax-subsidy scheme involves no taxes and no subsidies: $T_{t+j} = \tau_{t+j} = \theta = 0$ for all $j \geq 0$. Clearly, from equation (21) in the text, employment will in general be serially correlated -- there will be a business cycle.

---

*In the language of the solution to Exercise XIV.5B, $g_1 = 0$ is feasible, but not optimal.